Cognition
and Rationality
in Negotiation

Cognition
and Rationality
in Negotiation

Margaret A. Neale
Max H. Bazerman

THE FREE PRESS
A Division of Macmillan, Inc.
NEW YORK

Collier Macmillan Canada
TORONTO

Maxwell Macmillan International
NEW YORK   OXFORD   SINGAPORE   SYDNEY

The Free Press
A Division of Macmillan, Inc.
866 Third Avenue, New York, N. Y. 10022

Collier Macmillan Canada, Inc.
1200 Eglinton Avenue East
Suite 200
Don Mills, Ontario M3C 3N1

Printed in the United States of America

printing number

2 3 4 5 6 7 8 9 10

Library of Congress Cataloging-in-Publication Data

Neale, Margaret Ann.
    Cognition and rationality in negotiation/Margaret A. Neale, Max
H. Bazerman.
        p.   cm.
    Includes bibliographical references.
    ISBN 0–02–922515–9
    1. Negotiation.   2. Decision-making.   I. Bazerman, Max H.
II. Title.
BF637.N4N42   1991
158′.5—dc20   90–21585
                                                               CIP

Pages 22 and 28: The diagram (p. 22) and Figure 2.1 (p. 28) are reproduced from Max
Bazerman, *Judgment in Managerial Decision Making,* 2nd ed., pp. 115, 119. Copyright ©
1990 by John Wiley & Sons, Inc. Reprinted by permission of John Wiley & Sons, Inc.

Page 63: Figure 4.1 is reproduced from M. H. Bazerman, T. Magliozzi, and M. A. Neale,
"Integrative Bargaining in a Competitive Market," *Organization Behavior and Human Performance,* 1985, *34,* 294–313. Used by permission.

Page 72: Figure 4.2 is reproduced from W. F. Samuelson and M. H. Bazerman, "Negotiating
Under the Winner's Curse," in V. Smith (Ed.), *Research in Experimental Economics,* Vol. III
(Greenwich, CT: JAI Press, 1985), p. 116. Used by permission.

Page 85: Figure 5.1 is reproduced from S. B. Ball, M. H. Bazerman, and J. S. Carroll, "An
Evaluation of Learning in the Bilateral Winner's Curse," *Organizational Behavior and
Human Decision Processes,* in press. Used by permission.

Pages 164 and 165: Figures 9.1 and 9.2 are reproduced from G. Loewenstein, L. Thompson,
and M. H. Bazerman, "Social Utility and Decision Making in Interpersonal Contexts,"
Journals of Personality and Social Psychology, 1989, *57,* 426–441. Copyright 1989 by the
American Psychological Association. Reprinted by permission of the publisher.

To Al and Marla
for their continuing love, counsel, and support

Contents

Preface and Acknowledgments

This book is the product of a decade of our collaboration on the decision-making processes of negotiators. Our interest in this topic dates back to early conversations in 1980 in which one of us (Max as an assistant professor) was interested in decision making and the other (Maggie as a doctoral student) wanted to start working on negotiation. These discussions could have easily ended with a quick conclusion that our interests did not overlap. Instead, they led to a series of research studies that have evolved into (what we hope you will see as) an integrated decision perspective of negotiation.

The intellectual seeds of our research lie in the work of others. Howard Raiffa's *The Art and Science of Negotiation* (1982) has been a consistent source of insight concerning the potential for interdisciplinary interaction on the topic of negotiation. Raiffa's arguments are crucial to the perspective offered in our book. Danny Kahneman and Amos Tversky have been the leading researchers in developing an understanding of cognitive biases that affect judgment. Their exceptional work provides the primary analytical lens that we use in developing our arguments. As such, Howard, Danny, and Amos have been central figures in our intellectual development and the evolution of this research perspective over the last decade.

Our coauthors have helped us develop the specific arguments presented in this book. In fact, some were so critical to our emerging view of negotiation that their contributions are specifically acknowledged in a number of chapters in the book. The research highlighted in Chapter 5—Negotiator Experience and Expertise—was the result of continuing collaborations with Gregory Northcraft; Chapter 6—Group Negotiations—profited from the ongoing research contributions of Elizabeth Mannix and Leigh Thompson; and early empirical work on the study of markets and matching in negotiation (Chapter 7) was conducted in conjunction with Harris Sondak, and, as well, served as the basis for his dissertation.

Other coauthors have informed and shaped our research and broadened our perspective with their unique understanding of the negotiation process. Our associations with Jeanne Brett, Jack Brittain, John Carroll, Vandra Huber, George Loewenstein, Keith Murnighan, Robin Pinkley, Tom Tripp, Kathleen Valley, and Sally White have expanded the frame and application of our work to dispute resolution.

Many of our colleagues have also provided us with an enormous number of helpful comments on a previous draft of this manuscript. The impact of their comments can be seen in the dramatic changes that have been made in the content of this book. The quality (and number) of their comments leads us to hope that any existing copies of the first draft of this manuscript be burned at the earliest opportunity. These individuals include Hank Farber, Jennifer Halpern, Rod Kramer, Elizabeth Mannix, Keith Murnighan, Gregory Northcraft, Lee Ross, Harris Sondak, and Leigh Thompson. In addition, Kathleen Valley and Sally White have spent almost as much time as we have with this particular manuscript as they functioned in the dual roles of research collaborators and editors.

We have also been fortunate to have the support of a number of institutions. The J.L. Kellogg Graduate School of Management at Northwestern University has been a wonderful place to work on the topic of negotiation. The interest in negotiation created by Jeanne Brett, the support of the area by Dean Donald Jacobs, the spectacular group of doctoral students, and the creation of the Dispute Resolution Research Center (funded by the Hewlett Foundation and directed by Jeanne Brett) have made Kellogg a truly unique academic environment. We have also been supported by the Borg-Warner and J.L. Kellogg Distinguished Professorships. Our research has also benefited from the support of research grants provided by the National Science Foundation, National Institute for Dispute Resolution, Fund for Research in Dispute Resolution, Northwestern University Research Grants Committee, and Eller Center for the Study of the Private Market Economy at the University of Arizona. This writing of this book was completed while Max was a Fellow at the Center for Advanced Study in the Behavioral Sciences. His funding there was partially provided by the Russell Sage Foundation and the National Science Foundation.

Finally, we would wish to acknowledge our spouses Alfred Lindahl and Marla Felcher—two people whose contributions have been crucial to our understanding of negotiation in the real world. Both have provided an immense amount of understanding of our time-consuming commitment to our research and this project. They have listened to and helped revise our ideas, clarified our thinking, and read our manuscripts. We dedicate this book to them for without their support and commitment, the writing of this book and much of the research on which it is based could not have been realized.

Research on negotiation has a great deal to offer to the successful resolution of conflict in society. We hope that our contribution encourages others to study negotiation, and that the end result will be more rational decision making in both common and critical disputes that confront us at the individual, group, and societal level.

1

An Introduction and Overview

Negotiation has long been recognized as an activity that affects world peace and the survival of political and trade relations. During the past decade, negotiation has also come to be viewed as a central aspect of managerial life. During this time, there has been a proliferation of research in negotiation and dispute resolution by management theorists. This work has evolved separately from traditional labor relations and social psychological studies, areas which have waned in popularity (Kochan, Katz, & McKersie, 1986; Nisbett & Ross, 1980).

This book introduces a new research area that has emerged through the management sciences. In this research, the negotiation process is conceptualized as a multiparty decision-making activity, where the individual cognitions of each party and the interactive dynamics of multiple parties are interpreted as critical elements. The central argument of this book is that to negotiate most effectively negotiators need to make more rational decisions. Making such decisions requires that negotiators understand and reduce the cognitive errors that permeate their decision processes.

In the following pages, this chapter offers an interpretation of the recent practical and theoretical interest in management negotiations, reviews some of the current dominant dispute literatures, specifies the relative benefits of the decision-making perspective, and outlines the remaining chapters of the book.

THE CURRENT INTEREST
IN THE AREA OF NEGOTIATION

We believe that important societal factors have facilitated the recent wave of managerial interest in dispute resolution. Social and economic changes have made negotiating an important managerial activity, and scholars have sensed that the environment is ripe for useful knowledge. Management schools now offer courses in negotiation because they provide a unique opportunity to combine theoretical and practical interests. Consider the major trends of the past twenty years:

1. *Global marketplace.* Twenty-five years ago, American managers faced a simpler environment. Global competition did not pose a serious threat. American managers could negotiate on their own terms. But the industrial lead of the United States has eroded and more and more American managers are negotiating with foreign counterparts who follow very different negotiating norms.

2. *Corporate restructuring.* During the 1980s, we entered the era of corporate restructuring. The stable organizational forms of the past can no longer be assumed. Mergers, acquisitions, downsizing, and joint ventures have created thousands of new corporate arrangements. Career survival in a restructuring environment requires negotiation skills.

3. *Work-force mobility.* Unlike past generations of employees, frequent job shifts are now common. Employers do not feel the long-term commitment to the employee that characterized past relationships. Employees often feel little long-term commitment to the organization. White-collar workers often see a job as simply one stepping stone in an upwardly mobile career. That next step may or may not be with the same organization. New models of employment show employees actively negotiating their organizational existence.

4. *Service-sector economy.* In recent years there has been a shift from a manufacturing-based economy to a service-based economy. Service-sector negotiations are, on average, harder than manufacturing-based negotiations. They require buyers and sellers to agree on more ambiguous outcomes than negotiations over manufactured goods. The ambiguity of service-sector transactions necessitates more complex negotiations, and re-negotiations are significantly more common.

One implication of these trends is that future interest in negotiations research will depend upon researchers' abilities to create knowledge that responds to these concerns. As the global economy expands, as the service sector grows, as corporate restructuring continues, and as employees continue to be concerned with managing their own careers, the importance of negotiation skills for managers will remain. For negotiation research to maintain its popularity, researchers will need to provide information that helps managers successfully cope with these concerns. Our interpretation of the existing negotiation literature is that it offers a surprisingly limited amount of empirically-justified advice. We believe that a decision approach to negotiation offers an important new perspective for making negotiators more effective.

OUR PERSPECTIVE ON THE EXISTING RESEARCH LITERATURE

In this section, we review what we consider to be the three dominant research literatures in the field of negotiation. These include two psychologically-based literatures: (1) negotiators' individual attributes and (2) situational characteristics within negotiations; and one economically-based literature: game theory. We do not review these research domains in detail. Reviews can be found elsewhere (Rubin & Brown, 1975; Bazerman, Lewicki, & Sheppard, 1991; Roth, 1991). Rather, we summarize what we feel are the benefits and shortcomings of each perspective. In the next section, we discuss how the decision perspective overcomes many of these shortcomings.

Individual Attributes

During the 1960s and early 1970s, the majority of psychological research conducted on negotiations emphasized dispositional variables (Rubin & Brown, 1975). Dispositional variables, or traits, are those individual attributes such as demographic characteristics, personality variables, and motivated behavioral tendencies that are unique to individual negotiators. Demographic characteristics (e.g., age, gender, race, etc.), risk-taking tendencies, locus-of-control, cognitive complexity, tolerance for ambiguity, self-esteem, authoritarianism, and Machiavellianism were all major research topics in the 1960s negotiation literature (Rubin & Brown, 1975; Hermann & Kogan, 1977; Lewicki, Weiss, & Lewin, 1988).

Since bargaining is clearly an interpersonal activity, it seems logical that the participants' dispositions *should* exert significant influence on the process and outcomes of negotiations. Unfortunately, despite numerous studies, dispositional evidence is rarely convincing. When effects have been found, situational features imposed upon the negotiators often reduce or negate these effects. As a result, individual attribute variables do not typically explain much variance in negotiator behavior (Thompson, in press).

Consider the example of gender differences in negotiation. In literally hundreds of studies, there has been little consistent evidence to support a main effect for gender differences in negotiator performance (Lewicki & Litterer, 1985). Thompson (in press) argues that even the evidence that does exist must be viewed skeptically. She argues that studies have not been consistent in reporting gender differences. Many studies report them as a secondary analysis. The implication is that there may be an even larger number of studies that have tested gender differences, but have never reported their findings because of the lack of a statistically demonstratable effect.*

A number of authors have reached the conclusion that individual differences offer little insight into predicting negotiator behavior and negotiation outcomes.

"There are few significant relationships between personality and negotiation outcomes." (Lewicki & Litterer, 1985)

"From what is known now, it does not appear that there is any single personality type or characteristic that is directly and clearly linked to success in negotiation." (Hermann & Kogan, 1977)

One possible reason for the lack of success of individual-differences research could lie in the simplistic way that researchers have operationalized dispositional variables. Most individual differences have been assessed using pencil and paper measures (Thompson, in press). In contrast, the key dependent variables of interest in nego-

---

* Obviously, gender differences are but one example. They also represent a variable that is easy to collect, is often collected without being the main topic of a study, and is selectively reported when significant results emerge.

tiation are typically behavioral measures of performance. In the organizational behavior literature, Staw and Ross (1985) argue that given the documented inconsistency between attitudes and behavior and the unreliability of self-report measures, behavioral assessment of individual differences should yield more reliable and consistent results than prevailing methods.

Staw, Bell, and Clausen's (1986) research demonstrates such a method for investigating the effects of individual differences. In a study of job attitudes (an area where organizational researchers have previously failed to find important effects for individual differences), Staw et al. analyzed longitudinal data on individuals. They found a significant positive, and surprisingly large, correlation between individual job satisfaction in later adulthood and overall affective disposition in early adulthood and adolescence. These results were stable even when they controlled for socioeconomic level.

A recent review of the individual-difference literature in organizational behavior by Davis-Blake and Pfeffer (1989) argues that even this newer form of dispositional research has several shortcomings. These authors assert that the evidence for dispositions in the research by Staw et al. (1986) fails to define and measure dispositions distinct from measuring the effects of dispositions. Thus, Davis-Blake and Pfeffer do not dispute that behavioral consistency may exist. However, they argue that individual differences should imply the ability to define and measure dispositions separately from measuring the behaviors that dispositions are posited to predict.

In addition to the lack of predictability of individual-differences research, this literature has also been criticized for its lack of relevance to practice. Bazerman and Carroll (1987) argue that individual differences are of limited value because of their fixed nature—i.e., they are not under the control of the negotiator. They simply exist in one state or another. Furthermore, individuals, even so-called experts, in trying to formulate an opposing strategy are known to be poor at making clinical assessments about another's personality (Bazerman, 1990).

In summary, the current literature on dispositional variables in negotiation offers few concrete findings. While recent research offers potential, and new, directions for the study of dispositional variables (Weiss & Adler, 1984; Staw, Bell, & Clausen 1986), the usefulness of these directions in negotiation research requires clear evidence, rather than intuitive assertions, that dispositions are important to predicting the outcomes of negotiations.

Situational Characteristics

Situational characteristics are the relatively fixed, contextual components that define the negotiation. Situational research considers the impact of varying these contextual features on negotiated outcomes. Examples of situational variables include the presence or absence of a constituency, the form of communication between negotiators, the outcome payoffs available to the negotiators, the relative power of the parties, the deadlines, the number of people representing each side, and the effects of third parties.

Research on situational variables has contributed much to our understanding of the negotiation process and has directed both practitioners and academics to consider important structural components. As an example, situational research has found that the presence of observers to a negotiation can dramatically affect outcomes. This effect holds whether the observers are physically or only psychologically present. Further, whether the observers are an audience (i.e., those who do not have a vested interest in the outcome of the negotiation) or a constituency (i.e., those who do have a vested interest in the outcome of the negotiation) is of little importance in predicting the behavior of the negotiator (Rubin & Brown, 1975). In general, observers cause negotiators to exhibit greater advocacy on behalf of previously announced positions (Lamm & Kogan, 1970) and to foster a more competitive bargaining atmosphere (Vidmar, 1971).

One of the main drawbacks of situational research is similar to that of individual-differences research. Situational factors represent aspects of the negotiation that are usually external to the participants and beyond the individual's control. For example, in organizational settings, participants' control over third-party intervention is limited by their willingness to make the dispute visible and salient. If and when the participants do, their manager usually decides how and when he or she will behave as a third party and intervene (Murnighan, 1986).

The same criticism holds true for other situational factors, such as the relative power of the negotiators or the prevailing deadlines. While negotiators can be advised to identify ways in which to manipulate their perceived power, obvious power disparities that result from resource munificence, hierarchical legitimacy, or expertise are less malleable. Negotiators are often best served by developing strategies for addressing these power differentials instead of trying to change them.

Many psychologically based literatures have compared situational characteristics versus individual differences for predicting individuals' behaviors. Many authors argue that situation dominates (Davis-Blake & Pfeffer, 1989), and others argue that the answer lies in the interaction between situation and individual differences (Chatman, 1989). Our view is that situations are most useful if viewed from an interpretive perspective. We believe that it is not the objective, external aspects of the situation that directly affect negotiator judgment; rather, it is the way that the negotiator perceives the features and uses these perceptions to interpret and screen information. This view follows directly from the work of Kelley and Thibaut (1978), who suggest that negotiators psychologically transform the structure of the negotiation to create the "effective" game that is to be played.

Judgments are based on a negotiator's *interpretation* of the dispute situation. This interpretive process defines the context of the negotiation for the negotiator. Negotiators do more than just process (correctly or incorrectly) information about negotiations. They also perceive negotiations with contexts and react to their perceptions in ways that validate their initial perceptions. Acting on these perceptions can enact their environment (Weick, 1979). Thus, a negotiator's cognitions contextualize negotiations and the development of this perceptual context influences subsequent decision making. The judgmental processes that are described throughout this book operate within this perceptual context.

The perceptual context of a negotiator includes the nature, origins, and the use of available knowledge structures such as stereotypes, categorizations, norms, roles, schema, and scripts (Pennington & Hastie, 1985; Fiske & Taylor, 1984; Bazerman & Carroll, 1987). Mather and Yngvesson (1981) suggest that the framing of disputes invokes norms of behavior and orders the importance and relevance of available facts. The cognitive interpretation of the context, or framing of the dispute, by negotiators becomes particularly important in view of the role that scripts play in social interaction processes (Klar, Bar-Tal, & Kruglanski, 1988). Schank & Abelson (1977, p. 41) define a script as:

" . . . a structure that describes appropriate sequences of events in a particular context. A script is made up of slots and requirements about what can fill those slots—a predetermined stereotyped sequence of actions. . . . "

Thus, different interpretations of situations will elicit different scripts which, in turn, dictate which behaviors are either encouraged or prohibited, and even which aspects of a situation are perceived as relevant. A particular interpretation thus creates a whole set of actions and expectations.

The existing situational research in the negotiation literature suffers from a prescriptive void because it fails to consider this interpretive process. Further, while identifying how situational factors influence a negotiation, situational findings offer limited practical advice to the negotiator. These factors are typically not under his or her control.

The Economic Study of Game Theory

Economics is often distinguished from the other social sciences by the basic, theoretical assumption that people have stable, well-defined preferences and make choices that are consistent with those preferences. A central tenet of almost all economics is that a person will choose the course of action that maximizes his or her expected utility (Nash, 1950). Expected utility is defined to represent the transformation of psychological and material preferences into hypothetical units of outcome, which can be measured ordinally. Economics do not specify how this transformation is made. Their contention is simply that it can be made. Once made, economists study how individuals can make optimal choices in complex decision environments.

Within economics, game theorists study human choice behavior in multiparty contexts. They specify a game (i.e., a negotiated, outcome-oriented interaction) by defining the specific conditions that constrain the interaction; e.g., the number of times that the negotiators—also called "players"—get to make offers and the exact order in which the players will choose (Myerson, 1990; Shubik, 1982). Utility measures for the outcomes of each player are then attached to every possible combination of players' choices. Axiomatic analyses focus on predicting whether an agreement will be reached, and if one is reached, what its specific nature will be. Game theory's model of goal-oriented, fully informed, rational behavior has been the dominant economic theory of negotiation for almost a half century (von Neumann & Morgenstern, 1947).

Many economists and other social scientists are very optimistic about the role of game theory for describing competitive situations

(Myerson, 1990; Harsanyi, 1988). They believe that the theory describes behavior in competitive environments and provides optimal prescriptions to negotiators seeking advice. Yet, as was pointed out earlier, the economists' assumption of rationality is fundamental to these analyses and thus, forms a critical link to their validity. We believe that it is an assumption that must be questioned.

While most economic models assume that all decisions will be fully explained by rational behavior, the work of Roth and his associates (compare Roth, forthcoming) is a notable exception. Roth focuses on qualitative predictions derived from economic theory combined with behavioral models that expose some of game theory's predictive limitations. For example, Roth (forthcoming) notes: "A broad class of apparently quite different models, including all of the standard axiomatic models, yield a common prediction regarding risk aversion. Loosely speaking, they all predict that risk aversion is disadvantageous in bargaining." Roth's work confirms this qualitative prediction, but also shows substantial divergence from the specific point predictions that are made by game theory. His work demonstrates both the power of game theory to offer precise, falsifiable predictions and the benefit of integrating economics with other behavioral sciences.

Despite considerable empirical research documenting the failure of the rationality assumption by economists (e.g., Guth, Schmittberger, & Schwarze, 1982; Roth, forthcoming), political scientists (Axelrod, 1984), and decision researchers (Bazerman, 1990; Northcraft & Neale, forthcoming), economists continue to assume full rationality. We believe that this assumption detracts from their ability to describe real choice behaviors. Another criticism of game theory is that its emphasis on "mathematizing" negotiations ignores the dynamic flavor of the social interaction (Rapoport, 1959; Roth, forthcoming). Game theory focuses on the underlying structure of a negotiation and how players take advantage of their position within that structure. Taken at its most extreme, game theory suggests that the structure of the negotiation determines its outcomes. The behaviors and cognitions of players during negotiations simply represent the unfolding or "playing out" of the structure. Thus, as with the radical behaviorism of the 1960s (e.g., Skinner, 1971), game theory defines individual cognitions and actions as irrelevant. Similarly, game theory allows no explicit role for the social processes that behavioral scientists often argue characterize negotiation (Klar, Bar-Tal, & Kruglanski, 1988).

On the other hand, economic and game theoretic perspectives have made important contributions to negotiation research. First, such models offer powerful analytic tools for negotiators in highly structured interactions. Second, game theory has catalyzed a vast amount of empirical research aimed at validating its predictions. Because of its explicit assumptions, game theory has simultaneously been a goal and a foil against which much descriptive experimental research has been directed. The economic perspective has given negotiation researchers a unique benchmark of optimality to use in evaluating the processes and outcomes of a successful negotiation. Third, economic theories have provided many qualitative predictions that are very stable. In general, people do seek to maximize their perceived outcomes. The theory weakens in making specific point predictions and by ignoring systematic departures from rationality. Kuhn (1970) argues that an existing scientific theory stays in power until an alternative subsumes and improves upon that theory. Currently, no other complete theory of negotiation behavior is available.

OUR BASIC ARGUMENT

As outlined in the previous pages, we believe that the dominant psychological and economic approaches to negotiations research suffer from critical shortcomings. The individual-attribute literature has failed to measure dispositions adequately, so that no consistent findings are available. The situational literature has not considered the importance of the negotiator's perceptions in interpreting situational characteristics. The game theorists have no methodology for coping with the behavioral findings that individuals do not always interpret information and respond to situations in perfectly rational ways.

Together, these literatures have tended to focus on aspects of the negotiation process that are beyond the negotiator's control. Typically, the negotiator is confronted with a given opponent—including his, her, or their personality(ies). The situational features of the negotiation are often predetermined. The implications of impasse are known. We assert that the only aspect that is routinely within the control of the negotiator is how he or she makes decisions. Thus, rather than seeking to change the environment surrounding the negotiation, we believe that the greatest opportunity to improve negotiator performance lies in focusing on his or her decision-making activities. We outline our view in greater detail below.

Decision researchers from various disciplines have offered a variety of theoretical perspectives on how to improve decision making (Bell, Raiffa, & Tversky, 1989). One aspect that differentiates these different perspectives is the descriptive/prescriptive distinction. Behavioral researchers (e.g., psychologists, sociologists, and organizational behaviorists) focus on *describing* how people actually make decisions. More analytic fields (e.g., economics and decision analysis) advocate *prescribing* how to improve decision making. Unfortunately, very little interaction has occurred between the descriptive and prescriptive camps. A central argument of our perspective is that a useful model of negotiation and the individual decision making that occurs within it must include both description and prescription.

One important theoretical connection between these two camps is offered by Raiffa (1982), who advocates an "asymmetrically" prescriptive/descriptive approach. In this context, asymmetric means that his approach focuses on only one of the actors—the focal negotiator. The work of Raiffa and his colleagues (which is the essence of Chapter 2) takes a variety of negotiation contexts and identifies how decision analysis can be used to develop optimal prescriptions. This approach provides prescriptions for the focal negotiator based on the best possible description of the likely behavior of the opponent. A number of authors argue that this approach leads to better prescriptions than those offered by more traditional models (Lax & Sebenius, 1986; Applbaum, 1987).

We believe that Raiffa's work represents a turning point in negotiation research for a number of reasons. First, in the context of developing a prescriptive model, he explicitly realizes the importance of developing accurate descriptions of opponents—rather than assuming them to be fully rational. Second, his realization that negotiators need advice implicitly acknowledges that negotiators do not intuitively follow purely rational strategies. Most importantly, he has initiated the groundwork for dialogue between prescriptive and descriptive researchers. His work demands descriptive models which allow the focal negotiator to anticipate the likely behavior of the opponent. In addition, we argue that decision analysts must acknowledge that negotiators have decision biases that limit their ability to follow such prescriptive advice.

In this book, we introduce a body of recent research that we believe addresses some of the questions that Raiffa's work leaves behind. If the negotiator and his or her opponent do not act rationally, what systemic departures from rationality can be predicted? Building from work in behavioral decision theory, a number of deviations from rationality have been identified that can be expected in negotiations. Specifically, research on two-party negotiations suggests that negotiators tend to:

1. Be inappropriately affected by the positive or negative frame in which risks are viewed (Huber, Neale, & Northcraft, 1987; Neale & Bazerman, 1985b; Bazerman, Magliozzi, & Neale, 1985);

2. Anchor their number estimates in negotiations on irrelevant information (Tversky & Kahneman, 1974; Huber & Neale; 1986; Northcraft & Neale, 1987);

3. Over-rely on readily available information (Neale, 1984);

4. Be overconfident about the likelihood of attaining outcomes that favor themselves (Neale & Bazerman, 1985b; Bazerman & Neale, 1982);

5. Assume that negotiation tasks are necessarily fixed-sum and thereby miss opportunities for mutually beneficial trade-offs between the parties (Neale & Northcraft, 1990a; Bazerman, Magliozzi, & Neale, 1985);

6. Escalate commitment to a previously selected course of action when it is no longer the most reasonable alternative (Northcraft & Neale, 1986; Bazerman & Neale, 1983);

7. Overlook the valuable information that is available by considering the opponent's cognitive perspective (Samuelson & Bazerman, 1985; Bazerman & Carroll, 1987);

8. Retroactively devalue *any* concession that is made by the opponent (Stillenger, Epelbaum, Keltner, & Ross, 1990).

These tendencies seriously limit the usefulness of the rationality assumption of traditional prescriptive models, i.e., the belief that negotiators are accurate and consistent decision makers. Further, these findings better inform Raiffa's prescriptive model by developing more detailed descriptions of negotiator behavior.

The main drawback of this research is that it is in its early stages and has typically been limited to a stylized set of studies on dyadic negotiations. The goal of this book is to combine Raiffa's realistic prescriptive approach with more useful descriptions of human decision behavior. The intended result is an integrated decision approach to negotiation that sets the foundation for more relevant descriptive research and more beneficial prescriptive research. We believe that a focus on decision making is critical for making the theoretical link between descriptive and prescriptive models.

The Benefit of Prescriptive Models for Descriptive Research

The primary contribution that prescriptive models make to descriptive research is to provide a benchmark of optimality. The use of rationality-based analyses as a standard of performance to compare actual decision making against has fueled the growth and expansion of behavioral decision research (Kahneman, Slovic, & Tversky, 1982). This literature explores how decisions deviate from rationality—identifying the specific changes that are required to improve individual decision making (Bazerman, 1990).

Theoretical economists often claim that the rational model of individual behavior offers the only complete descriptive theory of decision making, and they argue that we should not throw out rational models as descriptive models until there is a replacement. In a Kuhnian (1970) sense, this argument suggests that we are in the middle of a scientific revolution, and that the rational model will stay in power until a legitimate successor is found. We disagree. First, we do not expect a concise replacement theory to be developed that incorporates all of the systematic deficiencies from rationality that have been identified (Murnighan & Bazerman, in press). Rather, what is offered by behavioral decision theory is a set of adjustments that must be made to rational models to improve their predictive power. A model that adjusts the basic rational model and incorporates known systematic biases offers a better description of actual behavior than the rational model operating alone. This argument follows from March and Simon (1958), who argue that individuals try to be rational, but they are bounded by cognitive limitations. Behavioral research is only beginning to identify these bounds.

The Benefit of Descriptive Research for Prescriptive Models

We have often been asked what we try to teach students in our MBA elective course on negotiation. Our answer highlights the ways in which we see descriptive findings as useful to developing better prescriptions. While our prescriptive goal is for students to learn to think about negotiations as Raiffa does (1982), it is also important for them (1) to develop cognitive skills in assessing the likely behavior of the opponent and (2) to identify what constraints might keep the negotiators and their opponents from acting rationally. As a result, we encourage students to improve their cognitive assessments of their opponents. We emphasize identifying what information is available about the other negotiator and addressing what a rational model would suggest about the other's future behaviors. In addition, we recommend a "judgmental limitation audit." The audit can specify a variety of anticipated deviations from rationality in the opponent's decision making (Chapters 3 and 4 develop this information in detail). Simultaneously, we encourage students to identify and overcome barriers impeding their own decision processes, so that they know what mistakes to avoid in implementing optimal prescriptive advice. Thus, descriptive research informs a prescriptive approach by providing necessary information on the impediments to individual rationality.

AN OUTLINE OF THINGS TO COME

This chapter has introduced the decision approach to negotiation that will be developed in this book. We do not offer a complete formal theory, because we do not believe that any model of cognition can be complete, yet detailed enough, to be useful at this time. Rather, we develop a framework for descriptive research that benefits from prescriptive analysis and provides useful prescriptive advice. The prescriptive advice, in turn, benefits from the descriptive research on cognitive biases and deviations from rationality. Obviously, we have only provided a skeletal framework, and without the detail, our perspective is of limited value. However, this overview may be useful in offering a structure within which the different pieces of the decision model will fit.

The book is divided into two parts. In the first half, we present our general argument for a decision perspective to negotiation and focus on two-party interactions. Chapter 2 outlines the essential characteristics of Raiffa's approach. We also clarify the deficiencies that exist in his initial formulation because of his limited attention to descriptive models. Chapter 3 uses behavioral decision theory to specify a number of individual-level biases that affect negotiator judgment. Chapter 4 adds additional biases to this list that are created by the competitive context of negotiations. Chapter 5 examines the effects of expertise and experience on the rationality of negotiator behavior.

In the second half, we consider the application of our perspective in more complex social systems. As such, the last four chapters are a series of essays examining the influence and applicability of a decision perspective to these more complex negotiation situations. Chapter 6 introduces multiparty negotiations, with a focus on coalition formation. Chapter 7 explores the common problem of matching buyers and sellers in market settings (i.e., finding a mate, pairing employees and employers, etc.). Chapter 8 focuses on the decision processes of third parties who often intervene in disputes. Finally, Chapter 9 returns to our perceptual approach to situational characteristics that was introduced earlier in this chapter. Here, we examine how social cognitive phenomena further influence the decision-making processes that are developed throughout the book.

2

Prescriptions from a Decision–Analytic Perspective

One of the key reasons for the growing popularity of negotiation research is the belief that researchers can provide useful prescriptive advice to negotiators. Unfortunately, as argued in the previous chapter, the more traditional negotiation research streams have not been directed toward this goal. With the exception of game theory, all of the research emphasizes the description of negotiation behavior. Little scientific attention is given to the question of how to convert descriptive information into prescriptive recommendations.

While game theory does claim prescriptive value, these prescriptions apply in the world of rational, supersmart people (Raiffa, 1982). Game theory does not address a world where "erring folks like you and me actually behave, but in how we should behave if we were smarter, thought harder, were more consistent, were all knowing" (Raiffa, 1982, p. 21). Further, the advice derived from game theory assumes a world in which not only the focal negotiator (the target of advice) behaves rationally, but also the negotiating opponent behaves rationally. If the other party systematically deviates from rationality, then the optimal advice must be adapted from that of a pure game theoretic approach.

The decision–analytic approach introduced in this chapter originates from Raiffa's (1982) "asymmetrically prescriptive/descriptive" approach which tries to give the best possible advice to real negotiators involved in real conflicts. Raiffa's approach is prescriptive for the party receiving advice, based on a realistic description of the opposing party. He argues that it is necessary to obtain the best possible description of the expected behavior of the opponent to derive optimal prescriptions for the focal negotiator.

Before proceeding, it is important to note that Raiffa does not provide an alternative theory of negotiation. Unlike game theory, his framework does not create a falsifiable set of propositions that specify relations among variables, with the purpose of explaining past behavior and predicting future phenomenon. Instead, Raiffa offers an analytic framework that is based on economic thought, but is also cognizant of the need for behavioral insight into the complexities that exist in actual negotiations. This framework offers the best available prescriptive advice for thinking rationally in a less than rational world. As a result, this chapter is more applied than the remainder of the book.

Rather than offer a comprehensive presentation of the decision-analytic perspective (Raiffa, 1982; Lax & Sebenius, 1986; Applbaum, 1987), this chapter uses Raiffa's framework to focus on a specific two-party conflict and examine the basic information that is needed for a systematic analysis of the negotiation. This chapter then analyzes the distributive and integrative aspects of negotiation. We close the chapter with an evaluation of the value and limitations of the existing decision–analytic approach.

THE BASIC ELEMENTS
OF A DECISION–ANALYTIC APPROACH

As with game theory, Raiffa's approach is based on the assessment of information sets which include each party's alternatives to a negotiated agreement, each party's outcome interests, and the relative importance of each of these interests for each party. Together, these three sets of information determine the structure of the negotiation game (Sebenius, 1989). These sets of information are described in detail below.

Alternatives to a Negotiated Agreement

Before negotiators begin any important negotiation, they should consider what will happen if no agreement is reached. That is, they should determine their "Best Alternative To a Negotiated Agreement" (BATNA) (Fisher & Ury, 1981). This is critical because the subjective expected value of a negotiator's BATNA provides a precise lower bound for the minimum requirements of a negotiated agreement. At impasse, a negotiator obtains his or her BATNA. Thus, he or she prefers any negotiated agreement that provides more value than the BATNA over impasse. This assessment should logically determine the negotiator's reservation point; i.e., the point where a negotiator is indifferent between a negotiated agreement and impasse.

Most people enter negotiations with some idea of what they want; they have a target. However, many negotiators fail to either establish their reservation point or discover their opponent's.

A reservation point is, in many ways, closely related to the negotiator's BATNA. For example, rather than buying a specific new car, a negotiator may decide to continue to use mass transit. Alternatively, his or her BATNA may be to buy the exact same car from another dealership and the reservation point is the price offered at the second dealership. Notice that the second alternative makes it far easier to determine the reservation point. Whether the next best alternative provides the negotiator with an easy-to-assess alternative or makes such a comparison difficult, the negotiator should always do his or her best to determine a BATNA and to estimate the value of an opponent's BATNA. While this may be difficult, such an analytical assessment provides a better basis for negotiation. Otherwise an unprepared, intuitive decision will determine whether the negotiator will "walk" if certain outcomes are not obtained.

The Interests of the Parties

A complete analysis of a negotiation must identify all of the parties' interests. Unfortunately, negotiators are not always fully aware of their own or their opponents' interests. Fisher and Ury (1981) emphasized the differences between interests and positions and stressed the importance of distinguishing between parties' underlying interests and their positions. A position is the stated requirement that a party demands from the other side. An interest is what the negotiator really desires even if it is not publicly stated. Sometimes a focus on deeper interests can identify a more useful set of concerns to the parties. Consider the following example:

Prior to the Camp David agreement between Israel and
Egypt, both parties described their interests as ownership of

the Sinai peninsula (Pruitt & Rubin, 1986). Both countries
tried to negotiate for control of the peninsula, a situation in
which it appeared that the two sides had directly opposing
goals. Egypt wanted return of the Sinai in its entirety, while
Israel, which occupied the territory since 1967, refused to return the land. Efforts at compromise failed. Neither side
found the proposal of splitting the Sinai acceptable.

In contrast, the final settlement was based on both parties having a
better understanding of their underlying interests. Land ownership
(Egypt) and military security (Israel) were the underlying interests;
control over the Sinai was each one's stated position.

The Relative Importance of Each Party's Interests

Negotiators frequently know that they have several interests in a
negotiation, yet they rarely evaluate the relative importance of each.
Clearly identified priorities are needed to be fully prepared to
negotiate. Effective trade-offs can then be created during negotiation by conceding less important issues to gain more on important
issues. In the Israel-Egypt dispute, Egypt cared more about ownership of the land, while Israel cared more about the security that the
land provided. The solution that emerged traded off these issues.
The agreement called for Israel to return the Sinai in exchange for
assurances of a demilitarized zone and new Israeli air bases.

Alternatives, interests, and the relative importance of each party's
interests provide the building blocks for thinking analytically about the
distributive and integrative aspects of a negotiation. A negotiator
should assess this information before entering any important negotiation. This information prepares the negotiator to analyze the two
primary tasks of negotiation which are: (1) integration, or enlargement
of the pie of available resources; and (2) distribution, the claiming of the
pie (compare Lax & Sebenius, 1986). In the next sections, the distributive and integrative elements of negotiation are discussed.

THE DISTRIBUTIVE DIMENSION OF NEGOTIATION

All negotiations involve the distribution of outcomes. Negotiations
with only a single issue are purely distributive in nature. The total

amount of resources to be divided is fixed; one party's gain is at the direct expense of the other party. To illustrate the ideas in this chapter, we use the "El-Tek" simulation adapted from Bazerman and Brett (1988). El-Tek demonstrates both the distributive and integrative dimensions of negotiation. We will consider the distributive perspective first.

El-Tek is a large conglomerate in the electrical industry with sales of over $3.1 billion. El-Tek is a decentralized, product-centered organization, in which the various divisions of the firm are expected to operate autonomously, and are evaluated on their divisional performance. Specific divisions are chartered to sell their products to customers outside the company to preclude competition among the divisions on sales to external customers.

Recently, the Audio Division (AD) developed a new magnetic material (Z-25). Within the corporate charter, however, it is precluded from selling its discovery outside the company. Nevertheless, the product is still valuable to AD, since it can sell the magnetic material within the corporation and use this magnet to increase the quality of its audio products (competitors would not have access since the product is not available for sale outside of El-Tek). AD has assessed that under this scenario it would earn $5 million from this magnet (over its two-year life); $1.75 million from selling magnets internally to El-Tek and $3.25 million from the product improvement to its audio components that would not be available to competitors.

While this $5 million is attractive to AD, and El-Tek more generally, the Magnetic Division (MD) could make far more if it owned this Z-25 magnet. MD has much better manufacturing capabilities and could sell the magnet to a vast market. In fact, MD projects that it could earn $14 million from this magnetic material. In contrast, without this magnetic material, MD would be using its manufacturing and selling capabilities on a product that is expected to yield a profit of only $4 million. The parties have agreed to discuss the possibility of AD selling the rights to the magnet to MD.

Ben Franklin offered some advice to our two parties: "Trades would not take place unless it were advantageous to the parties concerned. Of course, it is better to strike as good a bargain as one's bargaining position permits. The worst outcome is when, by over-reaching greed, no bargain is struck, and a trade that could have been advantageous to both parties does not come off at all" (Raiffa, 1982).

To determine if an advantageous bargain can be struck, the El-Tek situation can be analyzed through the concept of the bargaining zone (Walton & McKersie, 1965), as diagrammed below.

MD's Payment to AD to Purchase Rights

$2 million	$5 million	$10 million	$12 million
MDt	ADr	MDr	ADt

MDt = MD's target price (a low price it would be very happy to pay)

ADr = AD's reservation point (the potential earnings if it keeps the rights to itself)

MDr = MD's reservation point (the maximum it could gain by buying the rights and selling the magnet)

ADt = AD's target price (the high price it would very much like to receive)

The bargaining zone framework organizes the distributive aspect of a negotiation by combining the reservation points of each negotiator (i.e., the point where each negotiator is indifferent between not reaching a settlement, or impasse, and a settlement at that level). These points are represented by the two reservation points in the diagram above. Notice that they overlap. That is, there are a set of agreements (i.e., all points between $5 million and $10 million) that both parties prefer over impasse. When the reservation points of two parties overlap, there is joint surplus to be gained by the parties for reaching agreement; i.e., a positive bargaining zone exists. When the reservation points of the two parties do not overlap, a negative bargaining zone exists. In the case of a negative bargaining zone, no resolution is possible since there are no settlements that are accept-able to both parties.

If MD could convince AD that an offer of $5.5 million was final, AD would probably accept the offer. Similarly, if AD could convince MD that $9.5 million was the lowest amount that it would accept, MD would probably accept. Thus, one of the critical pieces of information in a negotiation is the other party's reservation point. If it becomes known to one party, the negotiator can push for a resolution that is only marginally acceptable to the other party. Extreme demands will not be effective if they are worse than the other side's BATNA. To be tough, a negotiator must first have information about the bargaining zone. If one side has too much greed or its aspirations are too high, it may rigidly demand an outcome that is beyond the other side's reservation point, leading to impasse. Greed can also inhibit finding a solution within the bargaining zone (e.g., AD holds to a demand of $8 million and MD holds to the offer of $7 million— both believing that the other side will "cave in").

Notice that any agreement within the bargaining zone creates a joint surplus of $5 million. Without the trade taking place, AD can earn $5 million from the magnet and MD can earn $4 million from an alternative project—equaling a total of $9 million to El-Tek. By completing a trade, they divide $14 million. Thus, distributive agreements can be very profitable for both sides. Sometimes a more careful assessment of the relative preferences or interests of the parties can produce even more joint profit than a purely distributive agreement can provide. This is the basis of the integrative dimension of negotiation.

THE INTEGRATIVE DIMENSION OF NEGOTIATION

The preceding discussion limited the El-Tek negotiation to only one issue—the distribution of money. One-issue negotiations are distributive by definition. If additional issues can be added, the search for ways to increase the amount of total benefit available to the parties becomes possible by capitalizing on differences in the parties preferences (Pruitt, 1983). Thus, the degree of integration attained by an agreement can be defined as a measure of the relative efficiency of the negotiated agreement in allocating the available resources. If another agreement exists that both sides would prefer, the existing agreement is *pareto* inefficient. An agreement is defined as *pareto* efficient when there is no other agreement that would make any party better off without decreasing the outcomes to any other party. With any *pareto* inefficient agreement, there exists an alternative that would benefit at least one party without injuring any party. Integrative agreements occur through the creative search for ways to increase the size of the total pie available for distribution to all parties

(Pruitt, 1983). They often involve the development of novel alternatives, which usually emerge from creative problem solving.

Back to El-Tek: Remember that by not selling the magnet to MD, AD could earn additional profits by using the magnet in its own products. Thus, before going into the negotiation, AD might explore the value of adding marketing restrictions to the sale of the magnet. For example, perhaps AD should calculate the information contained in Table 2.1. Outcome 1 shows the $5 million profit available to AD by keeping the product. Outcome 2 shows that if AD simply transfers the product to MD, AD's profit will be equal to the transfer payment (P). The remaining outcomes, 3 through 11, offer additional solutions by adding restrictions on MD, which prohibit it from selling magnets to AD's competitors or all El-Tek competitors for various time lengths. Notice that AD is more concerned with prohibiting sales to AD competitors than it is with prohibiting sales to all El-Tek competitors. Note also that the value of AD protection has diminishing returns due to obtaining product leadership in a relatively short period of time. The first six months are worth $2 million (outcome 3), and the next six months add only $500,000 (outcome 5), etc.

Many managers are uncomfortable simulating the El-Tek negotiation, because they are not accustomed to having a complete quantitative assessment of all issues in a negotiation. However, a well-prepared, effective negotiator must be able to make assessments of trade-offs across issues. A quantitative basis for making trade-offs operationalizes the requirement of knowing the relative importance of each party's issues.

Now let's assume that MD could assess the costs of having its sales restricted in the same manner as assessed by AD. We have arranged these estimates in Table 2.2. Table 2.3 combines the assessments of AD and MD. This combination allows us to look at how three underlying issues (transfer price, AD competitor protection, and El-Tek competitor protection) collectively affect the joint surplus available to the parties.

Outcome 2 of Table 2.3 shows the improvement of $9 million from simply transferring the product from AD to MD for a negotiated price. The remaining rows show the additional impact of various marketing restrictions on MD's sales efforts. Notice that all of the outcomes that include protection for all El-Tek competitors (outcomes 4, 6, 7, 9, 10, and 11 on Table 2.3) decrease the joint gain available from this product. Thus, collectively the two parties are

Table 2.1 Audio Division's Payoff Matrix

Outcome	*Lifetime Expected Net Profit to AD* (in millions)*
1. AD produces Z-25 and the product is sold internally only.	$5.
2. MD produces and no limitations are put on its distribution efforts.	P**
3. MD produces and is prohibited from selling to AD competitors for 6 months.	$2. + P
4. MD produces and is prohibited from selling to any El-Tek competitors for 6 months.	$2.1 + P
5. MD produces and is prohibited from selling to AD competitors for 12 months.	$2.5 + P
6. MD produces and is prohibited from selling to AD competitors for 12 months and from selling to other El-Tek competitors for 6 months.	$2.6 + P
7. MD produces and is prohibited from selling to any El-Tek competitor for 12 months.	$2.7 + P
8. MD produces and is prohibited from selling to AD competitors for 20 months.	$2.9 + P
9. MD produces and is prohibited from selling to AD competitors for 20 months and from selling to other El-Tek competitors for 6 months.	$3. + P
10. MD produces and is prohibited from selling to AD competitors for 20 months and from selling to other El-Tek competitors for 12 months.	$3.1 + P
11. MD produces and is prohibited from selling to any El-Tek competitor for 20 months.	$3.2 + P

*These figures include (1) profit from selling Z-25 internally and (2) profit earned by AD for selling products containing the Z-25 magnet at a premium.
**Transfer payment.

better off not creating restrictions regarding other El-Tek competitors. However, the joint benefit can be increased from the "clean" sale of outcome 2 by restricting MD's sales to AD's competitors for six months. While this reduces MD's profits (before paying AD) from $14 million to $13.1 million, AD's profit increases by $2 million, creating an additional $1.1 million of profit to divide. This profit is created by the fact that AD gains more from the six-month restriction

Table 2.2 Magnetic Division's Payoff Matrix

Outcome	Lifetime Expected Net Profit to AD (in millions)
1. AD produces Z-25 and the product is sold internally only.	$0
2. MD produces and no limitations are put on its distribution efforts.	$14.0 − p*
3. MD produces and is prohibited from selling to AD competitors for 6 months.	$13.1 − P**
4. MD produces and is prohibited from selling to any El-Tek competitors for 6 months.	$10.4 − P
5. MD produces and is prohibited from selling to AD competitors for 12 months.	$12.2 − P
6. MD produces and is prohibited from selling to AD competitors for 12 months and from selling to other El-Tek competitors for 6 months.	$9.5 − P
7. MD produces and is prohibited from selling to any El-Tek competitor for 12 months.	$6.8 − P
8. MD produces and is prohibited from selling to AD competitors for 20 months.	$11.0 − P
9. MD produces and is prohibited from selling to AD competitors for 20 months and from selling to other El-Tek competitors for 6 months.	$8.3 − P
10. MD produces and is prohibited from selling to AD competitors for 20 months and from selling to other El-Tek competitors for 12 months.	$5.6 − P
11. MD produces and is prohibited from selling to any El-Tek competitor for 20 months.	$2.0 − P

*Amount MD pays AD.
**Transfer payment.

than MD loses. Additional protection, however, decreases the joint profit since additional protection (e.g. outcome 5) costs MD more than it benefits AD.

We combine the distributive and integrative analysis of El-Tek graphically in Figure 2.1, which plots AD's profit on the vertical axis and MD's profit on the horizontal axis. Lines a and b are the reservation points discussed earlier. Line b is the no–agreement alternative of AD's keeping the magnet. Lines of 45 degrees can be

Table 2.3 Joint Profit–Sample Resolutions (in $Millions)

Outcome	*A.D.*	*M.D.*	*A.D. + M.D.*
1. AD produces and sells internally only.	5.0	0.0	5.0
2. MD produces; AD limit equals 00 months and El-Tek competitors limit equals 00 months.	P	14.0 − P	14.0
3. MD produces; AD limit equals 6 months and El-Tek competitors limit equals 00 months.	2.0 + P	13.1 + P	15.1
4. MD produces; AD limit equals 6 months and El-Tek competitors limit equals 6 months.	2.1 + P	10.4 − P	12.5
5. MD produces; AD limit equals 12 months and El-Tek competitors limit equals 00 months.	2.5 + P	12.2 − P	14.7
6. MD produces; AD limit equals 12 months and El-Tek competitors limit equals 6 months.	2.6 + P	9.5 − P	12.1
7. MD produces; AD limit equals 12 months and El-Tek competitors limit equals 12 months.	2.7 + P	6.8 − P	9.5
8. MD produces; AD limit equals 20 months and El-Tek competitors limit equals 00 months.	2.9 + P	11.0 − P	13.9
9. MD produces; AD limit equals 20 months and El-Tek competitors limit equals 6 months.	3.0 + P	8.3 − P	11.3
10. MD produces; AD limit equals 20 months and El-Tek competitors limit equals 12 months.	3.1 + P	5.6 − P	8.7
11. MD produces; AD limit equals 20 months and El-Tek competitors limit equals 20 months.	3.2 + P	2.0 − P	5.2

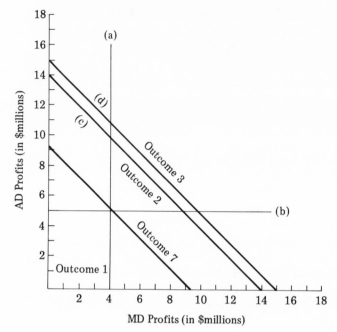

Figure 2.1 El-Tek

drawn for the various outcomes (2 through 11) to show the possible range of agreements after the transfer price (P) is negotiated. For example, the points on the outcome 2 line (c) all yield profits of $14 million, while the points on the outcome 3 line (d) yield profits of $15.1 million. More lines can be drawn for each of the possible settlements.

An agreement on the most northeasterly line is in the best interest of both negotiators. AD prefers being as close to MD's reservation point as possible on this line, while MD prefers being as close to AD's reservation point as possible. The task for the negotiators is to reach an integrative agreement, while doing as well as possible on the distributive issue (e.g., P). Often negotiators mistakenly focus on one dimension or another, rather than thinking about both dimensions simultaneously.

Someone in the role of AD who received a payment of $9.5 million out of the $14 million (on an outcome 2 agreement) might ask: "Why shouldn't I be happy with this agreement?" While this is a fine agreement for AD, MD could also have accepted an agreement that called for six months of protection and a payment of $8.3 million.

This would give MD \$4.8 million (rather than \$4.5 million), and would give AD \$10.3 million (rather than \$9.5 million).

In the El-Tek case, the set of outcome 3 agreements between the two parties' reservation points represents the *pareto* efficient frontier. As the example illustrates, even in a *pareto* efficient agreement, there is always a distributive issue concerning how to share the additional joint benefit.

In the El-Tek example, creating a more integrative agreement increases the joint benefit available to both parties. In other negotiations, no agreement may be possible without finding integrative trade-offs; for instance, if the BATNAs of AD and MD added up to more than \$14 million, but less than \$15.1 million. This was also the situation in the Egypt/Israel example: An agreement was possible only by switching from positions to interests, and trading off less important issues for more important issues. The sovereignty/security trade-off allowed for an agreement in a case where a distributive solution of dividing the Sinai was unacceptable to both parties.

Collecting the Information
to Create Integrative Agreements

So far we have focused on the elements of an integrative analysis, as if gathering full information on each party is a simple task. Negotiators must make decisions with uncertain information. A negotiator can select strategies to improve his or her informational position and increase the probability of reaching integrative agreements. Next, we will review five strategies for collecting that information.

Build Trust and Share Information. The easiest way to find the optimal integrative agreement in the El-Tek case is for both parties to share all information. It then becomes a simple arithmetic task to determine the outcome that maximizes joint benefit. Unfortunately, this is easier said than done. Negotiators often do not trust the other side and believe that such a strategy may give away critical information (such as reservation points) that could reduce the advantage in the distributive dimension.

However, consider this problem from El-Tek's global perspective. As the CEO of El-Tek, this is an ideal way for the two divisions to approach the task. It guarantees that the divisions will not lose corporate profitability by focusing on the distributive dimension. Trust between organizations, based on kinship, a close subculture, years of working together, or the potential for future interaction, is common. In these cases, the parties learn that they are both better off in the long run by creating integrative agreements. The benefit from the extra joint utility can more than offset the distributive gain that one party might achieve on a particular transaction with the use of more competitive tactics.

In some cases, parties may discuss a distribution rule in advance of sharing information. For example, AD may fear that it will be at a competitive disadvantage if MD knows that it can earn only $5 million on its own. One strategy is for AD and MD to agree to share any surplus benefit before sharing confidential information. For example, they might agree that AD gets 60 percent of the surplus. With this distributive understanding, they can then share information to create the optimal agreement under this distribution rule. If less than full trust exists, the parties could also agree to an independent party's review of all the financial assessments (e.g., this could be done by the corporate controller who might also have his or her particular interests in this dispute).

Ask Lots of Questions. In some cases, full information sharing will not be to a negotiator's advantage. For example, there may be information that will work against the negotiator if the other party obtains it. In addition, the other party will often be unwilling to agree to complete disclosure of confidential information. The simple strategy of asking many questions can provide a negotiator with significantly more information—even if the opponent refrains from answering many of the questions posed.

Most people tend to see negotiating as an opportunity to influence the other party. As a result, they do more talking than necessary and, instead of listening while the other side is talking, they concentrate on what they are going to say next. However, to negotiate effectively, a negotiator needs to understand the other party's interests. Such questions as "How much would MD lose if it did not sell to AD competitors?" "How much would a six-month restriction cost MD?" "How much would a twelve-month restriction cost MD?" are the basis for understanding the structure of the other side's interests. While an opponent may not answer all of these, information can be gained from what is not said as well as from what is said.

Give Away Some Information. Consider the situation in which there is low trust between the parties, and the opponent is not answering informational questions in any useful way. Giving away some information may be critical in breaking the information deadlock. While a negotiator might not wish to specify his or her BATNA, a negotiator may choose to offer information of comparatively minor importance. AD might volunteer that restricting sales to his or her competitors is more important in the early months than in the later months. AD has not revealed any information that MD can use unilaterally against him or her. However, this is useful information for MD to possess and may direct the negotiation in a way to identify and implement trade-offs.

Additionally, behaviors in negotiation are often reciprocated (Thompson, in press; Lewicki & Litterer, 1985; Walton & McKersie, 1965). When you scream at people, they tend to scream back. When you apologize to a negotiation opponent, they tend to reciprocate. When you give them information, they tend to return information. This act can create the information sharing necessary to create mutually beneficial agreements.

Make Multiple Offers Simultaneously. Many negotiators wish to state a position early in the negotiation to anchor the subsequent discussion. Unfortunately, this position is often made public before the focal negotiator knows about the relative interests and preference structure of the opponent. A negotiator needs to collect information before putting an offer on the table. In many cases, negotiators will not have all the necessary information when they are required to propose or respond to an offer. The common response in such a situation is to propose one offer; if it is turned down, however, the negotiator is not likely to learn very much.

Now consider the following alternative: AD offers MD the transfer of the magnet for (a) $9 million with no restrictions, (b) $7 million and a six-month restriction to AD competitors, or (c) $6.5 million and a twelve-month restriction to AD competitors. MD refuses all of these proposals. But AD asks which of these proposals is closest to acceptable. MD evaluates the proposals according to Table 2.2, and sees that the proposals provide a net profit of $5 million, $6.1 million, and $5.7 million, respectively. MD can now answer that of these unacceptable proposals, the second one is most reasonable. AD now has information to facilitate forming a *pareto* efficient agreement. Notice all three proposals by AD were equally valuable to AD. AD did not give away any information that would not be given away by making only one offer. Yet, AD appears more flexible and collects valuable information.

Search for Post-settlement Settlements. Howard Raiffa (1985) proposed the following:

We must recognize that a lot of disputes are settled by hard–nosed, positional bargaining. Settled, yes. But efficiently settled? Often not. . . . They quibble about sharing the pie and often fail to realize that perhaps the pie can be jointly enlarged. . . . There may be another carefully crafted settlement that both (parties) might prefer to the settlement they actually achieved. (p. 9)

In devising the concept of the post-settlement settlement (PSS), Raiffa (1985) offered a promising new approach to minimizing limitations on rationality in negotiation. His basic idea was that negotiators reaching a mutually acceptable agreement can later choose to allow a third party to help them search for a *pareto*-superior agreement—one that was better for both parties. Raiffa suggests that the negotiators may be more willing to allow a third party to create a superior agreement after an agreement is reached. During the PSS process, each negotiator reserves the right to veto the PSS proposed by the third party and revert to the original agreement.

We argue that negotiators, without the help of a third party, should also look for a PSS as a last step in assuring that parties reach an integrative agreement (Bazerman, Russ, & Yakura, 1987). After an initial agreement is reached, there may be ample opportunity for contract modification. If an agreement is reached and the participants are not confident that they have achieved a *pareto* efficient outcome, they may propose a process whereby both parties agree to be bound by the initial agreement if no better agreement is found. However, if a better agreement is found, the two parties will share the surplus. Thus, if AD and MD reached an agreement of a "clean" deal of the transfer of the magnet for $7 million with no limits, they could use a PSS process to share information better to create an agreement that would be worth $550,000 more to both sides ($5.55 million and six-month AD protection). A PSS process offers a last attempt for the parties to find a *pareto* efficient agreement when they fail to find one under the previously described strategies, with limited risk to either party.

These five strategies offer a variety of ideas for achieving fully integrative agreements. It is important to repeat that rarely will an integrative strategy eliminate the distributive aspect of negotiation, and any integrative advice is incomplete if it fails to consider the distributive dimension. However, by having frameworks for thinking about both dimensions, negotiators should be able to improve overall performance.

Using Differences to Create Integrative Agreements

Many negotiations break down because differences between the parties cannot be resolved. Negotiators simply fail to see that their differences can create opportunities rather than barriers (Lax & Sebenius, 1986). We highlight three such differences: assessments of the probability of future events, risk preferences, and time preferences.

Differences in Assessments of the Probability of Future Events. In El-Tek, MD had a set of assessments concerning the profitability of various outcomes ($14 million with no restrictions, $13.1 million with a six-month AD restriction, etc.). Assume that AD had its own assessment of the profitability that MD would receive from the product. Assume that AD believed that MD would earn $40 million with a six-month restriction and $40.9 million with no restrictions. Initially, this situation could create a barrier to agreement. AD might expect a payment of around $20 million, and MD would never pay that amount. If trust were lacking, there might be little that MD could do to convince AD of the accuracy of its forecast. Impasse would seem inevitable.

Now consider the following agreement: With six-months restriction, MD gets the first $9 million of profitability, and AD gets 80 percent of any profitability from the magnet over $9 million. This agreement would allow each of the parties to bet on their belief about future events. If MD's forecast is correct, this agreement would be much better for them than receiving 50 percent of the expected $15.1 million. If AD's forecast is correct, this agreement will also be better for them than receiving 50 percent of the expected $15.1 million. While the parties will not both be right, a trade based on differing expectations increases the likelihood of an agreement and is beneficial for the overall organization. This type of contract, a contingent contract, takes advantage of different beliefs and creates an opportunity for trade in which both parties believe that they will do very well.

Mark Twain noted that "it is difference of opinion that makes horse races" (Lax & Sebenius, 1986). Contingent contracts are bets that allow for agreement when the parties have different perceptions of the future. Essentially, a contingent contract creates multiple issues out of the single issue of payment. Rather than discussing what MD pays AD, the negotiation concerns what MD pays AD if X occurs, if Y occurs, if Z occurs, etc. The different weights that the parties place on these issues allow the trade to take place.

Differences in Risk Preferences. Both parties in El-Tek might agree on MD's forecast of future events, but both might also agree that these are only estimates. (In the format that the case was presented above, the numbers were described as fixed assessments.) They both agree that while MD expects to earn $13.1 million with a six-month restriction to AD competitors, the true outcome could be anywhere from $4.1 million to $22.1 million. Now let's add the assumption that AD is concerned that it receive at least the $5 million that it could earn on its own, and is unwilling to take any agreement that would risk earning below this level. MD, on the other hand, is willing to take risks if it is rewarded for risk taking. AD is comparatively more risk averse than MD. AD might reject an offer that split the profitability of the magnet equally, since the extreme negative situation would result in a profit below $5 million. Again, a trade-off is possible by giving AD more guaranteed money and MD more of the upside potential: AD gets six months of protection, the first $4 million of profitability, and 15 percent of the profitability above $4 million. AD gets its guarantee, and MD gets a higher expected return for taking the higher risk.

Rather than seeing one party's relative risk aversion as a problem, the parties use it as an opportunity to trade. One side gets a guarantee in return for increasing the expected value to the other side. More generally, different risk-sharing strategies can be developed to allow for trades that might not otherwise occur.

Differences in Time Preferences. Assume that MD is having a very poor year. It needs immediate profitability and is concerned that most of the fixed costs of manufacturing will be incurred on the front end. AD is more concerned with the overall profitability that it earns from the product. Assuming the product will be equally profitable over its two-year life, the transfer might be less attractive to MD if it were to split the profitability as the profit is earned. However, both sides might be happier with an agreement whereby MD gets 75 percent of the first year profitability and 20 percent of the second year profitability. AD gets 25 percent of the first–year profitability and 80 percent in the second year. MD gets the immediate return that it desires, and AD gets a slightly higher return for waiting.

Again, the parties are finding an issue to trade by focusing on the different time preferences that they have for receiving profitability.

When time-preference differences exist, future consequences can often be rearranged in a way that gives earlier return to the more impatient party. These differences in time preference might be due to individual differences, cultural differences, or the specific situations of the parties. Regardless, they should be seen as an opportunity, not as barriers to agreement.

The three topics in this section all focus on situations where a "troublesome" difference can be used as an opportunity to create benefit. As with the trade-offs discussed earlier in the chapter, this benefit may be the ability to reach an agreement that would not otherwise occur, or may simply create a preferable agreement.

Strategies for Creating Integrative Agreements

Raiffa's decision–analytical approach is unique among prescriptive researchers in its acknowledgement of both the non-rationality of negotiator behavior and the need for descriptive research of negotiator behavior. A parallel approach for developing prescriptions for integrative agreements is offered by descriptive researchers who have offered advice based upon empirical research (Pruitt, 1983). While Pruitt, for example, does not use the benchmark of rational behavior as the basis for his prescriptions, he identifies five strategies in the form of prescriptions to facilitate negotiators' reaching integrative agreements. The strategies contained in these prescriptions are useful for a more complete understanding of the development of integrative agreements.

Trading off existing issues is the most common way of creating joint gain. In this section, we will examine Pruitt's prescriptions for creating integrative agreements. To facilitate the description of each of these strategies, we will work through another example that illustrates strategic prescriptions beyond those identified in El-Tek. Consider the following:

ABC Inc., a consumer-oriented manufacturer, has identified an outstanding recruit from a high-caliber competitor. In fact, two departments are interested in hiring this recruit: marketing and sales. Both departments desire this individual's skills as a systems analyst, and value her background in consumer goods. Like many organizations, ABC is rap-

idly computerizing its internal systems. However, the
number of individuals trained in both the nature of the industry and computer systems is limited. The immediate
problem concerns how to deal internally with the mutual
desire of the two departments to hire this recruit. How
should the two departments deal with the conflict?

A couple of obvious solutions exist. The two departments could use a
free-market approach and compete against each other in trying to
hire the recruit. However, ABC is likely to end up paying more than
necessary to hire the recruit, and the process is likely to seem
peculiar to the recruit. Another obvious alternative is to compromise. One example would be to split the recruit's time, 50 percent in
marketing and 50 percent in sales. However, this leads to a number
of administrative problems. At least one of the parties is likely to feel
that 50 percent of the time is insufficient.

Both of these solutions *assume* that the two departments must
split a fixed resource. The search for integrative agreements is a
search for creative solutions that lie beyond distributive assumptions. Pruitt (1983) presented five potential integrative solutions for
this type of problem.

Trading Issues. Trading issues asks each party to concede on low-
priority issues in exchange for concessions on higher-priority issues.
In the recruiting example, assume that the computerization issues
facing both departments are twofold: (1) the long-term need to hire
qualified computer professionals and (2) the immediate need to
handle the work merger of the sales and marketing databases. Obviously, the recruit would be valuable to either department. However,
the primary interests of the two parties may be different. For example, marketing may be primarily concerned about developing a
high-quality group of computer professionals, while sales may be
primarily interested in handling the immediate database merger
with maximum efficiency. Thus, an agreement could allow the marketing department to hire the recruit, but also give them full responsibility for the database merger (thereby reducing the workload of
the sales group).

Nonspecific Compensation. In nonspecific compensation, one party
gets what it wants and the other party is paid on some unrelated
issue. Compensation is defined as nonspecific when the "unrelated"
issue is external to the main issue being negotiated. For example,
assume that the sales and marketing departments also had been

arguing about an issue unrelated to the defined dispute (e.g., which department should pay for acquiring the new database). A non-specific compensation agreement might allow the sales department to hire the recruit and also pay the entire bill for acquiring the mutually desired database.

Nonspecific compensation is conceptually very similar to trading issues. Under nonspecific compensation, additional issues are included to create the potential for a trade-off. Thus, nonspecific compensation can be viewed as trading issues within a broader definition of the conflict.

Cost-cutting. The cost-cutting strategy calls for one party to get what it wants and for the other party to have its costs associated with the concession reduced or eliminated. High joint benefit results not because one party "wins," but because the other party suffers less. Assume that the recruit is a highly priced, highly skilled individual. In addition, assume that the marketing department really values these skills, but the sales department simply needs added personnel with computer skills. An integrative agreement could be arranged that called for marketing to hire the recruit, and for the marketing department to transfer a lower skilled employee (with a lower salary) to the sales department.

Cost-cutting often takes the form of specific compensation, where the party who makes the major concession receives something to satisfy the precise goals that were frustrated by the concession. Thus, cost-cutting is also conceptually similar to trading issues in terms of the existence of some trade-off. However, it is a unique strategy because of its emphasis on reducing or eliminating the costs to one party while the other party achieves its objectives.

Obtaining Added Resources. The recruiting problem, as with many conflicts, is largely due to a resource shortage. The number of skilled recruits currently identified is insufficient to meet the needs of the organization. Another approach to integrating the interests of two parties when the conflict is one of resource shortage is to expand the available resources. Can they use similar recruiting procedures to identify another recruit? If so, each department can achieve its objective.

Obtaining added resources is a useful strategy when additional resources exist, but premature assumptions about the nature of the conflict usually block an extended search for added resources. This strategy is only viable when the parties' interests are not mutually exclusive. That is, there is nothing about the marketing department's interest in hiring a consumer-oriented systems analyst that conflicts with the sales department's interests. In contrast, many conflicts can be categorized by the parties having mutually exclusive interests. In these cases, obtaining added resources is unlikely to be a successful integrative strategy.

Bridging. Bridging is the development of a new solution created by focusing closely on both parties' interests. Here, neither side achieves its initially stated objective (or position). Instead, the parties search for creative options that are hidden by assumptions about the nature of the conflict. For example, assume that both sales and marketing want the following from hiring the recruit: (1) some of the employee's skills; (2) the ability to use these skills over an extended period of time; and (3) performance of the department's share of the work associated with merging the sales and marketing databases. One bridging solution would consist of hiring the recruit into a staff position in the Management Information Systems Department, with the understanding that she would initially work on the sales/marketing database merger. She would also be available for special future projects in both sales and marketing.

Bridging involves a reformulation of the conflict and necessitates a clear understanding of the underlying interests of the parties. The search for bridging solutions is achieved by removing the parties from their immediate definitions of the conflict, identifying their interests, and brainstorming for a wide variety of potential solutions.

Each of Pruitt's five strategies for identifying integrative agreements requires that at least one party escape the existing definition of the conflict. Either side or a third party can use these strategies to develop integrative alternatives. Thus, the search for creative solutions that lie outside the assumptions of the conflict is a useful approach to increasing the joint resources obtained by the conflicting parties.

NEGOTIATION AND THE
DECISION–ANALYTIC APPROACH

The goal of this chapter was to provide an overview of the prescriptive thinking that is offered by a decision–analytic approach. This approach offers a framework for thinking rationally in a world that is less than fully rational. We believe that this is the best available framework for giving negotiation advice and teaching people to negotiate more effectively. This basic structure will be emphasized throughout the book to integrate the prescriptive and descriptive approaches to negotiation. However, this approach does not represent a paradigm shift from economic thought because no alternative theory is offered. Rather, this approach subsumes a game—theoretic approach to the realities that exist in negotiations.

As noted in Chapter 1, a fundamental contribution of the decision-analytic approach is the explicit recognition of the importance of descriptive research. Chapters 3 and 4 will continue the dialogue between prescriptive and descriptive researchers that was initiated here. The next chapters will enrich this decision—analytic perspective by offering concrete predictions concerning the behavior of actual negotiators.

Chapters 3 and 4 address many of the questions that Raiffa's asymmetric prescriptive/descriptive approach leaves unanswered. If the parties do not act rationally, what systematic departures from rationality can be expected or predicted? How can negotiators anticipate the actual behavior of the opponent and how do they identify and overcome barriers (biases) that might prevent them from following decision—analytic advice? These chapters will offer a set of falsifiable predictions concerning the cognitive limitations that can be expected as adjustments to a model of rational expectations and behavior.

3

Individual Biases in Negotiations

The previous chapter introduced the decision–analytic approach to negotiation. One of the shortcomings of this approach is its inability to specify the less rational behaviors that can be expected from the focal negotiator and the opponent. A framework for thinking about prescriptions in a world of imperfectly rational actors requires an understanding of how individuals actually make decisions. Toward this end, Chapters 3 and 4 describe the systematic deviations from rationality that a negotiator can expect from his or her own behavior—a descriptive aspect that the decision–analytic approach does not address. In this chapter, we introduce the literature of behavioral decision theory, and argue that many of its findings explain a great deal of the irrationality that we observe in negotiation. Chapter 4 extends these arguments by looking at additional biases that are created within the competitive context of the negotiation task.

As a first step to examining how individuals deviate from rationality, it is useful to consider what a rational decision process resembles. The following six-step process offers an outline of what should occur (implicitly or explicitly) when applying rational decision making to a problem (Bazerman, 1990).

1. *Defining the problem.* Many times decision makers act without an adequate understanding of the problem to be solved. When this occurs, the wrong problem may be solved. Accurate judgment is required to identify the appropriate definition of the problem.

2. *Issue identification.* Most decisions require the decision maker

to accomplish more than one objective. Thus, in buying a car, a decision maker may, simultaneously, want to maximize fuel economy, minimize cost, and maximize comfort. The rational decision maker will identify all relevant criteria in the decision process.

3. *Criteria weighting.* The criteria identified above are of varying importance to a decision maker. The rational decision maker will know the relative value he/she puts on each of the criteria identified (i.e., the relative importance of fuel economy, versus cost, versus comfort, etc.).

4. *Alternative generation.* The fourth step in the decision-making process requires identification of possible courses of action. An optimal search is one that continues until the cost of the search outweighs the value of the added information.

5. *Rating each alternative on each criterion.* How well will each of the alternative solutions achieve each of the defined criteria? The rational decision maker will carefully assess the potential consequences of selecting each of the alternative solutions on each of the identified criteria.

6. *Computing the optimal decision.* Computing the optimal decision consists of multiplying the expected effectiveness of each choice times the weighting of each criteria times the rating of that criteria for each alternative solution. The solution with the highest expected value should then be chosen.

The model of decision making presented above assumes that decision makers follow these six steps (Friedman, 1957). In the extreme, the rational decision maker is assumed to: (1) perfectly define the problem, (2) know all relevant alternatives, (3) identify all criteria, (4) accurately weigh all of the criteria according to his/her preferences, (5) accurately assess each alternative on each criterion, and (6) accurately calculate and choose the alternative with the highest perceived value. This rational model provides very good guidance for thinking about what an optimal decision process might look like.

The rational model is based on a set of assumptions that prescribe how a decision *should* be made rather than describing how a decision *is* made. In his Nobel Prize-winning work, Simon (1957; March & Simon, 1958) suggested that individual judgment is bounded in its rationality and that the decision-making process becomes more accessible when a descriptive, rather than prescriptive, approach is taken. While the bounded-rationality framework views individuals as attempting to make rational decisions, it acknowledges that decision makers often lack important information to complete the necessary six-stage process. Time and cost constraints limit the quantity and quality of available information. Further, decision makers retain only a limited amount of information in their usable memory. Finally, limitations on intelligence and perceptions constrain the ability of decision makers to make the necessary calculations and identify the optimal choice from the available information.

March and Simon (1958) suggest that decision makers will forego the best solution in favor of one that is acceptable or reasonable. That is, decision makers often "satisfice." They do not examine all possible alternatives. They simply search until they find a solution that meets a certain, acceptable level of performance.

Although the concepts of bounded rationality and satisficing are important in identifying that judgment deviates from rationality, they do not describe how judgment will be biased. Fifteen years after the publication of Simon's work, Kahneman and Tversky continued what March and Simon had begun. They provided critical information about specific, systematic biases that influence judgment; they also suggest that decision makers rely on a number of simplifying strategies, called cognitive heuristics, to make decisions. While these strategies are a mechanism for coping with the complex environment surrounding decisions, their use can sometimes lead to severe decision errors.

BIASES IN NEGOTIATOR COGNITION

Recent research in behavioral decision theory has identified a variety of ways in which cognitive heuristics have influenced decision making, in general, and negotiator performance, specifically. The appropriate use of these heuristics results in more efficient cognitive processing and decision making. However, when used inappropriately, these cognitive heuristics can systematically bias negotiator performance. Negotiation researchers have identified four cognitive heuristics that have been shown to produce biased negotiator performance: framing, anchoring and adjustment, availability, and overconfidence. These biases and the related research are reviewed in the following sections.

Framing

Tversky and Kahneman (1981) presented a group of subjects with the following problem: The United States is preparing for the outbreak of an unusual Asian disease that is expected to kill 600 people. Two alternative programs are being considered. Which would you favor? Half of the subjects (Group I) were presented with the following two options from which to choose: (1) If Program A is adopted, 200 people will be saved. And (2) if Program B is adopted, there is a one-third probability that all will be saved and a two-thirds probability that none will be saved. The other half of the subjects (Group II) received the following two options from which to choose: (1) If Program A is adopted, 400 people will die. And (2) if Program B is adopted, there is a one-third probability that no one will die and a two-thirds probability that all will die.

Of the 158 respondents in Group I, 76 percent chose Program A, while 24 percent chose Program B. Thus, it seems that for Group I, the prospect of saving 200 lives for certain was more valued than a risky prospect, which had equal expected value. Of the 169 respondents in Group II, 13 percent chose Program A, while 87 percent chose Program B. The subjects in this group expressed a strong preference for the risky, rather than certain, alternative. The prospect of 400 people dying for certain was less valued than a lottery of equal expected value.

It is obvious that the decisions required of the two groups were identical. However, in changing the description of the options from lives saved (a gain) to lives lost (a loss), subjects expressed very different preferences. This pattern of responses is consistent with the predictions of Prospect Theory that suggest that individuals are risk-averse when confronting potential gains and risk-seeking when confronting potential losses (Kahneman & Tversky, 1979).

The impact of framing on negotiators arises in evaluating an alternative (vis-a-vis some referent point) as a potential gain or a potential loss. Negotiators behave in a more risk-averse fashion when evaluating potential gains, and in a more risk-seeking manner when evaluating potential losses. In negotiation, the risk-averse course of action is to accept an offered settlement; the risk-seeking course is to hold out for future, potential concessions. In translating the framing heuristic to the framing bias in negotiation, one must first consider that the particular frame a negotiator employs is based upon the selection of a referent point. Consider the following example:

The union claims it needs a raise to $12 per hour for its members and that any lesser raise would represent a loss to members, given the current inflationary environment. Management, in contrast, claims that it cannot pay more than $10 per hour and that any greater raise would result in unacceptable losses to the company.

Imagine what would happen if each side had the option of settling for $11 per hour or going to arbitration. Since each party is viewing the negotiation in terms of what they will lose, each is likely to respond in a risk-seeking manner by declaring impasse and invoking arbitration.

If we present the same objective situation framed in terms of gains, a different solution to the dispute may emerge. It might be more advantageous if the union views anything above the current wage of $10 per hour as a gain, and management views anything under $12 per hour as a gain. Then the parties will be risk-averse and more likely to settle at some point between $10 and $12 per hour and avoid the uncertainty of arbitration.

In a study of the impact of framing on collective bargaining outcomes, we (Neale & Bazerman 1985b) used a five-issue negotiation with subjects playing the roles of management or labor negotiators. The framing manipulation was accomplished by manipulating each negotiator's referent. Half of the subjects were randomly assigned to the negatively framed condition. That is, they were told that any concessions they made from their initial offers represented losses to their constituencies. The other half of the subjects were randomly assigned to a positively framed condition. They were told that any agreements they were able to reach which were better than the current contract were gains to their constituencies. We found that negatively framed negotiators were less concessionary and reached fewer agreements than positively framed negotiators. In addition, negotiators who had positive frames perceived the negotiated outcomes as more fair than those who had negative frames.

Bazerman, Magliozzi, and Neale (1985) also discovered that the frame of buyers and sellers systematically affects behavior. Negotiators were led to view transactions in terms of either (1) net profit or (2) total expenses deducted from gross profits. The net profit, or gain condition, payoff tables are shown in Table 3.1. To create the loss condition, this table was converted into expenses that the subject

Table 3.1 Buyer and Seller Schedules for Positively and Negatively Framed Negotiations

	Seller net profit schedule			Seller expense schedule (gross profit = $8000)		
	Delivery Time	Discount Terms	Financing Terms	Delivery Time	Discount Terms	Financing Terms
A	$ 000	$ 000	$ 000	$ −1600	$ −2400	$ −4000
B	200	300	500	−1400	−2100	−3500
C	400	600	1000	−1200	−1800	−3000
D	600	900	1500	−1000	−1500	−2500
E	800	1200	2000	−800	−1200	−2000
F	1000	1500	2500	−600	−900	−1500
G	1200	1800	3000	−400	−600	−1000
H	1400	2100	3500	−200	−300	−500
I	1600	2400	4000	000	000	000

	Buyer net profit schedule			Buyer expense schedule (gross profit = $8000)		
	Delivery Time	Discount Terms	Financing Terms	Delivery Time	Discount Terms	Financing Terms
A	$4000	$2400	$1600	$ 000	$ 000	$ 000
B	3500	2100	1400	−500	−300	−200
C	3000	1800	1200	−1000	−600	−400
D	2500	1500	1000	−1500	−900	−600
E	2000	1200	800	−2000	−1200	−800
F	1500	900	600	−2500	−1500	−1000
G	1000	600	400	−3000	−1800	−1200
H	500	300	200	−3500	−2100	−1400
I	000	000	000	−4000	−2400	−1600

would have deducted from the $8,000 gross profit received for each completed transaction. Since net profit is equal to gross profit minus expenses, the buyer's and seller's net profits are objectively equivalent to the buyer's and seller's expenses. For example, the seller's profit for A-E-I is $5,200, the sum of 0 + $1,200 + $4,000. This same transaction would result in expenses of $2,800, the sum of $1,600 + $1,200 + 0. When $2,800 is subtracted from the $8,000 gross profit, the same net $5,200 is received. While both frames of the schedule yield the same objective profit, positively framed negotiators were more concessionary. In addition, positively framed negotiators completed significantly more transactions than their negatively framed counterparts (Bazerman, Magliozzi, & Neale, 1985; Neale & Bazerman, 1985b; Neale & Northcraft, 1986). Because they completed more transactions, their overall profitability for the market was higher, although negatively framed negotiators completed transactions of greater mean profit (Neale, Huber, & Northcraft, 1987).

What determines whether a negotiator will have a positive or negative frame? The answer probably lies in the selection of a referent. Consider the reference points available to a union negotiator in negotiating a wage: (1) last year's wage, (2) management's initial offer, (3) the union's estimate of management's reservation point, (4) the union's reservation point, or (5) the union's publicly announced bargaining position. As the referent moves from 1 to 5, the union negotiator progressively moves from a positive frame to a negative frame. What is a modest *gain* compared to last year's wage is a *loss* compared to the publicly announced goals. For example, workers currently making $10 per hour and demanding an increase of $2 per hour can view a proposed increase of $1 per hour as a $1 per hour gain in comparison to last year's wage (Referent 1) or as a $1 per hour loss in comparison to the stated bargaining position (Referent 5).

Framing has important implications for the tactics that negotiators use. The framing effect suggests that to induce concessionary behavior from an opponent, a negotiator should create referents that lead the opposition to a positive frame and couch the negotiation in terms of the other's potential gains. In addition, the negotiator should make it salient to the opposition that the opponent is in a risky situation where a sure gain is possible.

Similarly, the impact of framing can have important implications for mediators. To the extent that the strategy of a mediator is to reach an agreement through compromise, a mediator should strive to have both parties view the negotiation in a positive frame. This is tricky, however, since the same referent that will lead to a positive frame for one negotiator is likely to lead to a negative frame for the other negotiator. This suggests that when the mediator meets with each party separately, he or she needs to present different perspectives to create risk-aversion in each party. Again, if the mediator is to affect the frame, he or she also wants to emphasize the realistic risk of the situation. This tactic creates uncertainty and can lead both sides to prefer a sure settlement.

Anchoring and Adjustment

Studies have found that people estimate values for unknown objects or events by starting from an initial anchor value and adjusting from there to yield a final answer. These anchors are typically based upon whatever information, relevant or irrelevant, is available. Slovic and Lichtenstein (1971) found that an arbitrarily chosen reference point will significantly influence value estimates, and that those estimates will be insufficiently adjusted away from this reference point. In a demonstration of this effect, Tversky and Kahneman (1974) had subjects estimate the percentage of African countries in the United Nations. Each subject was given a starting point by spinning a (fixed) random number wheel. Subjects then had to decide whether the number generated by spinning the wheel was higher or lower than the correct percentage and then give a best estimate of the correct percentage of African countries in the U.N. Despite the fact that the wheel-generated number had nothing to do with the percentage of African countries in the U.N., the number significantly influenced subjects' subsequent estimates. The median estimate of subjects given a wheel-generated number of 10 was 25, while the median estimate of subjects given a wheel-generated number of 65 was 45. Further, offering subjects financial incentives for accuracy did not significantly change the anchoring of their estimates.

In the Tversky and Kahneman (1974) example, the number generated by the wheel was clearly nondiagnostic. In another study, Joyce and Biddle (1981) also provide empirical support for anchoring and adjustment with more diagnostic information in the decisions of practicing auditors at Big Eight accounting firms. Specifically, subjects in one condition were asked:

It is well known that many cases of management fraud go un-detected even when competent annual audits are performed. The reason, of course, is that Generally Accepted Auditing Standards are not designed specifically to detect executive-level management fraud. We are interested in obtaining an estimate from practicing auditors of the prevalence of executive-level management fraud as a first step in ascertaining the scope of the problem.

1. Based on your audit experience, is the incidence of significant executive-level management fraud more than 10 in each 1,000 firms (i.e., 1 percent) audited by Big Eight accounting firms?

   A. Yes, more than 10 in each 1,000 Big Eight clients have significant executive-level management fraud.

   B. No, fewer than 10 in each 1,000 Big Eight clients have significant executive-level management fraud.

2. What is your estimate of the number of Big Eight clients per 1,000 that have significant executive-level management fraud?

   (Fill in the blank below with the appropriate number.) _____ in each 1,000 Big Eight clients have significant executive-level management fraud.

The second condition differed from the first only in that subjects were asked whether the fraud incidence was more or less than 200 in 1,000, rather than 10 in 1,000. Subjects in the former condition estimated an average fraud incidence of 16.52 per 1,000 compared to 43.11 per 1,000 in the second condition. Thus, even professional auditors fall victim to anchoring and adjustment.

Susceptibility to this bias can influence the negotiation process in a number of ways. First, it can provide a partial explanation for the importance of initial offers in bargaining. Rubin and Brown (1975) note that early moves are critical to constructing the parameters of the negotiation. Research has shown that final agreements are more strongly influenced by initial offers than by subsequent concessionary behavior (Liebert, Smith, Hill, & Keiffer, 1968; Yukl, 1974).

Second, it can explain one of the causes for impasse when a positive bargaining zone exists. Negotiators sometimes fail to reach an agreement when a potential agreement exists that makes both parties better off than their next best alternative. One of the reasons for this outcome is that negotiators may often confuse targets with reservation prices. A rational negotiator should prefer any agreement that is marginally better than his/her reservation price. However, if negotiators only assess their targets—what they want to see occur—then, once set, this target can become an anchor from which the negotiator does not sufficiently adjust. A rational negotiator may use a realistic target as a goal. However, he or she must also be ready to forego that goal to accept an agreement between the goal and reservation point when the goal is not possible. Unfortunately, most negotiators do not use such contingent planning in their strategies (Roloff & Jordan, 1989).

Since issues under negotiation are typically of uncertain or ambiguous value, an initial offer can anchor subsequent moves by both sides. The other side often anchors a negotiation by its early demands. Once negotiators respond to these demands with suggested adjustments, this act gives credibility to that anchor. Thus, tough-to-soft is more successful strategy than its counterpart (soft-to-tough) because it takes advantage of the anchoring effects of high initial offers (Chertkoff & Conley, 1967; Coker, Neale, & Northcraft, 1987). If the other party provides an unacceptable anchor, the negotiator must re-anchor the process—even if it means threatening to walk away from the table rather than acknowledge an unacceptable starting point for the negotiation.

Within individual negotiators, anchoring and adjustment can also affect outcomes through performance and goal setting. Adjusting the negotiator's perception of possible goals or limits may shape what a negotiator believes are attainable or even acceptable outcomes. Huber and Neale (1986) studied the impact of goal setting on negotiator behavior in a competitive market simulation with three goal levels (easy, challenging, and difficult). They found that subjects who were originally assigned easy goals set harder new goals, while subjects originally assigned harder goals chose easier, new goals. In spite of the adjustments, the harder goals chosen by the easy-goal subjects were significantly easier than the easier goals chosen by the difficult-goal subjects. Thus, initial goal levels anchor performance goals and have a considerable impact on future expectations of performance.

Availability

Tversky and Kahneman (1974) argue that when an individual judges the frequency of an event by the availability of its instances, an event whose instances are more easily recalled will appear more numerous than an event of equal frequency whose instances are less easily recalled. They cite as evidence of this bias a laboratory study in which individuals heard lists of names of well-known personalities of both sexes and were asked to determine whether the lists contained the names of more men or women. Different lists were presented to two groups. One group heard lists of the names of women who were relatively more famous than the listed men, but included more men's names overall. The other group heard lists of the names of men who were relatively more famous than the listed women, but included more women's names overall. In each case, the subjects incorrectly guessed that the sex of the more famous personalities was the more numerous.

These findings suggest that decisions makers are prone to overestimate unlikely events—if memory associations with that event are particularly vivid. For instance, if someone were to witness a house burning, the impact on his/her subjective probability of such accidents occurring is likely to be greater than the impact of reading about a fire in the local newspaper. The vividness of direct observation of the event makes it more salient to the observer—as does the vividness of famous names in the previous example. Slovic and Fischhoff (1979) discuss the implications of the availability heuristic on the perceived risks of new technologies, such as nuclear power. They point out that any discussion of the potential hazards, regardless of likelihood, will strengthen the memorability of those hazards and increase their perceived risks.

There are three notable misapplications of the availability heuristic. These are biases due to (1) ease of retrievability, (2) established search patterns, and (3) illusory correlations. Bias due to ease of retrievability occurs when some information is particularly vivid or salient to an individual and is more easily recovered from memory. The examples in the preceding paragraph offer evidence of this phenomenon. Recency, in addition to vividness, of an event will often enhance the ease of recall and increase its perceived likelihood of occurrence.

Bias due to established search patterns results from overreliance on the way in which events or facts are stored in memory. For example, when individuals are asked to judge the frequency of words beginning with the letter "r" relative to words that have "r" as the third letter, they overwhelmingly guess that the former are more frequent than the latter. In reality, the opposite is true. However, it is easier for people to search their memory for words that begin with "r" than for words that have "r" as the third letter. Consequently, they can call to mind many more examples of the former and few examples of the latter. From this biased search, they derive incorrect conclusions about frequency.

The third way in which the availability heuristic results in biases is through illusory correlations. People frequently misjudge the likelihood of two events occurring together if their co-occurrence fits into some stereotypical pattern. As an example, subjects in one study were shown to overestimate the frequency of which a clinical diagnosis (e.g., suspiciousness) was associated with features of a drawing (e.g., peculiar eyes) made by a subject (Chapman & Chapman, 1967). This correlation persisted even when the true correlation between symptom and diagnosis was actually negative. The judgment of how frequently two events co-occur is often based on the strength of the associative bond between them. When the cognitive, associative bond is strong, the conclusion is that these events are frequently paired. Thus, the illusory correlation between suspiciousness and drawing of peculiar eyes occurs because suspiciousness is more closely associated with the eyes than with any other body part.

The availability of past and present information plays an important role in the negotiator's evaluation of alternatives (Tversky & Kahneman, 1973). From a negotiation perspective, the rational negotiator should be able to draw on past experiences and present information to assess the consequences of various actions. Unfortunately, not all of a negotiator's past experiences are likely to be coded in memory in an equivalent manner. Not all of his/her related experiences are likely to be so easily recalled. As an example, Northcraft and Neale (1986) found that because opportunity costs are much less concrete than out-of-pocket costs, they are much less likely to be included in financial decision making during negotiations.

Research has also shown that when information is presented in a colorful or emotionally vivid manner (controlling for the amount of information), the vivid information exerts a much greater impact on the final decision than equally informative, but pallid, information (Wilson, Northcraft, & Neale, 1989; Taylor & Thompson, 1982). These findings suggest that there is a potential for manipulating negotiation outcomes through the control of information—both the amount and mode of presentation. In a laboratory study of bargaining, Neale (1984) found that manipulating the availability of personal and organizational costs produced systematic changes in negotiator behavior. When the personal costs of reaching a (poor) settlement were made salient (such as the cost of a negative evaluation by a constituency), negotiators were generally less likely to settle. When the costs of resorting to third-party intervention were made salient (such as the cost in dollars and time commitment of arbitration), negotiators were more likely to settle.

Overconfidence

Einhorn and Hogarth (1978) assert that decision makers demonstrate unwarranted levels of confidence in their judgment abilities. As an example, realistically confident individuals should produce accurate judgments 75 percent of the time they claim to be 75 percent certain of their assessments. In reality, when subjects respond to a large group of two-option questions for which they claim to be 75 percent certain, their answers tend to be correct only 60 percent of the time. For confidence judgments of 100 percent, it is not uncommon for subjects to be correct only 85 percent of the time (Fischhoff, 1982). Fischhoff, Slovic, and Lichtenstein (1977) found that subjects who assign odds of 1,000:1 are correct only 81 to 88 percent of the time. For odds of 1 million:1, their answers are correct only 90 to 96 percent of the time. Hazard and Peterson (1973) have identified overconfidence among members of the armed forces, while Cambridge and Shreckengost (1980) have found extreme overconfidence in CIA agents.

The most well-established finding in this literature is the tendency of people to be most overconfident of the correctness of their answers when asked to respond to questions of moderate-to-extreme difficulty (Fischhoff, Slovic, & Lichtenstein, 1977; Koriat, Lichtenstein, & Fischhoff, 1980; Lichtenstein & Fischhoff, 1977, 1980). That is, as the subject's knowledge of a question decreases, the subject does not correspondingly decrease his/her level of confidence. However, subjects typically demonstrate no overconfidence, and often some underconfidence, in answering questions with which they are familiar (Einhorn & Hogarth, 1978).

Many different explanations are offered for the existence of overconfidence. Tversky and Kahneman (1974) explain overconfidence in terms of anchoring. They argue that when individuals are asked to set a confidence range around an answer, their initial estimate serves as an anchor that biases their estimation of confidence intervals in both directions. As explained earlier, adjustments from an anchor are usually insufficient—resulting in an overly narrow confidence band.

Farber and Bazerman (1986, 1989; Farber, 1981) argue for divergent expectations as the cause of overconfidence. They suggest that in third-party negotiations, each side is optimistic that the neutral third party will adjudicate in its favor. Consider the situation where: (1) the union is demanding $8.75 per hour, (2) management is offering $8.25 per hour, and (3) the "appropriate" wage is $8.50 per hour. Farber suggests that the union may typically expect the third party to adjudicate at a wage somewhat over $8.50, while management may expect a wage somewhat under $8.50. Given these divergent expectations, neither side may be willing to compromise at $8.50. Both sides will incur the costs of impasse. The parties will do no better, in the aggregate, through the use of a third party who will assign the "appropriate" $8.50 wage. Further, negotiators in final-offer arbitration consistently overestimate the probability that their side's final offer will be accepted (Neale & Bazerman, 1983; Bazerman & Neale, 1982). Since there is only a 50 percent chance of all final offers being accepted, the average subject estimated that there was a much higher probability that his or her offer would be accepted.

Overconfidence may also inhibit settlements, despite the existence of a positive bargaining zone. When a negotiator is overconfident that a particular favorable outcome will be achieved, his or her reservation point becomes more extreme. His/her incentive to compromise is then reduced. If a more accurate assessment is made, the negotiator is likely to feel uncertain about the probability of success and is more likely to compromise. Based on the biasing impact of overconfidence, we found that accurately confident negotiators were more concessionary and completed a higher proportion of agreements than overconfident negotiators (Neale & Bazerman, 1985b). Further, negotiators who assign higher probabilities of success are less concessionary than those assigning lesser probabilities. Here, the high-probability negotiators were less willing to compromise and experienced a higher number of negotiations that ended in impasse (Bazerman & Neale, 1982).

In their review of the overconfidence literature, Lichtenstein, Fischhoff, and Phillips (1982) suggest two viable strategies for eliminating overconfidence. Giving people feedback about their over-

confidence *based on their judgments* has been moderately successful at reducing this bias. Second, Koriat, Lichtenstein, and Fischhoff
(1980) found that asking people to explain why their answers might
be wrong (or far off the mark) can decrease overconfidence by getting
subjects to see contradictions in their judgment.

UNEXPLORED BIASES IN NEGOTIATION

The above findings from the literature on behavioral decision theory—framing, anchoring and adjustment, availability, and overconfidence—provide an initial list of the information processing mistakes to which negotiators are prone. These effects have been
documented empirically in negotiation research. While by no means
exhaustive, this section offers other ideas from the literature about
other types of cognitive biases that may be useful in understanding
negotiator cognitions. In each case, there is empirical evidence
about individual cognition; however, we are lacking the empirical
evidence to generalize the impact of these biases to the negotiation
context. Three other cognitive effects that are considered are: the
law of small numbers, the confirmatory evidence bias, and biased
causal accounts.

Law of Small Numbers

Another interesting finding from the research done by Kahneman
and Tversky (1972, 1973) is that subjects tend to ignore the role of
sample size in assessing the validity of new information. Even when
this data is emphasized in the formation of the problem, subjects
tend to be more influenced by other characteristics of the situation
than by sample size. Consider the following research problem
(Tversky & Kahneman, 1974):

> A certain town is served by two hospitals. In the larger hospi-
> tal about forty-five babies are born each day and in the
> smaller hospital about fifteen. As you know, about 50 percent
> of all babies are boys. However, the exact percentage varies
> from day to day. Sometimes it may be higher than 50 percent,
> sometimes lower. For a period of one year, each hospital re-
> corded the days that more than 60 percent of the babies born

were boys. Which hospital do you think recorded more such days?

The larger hospital? (21)
The smaller hospital? (21)
About the same? (53)
(That is, within 5 percent of each other)

The values in parentheses represent the number of individuals who chose each answer. From sampling theory we know that the expected number of days that more than 60 percent of the babies born are boys is much greater in the small hospital, since a large sample is less likely to stray from the known mean of 50 percent. However, most subjects judge the probability to be the same in each hospital, effectively ignoring sample size.

Tversky and Kahneman's (1971) work shows that misconceptions of chance affect gamblers, sports fans, and laypersons. Even research psychologists fall victim to the "law of small numbers." They believe that sample events should be far more representative of the population from which they are drawn than simple statistics would dictate. These researchers put too much faith in the results of initial samples and grossly overestimate the replicability of empirical findings. This suggests that the "law of small numbers" may be so well institutionalized in our decision processes, that even scientific training and its emphasis on the proper use of statistics may not effectively eliminate its biasing influence.

For negotiators, this bias may have its most dramatic impact on learning from experience. We will consider the specific problems associated with learning from experience in detail in Chapter 5. However, for now, consider the impact of developing an understanding of effective negotiating strategies solely by extrapolating from one's own experience. For example, if a negotiator were to develop a preferred style of negotiating based upon the outcome of his or her early negotiating experiences (representing a relatively limited sample size), then the likelihood of his or her developing a sophisticated, contingency-based set of negotiating skills is very low. It is likely that whatever schema a negotiator develops will be incorrect (based upon the small sample size). For example, what might emerge is a rather simplistic perspective on how to negotiate successfully. As we will explore in the next chapter, the bias of the "fixed pie" may be the consequence of the belief in the law of small numbers.

Confirmatory Evidence Bias

Hypothesis testing sometimes results in *confirmatory evidence bias*. When people hold certain beliefs or expectations, they tend to ignore information that disconfirms those beliefs. The initial demonstration of this tendency was provided in a series of projects by Wason in the 1960s. In his first study, Wason (1960) presented subjects with the three-number sequence 2-4-6. The subject's task was to discover the numeric rule that the three numbers conformed. To determine the rule, subjects were allowed to generate other sets of three numbers that the experimenter would classify as either conforming or not conforming to the rule. At any point, subjects could stop when they thought that they had discovered the rule.

Wason's rule was "any three ascending numbers"—a solution that required the accumulation of disconfirming, rather than confirming, evidence. Let's suppose you thought the rule included "the difference between the first two numbers equaling the difference between the last two numbers" (a common expectation). To discover how the true rule differs from this rule, you must try sequences that do *not* conform to your hypothesized rule. Trying the sequences 1-2-3, 10-15-20, 122-126-130, etc., will only lead you into the confirmation trap. In Wason's (1960) experiment, only six out of twenty-nine subjects found the correct rule the first time they thought they knew the answer. He concluded that obtaining the correct solution necessitates "a willingness to attempt to falsify hypotheses, and thus to test those intuitive ideas which so often carry the feeling of certitude" (p. 139).

In a study by Lord, Ross, and Lepper (1979), subjects were selected based upon their support or opposition to capital punishment. The subjects were presented with two (purportedly) authentic empirical studies. One provided support for their position; the other opposed their position. At various points during the reading of these two studies, subjects were asked to evaluate the studies. These ratings revealed how strongly subjects were able to interpret new information in a way that strengthened their original position. Both the proponents and opponents of capital punishment rated the study that supported their beliefs as more convincing and better conducted than the study that opposed their beliefs. Further, the net effect of reading these two studies was to polarize further the beliefs of the two groups. Lord et al. found that potentially confirmatory evidence is more likely to be taken at face value while potentially disconfirmatory information is likely to be subjected to careful scrutiny.

Ross and Anderson (1982) showed that when individuals form initial impressions about self, others, or some other relationship, they are likely to base that impression on some set of salient information from memory. These findings imply that information is likely to be recalled only to the extent that it is consistent with or matches the initially formed impression. This notion is not new to social scientists. Rosenthal and Jacobson (1968) identified the "Pygmalion" effect to explain their finding that teachers' expectations about students' performances had a significant impact on students' actual performances.

Is this bias curable through training? Einhorn and Hogarth (1978) documented the tendency to search for confirmatory information in a sample of twenty-three statisticians. Their findings suggest that the tendency is not eliminated by formal scientific training that emphasizes the importance of disconfirming hypotheses.

Although there has been no specific empirical consideration of how the confirmatory bias influences negotiator performance, its effect could be to exacerbate many of the biases described previously. As introduced earlier, the overconfidence bias influences negotiator performance by reducing information search. Thus, it is likely that the limited information search that is conducted by negotiators will tend to focus on gathering support for already-held expectations about the negotiating situation, opponent, and interaction.

Negotiators tend to enter negotiations with one strategy for reaching agreement. They assume that their negotiation plan will work, and they develop their strategy accordingly. A very different view, and perhaps more useful one, is to realize that one's initial strategy may not work and seek to disconfirm the initial strategy through the search for new information. To the extent that a negotiator is not open to disconfirming information, he or she may be unable to adapt to the unexpected circumstances that occur in negotiations.

Judgments of Causation

McGill (in press) provides evidence that the explanations that individuals provide for specific outcomes can influence their subsequent behaviors. As an example of this phenomenon, she argues that an individual who attributes a severe cold to smoking cigarettes might decide to quit the habit. Another smoker might explain the same cold by noting that she had become run down prior to catching the cold. Thus, in one case, the individual might quit smoking, and in the other, the individual might continue to smoke, but decide to get additional rest.

Causal accounts are important because of their potential impact on behavior. There is evidence that suggests that subtle changes in an individual's representation of the event can produce large differences in the causal explanations (Einhorn & Hogarth, 1986; McGill, 1989). In a series of studies, McGill (in press) found that the order in which subjects examine information about the event and the temporal ordering of the causal-judgment request can substantially alter an individual's causal judgment.

Such differences in attributions of causality are critical in the development of disagreements and disputes. To the extent that individuals view the cause of the dispute as arising from different factors, the strategy of negotiation may be more or less likely to be invoked. Further, agreement on a specific resolution may be difficult to attain depending upon the disparity between causal accounts. For example, if a individual is trying to determine whether the "true" cause of poor workmanship is a function of employee indifference or inadequate training, the resulting choice is likely to be different, depending on whether one is the employer or the employee (Festinger, 1957).

Influencing causal judgments and the resulting impact on future behavior can also have dramatic impact on the dispute-resolution activities of third parties. For example, the causal judgments of arbitrators can have a significant impact on the remedies they impose upon disputants. Lawyers in personal injury cases may find that neither side disputes the facts of the case. What is in dispute, and what the jury must decide, is what factors caused the accident. Was it the road condition and the pedestrian's behavior (as the defendant's lawyer might argue) or was it the bad brakes and the driver's lack of experience (as the plaintiff's lawyer might claim)? Clearly, future research on negotiation should explicitly consider the impact of causal judgments on the behavior of disputants.

CONCLUSIONS

This chapter offers a framework for thinking about prescriptions for decision makers in a world of imperfectly rational actors. We have focused on identifying some of the decision biases that influence individual negotiators' decision-making processes. This grounding offers a more complete understanding of how individuals actually process information and make decisions. From findings in the literature of behavioral decision theory, we have begun to expand upon the current understanding of the behaviors that the focal negotiator can expect from his or her opponent. In addition, we have begun to build a list of concerns that a negotiator should have regarding his or her own decision making. What remains to be explored in the next chapter are the particular biases that uniquely influence the dyadic decision maker within the competitive negotiation context.

4

Negotiation Biases

Chapter 3 introduced the findings of behavioral decision theory to identify how negotiator judgment deviates from rationality. This chapter continues that theme. Here, we focus on systematic deviations from rationality that are unique to the competitive nature of negotiations.

The biases identified in the preceding chapter are based on the heuristics that humans use to simplify their decision processes in individual decision contexts. In this chapter, we argue that negotiation is a very complex social phenomenon that makes more difficult judgmental demands. In addition to being prone to the judgmental errors identified previously, the negotiator is also at risk with additional judgmental biases as he or she attempts to cope with the complexities of the negotiation interaction. Specifically, this chapter examines the mythical fixed-pie of negotiations, the nonrational escalation of conflict, ignoring the cognitions of others, and reactive devaluation.

The Mythical Fixed-Pie of Negotiations

As stated in Chapter 2, integrative agreements are non-obvious solutions to conflict that yield higher joint benefit than purely distributive agreements. However, negotiators often fail to reach integrative solutions partially resulting from a systematic intuitive bias to assume that their interests necessarily and directly conflict with the other party's interests. "What is good for the other side is bad for us" is a common and unfortunate perspective that most people have of the negotiation process.

The fundamental assumption of a fixed-pie may be rooted in social norms that lead us to interpret most competitive situations as win-lose. This win-lose orientation is manifested in our society in athletic competition, admission to academic programs, corporate promotion systems, and so on. Individuals tend to generalize from these objective win-lose situations and create similar expectations for other situations that are not necessarily win-lose. Faced with a mixed-motive situation, requiring both cooperation and competition, it is the competitive aspect that becomes salient—resulting in a win-lose orientation and a distributive approach to bargaining. This, in turn, results in the development of a strategy for obtaining the largest share possible of the perceived fixed-pie. Such a focus inhibits the creative problem solving necessary for the development of integrative solutions.

The tendency of negotiators to initially approach bargaining with a mythical fixed-pie perception has been illustrated in the Bazerman, Magliozzi, and Neale (1985) study discussed in Chapter 3. Recalling this market task, the profit available to sellers and buyers for various levels of the three issues on a per-transaction basis was shown in Table 3.1. Note that buyers achieve their highest profit levels and sellers their lowest profits at the "A" level; whereas sellers achieve their highest profits and buyers their lowest profits at the "I" levels. A negotiated transaction consisted of the two parties agreeing to one of the nine levels for each of the three issues. As can be observed, a simple compromise solution of E-E-E results in a $4,000 profit to each side. However, if the parties are able to reach the fully integrative solution of A-E-I (by trading issues), then each receives a profit of $5,200.

The fixed-pie bias predicts that negotiators will approach this competitive context with a win-lose orientation and only relax this assumption when provided with considerable evidence to the contrary. This hypothesis was supported by the results. Figure 4.1 plots the average of buyer and seller profit for all agreements (sample size equals 942 transactions) reached in each five-minute segment of the market (aggregated across six runs of the market simulation). The diagonal line in this figure shows the joint profits to the two parties if they make simple compromises (e.g., E-E-E). The curved line shows the *pareto* efficient frontier available to the negotiators. Negotiators start the simulation with agreements predicated on the mythical fixed-pie bias (i.e., the transactions approach the distributive point of $4,000 each). As the negotiators gain experience, the myth fades and integrative behavior increases (i.e., the transactions approach the fully integrative point of $5,200 each).

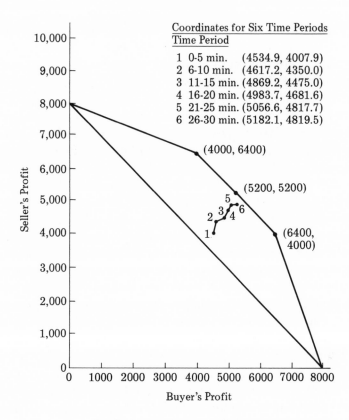

Figure 4.1 Average Profit for Buyers and Sellers of Transactions Completed in Each Segment of the Market (aggregated across markets)

We infer from these results that inefficient agreements result from the parties initially assuming a fixed-pie. While the data is certainly consistent with this explanation, no direct measure of negotiator perceptions was obtained in these experiments. In a clever set of experiments, Thompson (1990a, 1990b; Thompson & Hastie, 1990) assessed each negotiator's perceptions of the other party's payoffs in an integrative bargaining task. She had negotiators estimate the payoffs of the other party for a series of issues. Her results largely confirm our speculation above: Negotiators assumed that their opponent's preferences were diametrically opposed to their own. They entered negotiations assuming that the other's preferences were the reverse of their own, and they assumed that the other party's relative weighting for each issue was the same as their own.

Thompson (1990a) also examined the learning that takes place in a

negotiation about the relative structure of the opponent's preferences. She had subjects assess the other party's payoffs before the
negotiation, after five minutes of negotiation, and after completing
the negotiation. Her results document that (1) many subjects continue to maintain a mythical fixed-pie throughout a negotiation, (2)
most of the learning of the other party's true preferences occurs
within the first five minutes of the negotiation, and (3) the ability to
unravel the mythical fixed-pie leads to better individual and joint
outcomes.

As well, Thompson (1990a) investigated another, similar bias to
the fixed-pie bias—that of the *incompatibility bias*. While the nature
of the fixed-pie bias is that negotiators assume that the structure of
the negotiation is such that the choice is to win or lose, Thompson
suggests that negotiators make a second assumption that they have
no common interests. Even when the two sides want the same
outcome, negotiators often settle for a different outcome because
they assume that they must compromise to get agreement. That is,
they assume that their interests are incompatible with the other
side's interests. While the fixed-pie bias prevents parties from finding effective trades across issues, the incompatibility bias prevents
negotiators from identifying issues for which no real conflict exists.

When the parties had two compatible issues out of eight,
Thompson (1990a) found that 39 percent of all dyads failed to agree
on the mutually preferred outcome for at least one of the two
compatible issues. In a related study in which the parties had one
compatible issue out of five, Thompson (1990b) found that 25 percent of the dyads failed to reach an optimal agreement on that
compatible issue. She concludes that even when negotiators reach
an optimal agreement on compatible issues, they do not realize that
the other party has also benefitted from the arrangement. Simply,
negotiators often erroneously believe that they are coming out ahead
of the other party. This misperception may provide negotiators with
inflated confidence in their persuasive and bargaining abilities,
which can lead parties to engage in more contentious behavior
(Thompson, 1990a; Neale & Bazerman, 1985b).

Individuals often fail to solve problems because of the assumptions
they place on the problem. They miss the optimal solution for a
problem, not because they choose a different alternative, but because they never imagine that the optimal choice exists. The mythical fixed-pie and incompatability biases clearly fall into this category.
People are not opposed to trade-offs or common interests. Rather,

they make assumptions about the structure of the other party's interests that inhibits the search for such trade-offs or commonalities. A fundamental task in training negotiators lies in identifying and eliminating these false assumptions and institutionalizing the creative process of integrative bargaining.

Considering the assumption of the fixed-pie, the tasks used in much of the experimentation may overemphasize the importance of trade-offs. That is, finding the trade-offs may be more important in these tasks—as a percent of the total benefit available in the negotiation—than in most real world negotiations. However, this would also imply that the trade-offs in these laboratory studies will be easier to find than trade-offs in the real world. Thus, the importance of trade-offs may be overdramatized in these studies, but the evidence about the difficulty of finding the trade-offs is likely to be conservative.

We offer one final comment to document the pervasiveness of the fixed-pie assumption in our culture. In the labor-relations context, many experienced negotiators recommend that it is important to "start with the easy issues first." This is an institutionalized part of the folklore of the labor-management negotiation process. Unfortunately, it may be bad advice. While it may make the initial stages of the negotiation easier, it may increase the likelihood of impasse. It delays the true conflict, while eliminating possible trade-offs that may create joint gain for the parties. Once resolved, an issue is rarely resurrected to create a trade-off with a later issue. Such poor advice survives because people can recall confirmatory evidence of how the strategy changed the atmosphere of past negotiations. The barrier to trade-offs that the strategy creates is never seen, because it lies outside the scope of the negotiation as defined by the "easy-issues-first" negotiators.

The Nonrational Escalation of Conflict

Consider the following situation described in Bazerman (1990):

It is 1981. PATCO (Professional Air Traffic Controllers Organization) decides to strike to obtain a set of concessions from the U.S. government. The union is willing to "invest" in a temporary loss of pay during the strike to obtain concessions. No government concessions result or appear to be forthcoming. PATCO is faced with the option of backing off

and returning to work under the former conditions or increasing its commitment to the strike to try to force the
concessions it is seeking.

One explanation of what happened to PATCO is that it committed
resources to a course of action, then faced a decision of whether to
escalate commitment or back out of the conflict. The escalation
literature predicts that PATCO was far more likely to persist in its
course of action than a rational analysis would have dictated—which,
in fact, it did.

Escalation can occur without competition. For example, Staw
(1976, 1981) has documented that individuals tend to nonrationally
escalate commitment to previous decisions. This stream of research
has shown that individuals who make an initial decision are likely
to make further decisions in a biased way to justify their earlier
decisions (Staw & Ross, 1978; Teger, 1980; Bazerman, Beekun, &
Schoorman, 1982; Bazerman, Guiliano, & Appelman, 1984;
Brockner & Rubin, 1985; Schoorman, 1988). Typically, this research
compares the decisions of an individual (or group) who was responsible for an initial decision to a control group that inherits the latter
decision from a previous decision maker. Both groups are then asked
to make a subsequent decision to commit further resources to the
previously selected course of action. A consistent result is that
individuals who made the initial decision commit significantly more
resources to the previously chosen action than individuals who did
not make the initial decision. A consequence of this phenomenon is
that resources end up being committed in a way that justifies previous actions, whether or not the rationale for those initial commitments is still valid.

While escalation is certainly relevant outside the competitive
context, competition creates a context that is ideal for encouraging
negotiators to nonrationally escalate commitment to previous actions. Consider the following situation: You are in a room with thirty
other individuals and the person at the front of the room takes out a
$20 bill from his/her pocket and announces the following:

> "I am about to auction off this $20 bill. You are free to partici-
> pate or just watch the bidding of others. People will be in-
> vited to call out bids in multiples of $1 until no further
> bidding occurs; at which point the highest bidder will pay the
> amount bid and win the $20. The only feature that distin-

guishes this auction from traditional auctions is a rule that the second highest bidder must also pay the amount he/she bid, although he/she will obviously not win the $20. For example, if Bill bid $3 and Jane bid $4, and bidding stopped, I would pay Jane $16 ($20–$4) and Bill, the second highest bidder, would pay me $3."

Would you be willing to bid $2 to start the auction?

This auction has been run with undergraduate students, graduate students, and executives. The pattern is always the same. The bidding starts out fast and furious until the bidding reaches the $10–to–$17 range. At this point, everyone except the two highest bidders drops out of the auction. The two bidders then begin to feel the trap. One bidder has bid $16 and the other $17. The $16 bidder must either bid $18 or suffer a $16 loss. The uncertain option of bidding further (a choice that might produce a gain if the other bidder quits) seems more attractive than the current sure loss, so he/she bids $18. This continues until the bids are $19 and $20. Surprisingly, the decision to bid $21 is very similar to all previous decisions—you can accept a $19 loss or continue and reduce your loss if the other person quits. Of course, the rest of the group roars with laughter when the bidding goes over $20—which it virtually always does. Obviously, the bidders are acting irrationally. But where did the irrational bids begin?

The dollar-auction paradigm was first introduced by Shubik (1971), an economist and game theorist. (We have adjusted the auction from $1 to $20 to account for inflation and to earn a little extra cash.) Teger (1980) has used the paradigm extensively for the experimental investigation of why individuals escalate commitment to previously selected actions. He argues that subjects naively enter the auction expecting the bidding not to exceed $1—"After all, who would bid more than one dollar for one dollar?" The potential gain, coupled with the possibility of winning the auction, are enough reason to enter the auction. Once the subject is in the auction, it takes only a little bit of extra money to stay in the auction rather than accept a sure loss. This reasoning, along with a strong need to justify why the bidder entered the auction to begin with, are enough to keep most bidders bidding for an extended period of time.

Careful examination of the dollar-auction game shows that choosing to bid at all creates the problem. It is true that one more bid may get the other person to quit. However, if both bidders feel this way, the result can be catastrophic. Yet, without knowing the expected bidding patterns of the opponent, we cannot conclude that bidding is clearly wrong. Successful decision makers must learn to identify traps, and the key to the problem lies in identifying the auction as a trap and never making even a very small bid.

Similar traps may exist in business, war, and other facets of our lives. Teger (1980) concludes that the Vietnam War was a clear application of the dollar-auction paradigm. Two gasoline stations staging a price war can also create the dollar-auction trap. Both parties may suffer tremendous costs in an effort to win the price war, and as with the dollar auction, neither side is likely to actually win the competition.

A highly visible application of escalation can be seen in the airline industry. Perhaps the most innovative marketing program in the history of the airlines was American Airlines' introduction of the Frequent Flyer program in 1981. The idea was that business flyers (or anyone else who flew frequently) could earn miles for the flights that they took and use these miles for travel awards. The logic was to provide an incentive to the traveler to be loyal to American Airlines. Soon every airline in the industry had a program. Over the years, individual airlines increased their commitments by offering double miles to their most frequent passengers, miles for hotel stays and car rentals, low-mileage awards for less frequent, frequent fliers, etc. The other airlines always followed. By 1987, analysts estimated that the airlines owed their passengers between $1.5 billion and $3 billion in free trips.

Delta was faced with an additional problem—United and American were picking up market share from these programs because passengers had an incentive to be a member of a program with an airline that flew to the largest number of cities. Since United and American fit this profile, they were getting the largest number of frequent flyers. To solve the problem, on December 15, 1987, Delta announced that all passengers who charged their tickets to American Express would get *triple* miles for all of 1988. Presumably, passengers would switch their loyalty for triple miles. What happened instead was that all major airlines announced triple miles, and a number of other benefits were added that kept dramatically escalating a bad situation throughout the remainder of 1988. Airline debt went up geometrically from the 1987 debt estimates.

Interestingly, a parallel escalatory war had been solved in a visible episode just prior to the airline debacle. In the summer of 1986, all three U.S. auto companies were engaged in an escalatory war of rebate programs that was eliminating profits. They added the option of discount financing as an alternative to a rebate. The industry was losing money as rebate volume increased. Each company faced the problem of how to stop its program without losing market share to the other two firms.

Lee Iacocca, the CEO of Chrysler, came up with a solution. He communicated to the press that all the companies had programs scheduled to expire in the near future and that he had no plans of continuing with the program. However, if either of the other two announced a continuation of their plans, he would be forced to meet or beat any promotion that was offered. He was announcing an opportunity to end the war if the others cooperated, but threatened retaliation if the others continued. The other two car companies got the message, and the rebate/financing program stopped for a significant period of time. We will never know what would have happened if United or American had made the announcement that Iacocca made before Delta announced triple miles.

Bazerman (1990) argues that nonrational escalation occurs for several reasons. First, once negotiators make an initial commitment to a course of action, they are more likely to notice information that supports their initial evaluation. Second, a negotiator's judgment of any new information will be biased to interpret it in a way that justifies the existing position. Third, negotiators often make subsequent decisions to justify earlier decisions to themselves and others. This tendency is supported by the need for cognitive balance (Festinger, 1957), which requires that an individual cannot maintain two opposing beliefs. Finally, the competitive context adds to the likelihood of escalation. Unilaterally giving up or even reducing demands seems like defeat, while escalating commitment leaves the future uncertain. The framing effect tells us that an uncertain future is typically more desirable than a certain loss of similar value. Thus, at the margin, most of us will escalate commitment to the conflict, rather than accepting the sure loss of retreating. Unfortunately, if both sides have this view, an escalatory war can be created.

It is easy to see the how the negotiation process exacerbates the nonrational escalation of commitment. This process commonly leads both sides to make extreme initial demands. The escalation literature predicts that if negotiators become committed to these initial public statements, they will nonrationally adopt a nonconcessionary stance. To the extent that a negotiator believes that he or she "has too much invested to quit," inappropriate stubbornness is the likely behavior. Further, if both sides incur losses as a result of a lack of agreement (e.g., a strike), their commitment to their positions is likely to increase, and their willingness to change to a different course of action (i.e., compromise) is likely to decrease. For example, one interpretation of the decision of the "hard-liners" in China to fire on the students in the spring of 1989 rests on nonrational escalation of commitment. Virtually all analysts agree that this decision was irrational from any political viewpoint. However, the hard-liners had made public commitments to stop the student protests. When nothing else worked, they escalated their commitment, killed many people, and weakened their political standing within the international community.

An important result for the negotiation process from the escalation literature is that public announcement increases the tendency to escalate nonrationally (Staw, 1981). Once the general public (or one's constituency) is aware of the commitment, the decision maker is far less likely to retreat from his/her previously announced position. This suggests that escalation can be reduced if negotiators and third parties avoid the formation of firmly set, public positions. Implementation of this recommendation is, however, contradictory to how negotiators typically behave when they represent constituencies (e.g., labor leaders, political leaders, representatives of management). It may be that it is in the best interest of the constituency for a negotiator to not make public commitments. However, this is likely to conflict with the constituency rewarding negotiators for showing their strength by making public commitments. Thus, what is best for the constituency is not necessarily what the constituency rewards.

Ignoring the Cognitions of Others

Consider the following problem from Samuelson and Bazerman (1985):

In the following exercise you will represent Company A (the acquirer), which is currently considering acquiring Company T (the target) by means of a tender offer. You plan to tender in cash for 100% of Company T's shares but are unsure how high a price to offer. The main complication is this: the value of Company T depends directly on the outcome of a major oil exploration project it is currently undertaking. Indeed, the

very viability of Company T depends on the exploration outcome. If the project fails, the company under current management will be worth nothing—$0/share. But if the project
succeeds, the value of the company under current management could be as high as $100/share. All share values between
$0 and $100 are considered equally likely. By all estimates,
the company will be worth considerably more in the hands of
Company A than under current management. In fact, whatever the ultimate value under current management, *the company will be worth fifty percent more under the management
of A than under Company T*. If the project fails, the company
is worth $0/share under either management. If the exploration
project generates a $50/share value under current manage-
ment, the value under Company A is $75/share. Similarly, a
$100/share value under Company T implies a $150/share value
under Company A, and so on.

The board of directors of Company A has asked you to determine the price they should offer for Company T's shares.
This offer must be made *now, before* the outcome of the drilling project is known. From all indications, Company T would
be happy to be acquired by Company A, *provided it is at a
profitable price*. Moreover, Company T wishes to avoid, at all
cost, the potential of a takeover bid by any other firm. You expect Company T to delay a decision on your bid until the results of the project are in, then accept or reject your offer
before the news of the drilling results reaches the press.

Thus, *you (Company A) will not know the results of the exploration project when submitting your price offer, but Company T will know the results when deciding whether or not to
accept your offer. In addition, Company T is expected to accept any offer by Company A that is greater than the (per
share) value of the company under current management.*

As the representative of Company A, you are deliberating
over price offers in the range of $0/share (this is tantamount to
making no offer at all) to $150/share. What price offer per
share would you tender for Company T's stock?

In this "Acquiring a Company" problem, one firm (the acquirer)
may offer to buy another (the target). However, the acquirer is
uncertain about the ultimate value of the target firm. They only
know that its value under current management is between $0 and

$100, with all values equally likely. Since the firm is expected to be worth 50 percent more under the acquirer's management than under the current ownership, it appears to make sense for a transaction to take place. While the acquirer does not know the actual value of the firm, the target knows its current worth exactly. What price should the acquirer offer for the target?

The problem is analytically quite simple (as will be demonstrated shortly), yet intuitively quite perplexing. The responses of 123 MBA students from Boston University are shown in Figure 4.2. The table shows the dominant response was between $50 and $75. How was this decision reached? One common but erroneous explanation is: On average, the firm is worth $50 to the target and $75 to the acquirer. Consequently, a transaction in this range will, on average, be profitable to both parties.

Now consider the solution. If the acquirer offers any positive value, $X, and the target accepts, the current value of the company is worth anywhere between $0 and $X. As the problem is formulated, any value in that range is equally likely. Therefore, the expected value of the offer is equal to $X/2. Since the company is worth 50 percent more to the acquirer, the acquirer's expected value is 1.5($X/2), which equals only 75 percent of the offer price. Thus, on the average, the acquirer obtains a company worth 25 percent less than the price it pays when an offer is accepted. For any value

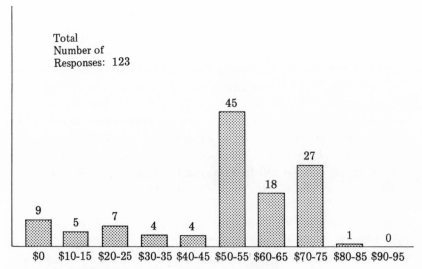

Figure 4.2 The Distribution of Acquirer Offers

of $X, the best the acquirer can do is to not make an offer ($0 per share).

The paradox of the situation is that even though the firm is worth more to the acquirer than to the target, any offer above $0 leads to a negative expected return to the acquirer. The source of this paradox lies in the high likelihood that the target will accept the acquirer's offer when the firm is least valuable to the acquirer—i.e., when it is a "lemon" (Akerlof, 1970). As a result, the "winning" bidder, on average, loses money: he or she suffers the "winner's curse."

The answer to this problem is so counterintuitive that only 9 of 123 subjects correctly offered $0 per share. Replications with masters students in management at Massachusetts Institute of Technology, have shown similar results. Finally, even subjects who were paid according to their performance exhibit the same pattern of responses (Samuelson & Bazerman, 1985; Bazerman & Carroll, 1987).

Most individuals have the analytical ability to understand the solution that the optimal offer is $0 per share. Yet without assistance, most individuals make a positive offer. Thus, individuals systematically exclude information from their decision processes that they have the ability to include. As with the fixed-pie and incompatibility biases, they are blocked from perceiving the total range of solutions to the problem. They fail to realize that the expected return is conditional on acceptance by the other party. The other party will only accept when it is in his/her best interests, which is most likely to occur when it is least desirable for the party making the offer. Subjects who make this mistake systematically are ignoring the cognitions of the other party.

A study using verbal protocols has documented the tendency to ignore the cognitions of others and has found that it largely results from individuals developing strategies to simplify competitive decisions (Carroll, Bazerman, & Maury, 1988). Rather than rationally analyzing a problem, negotiators make a number of assumptions about the opponent to reduce the problem's complexity. In this process, they ignore the contingent processing of the opponent. Carroll, Delquie, Halpern, and Bazerman (1990) have shown that training is possible to reduce this bias in negotiation. However, the amount of improvement that is possible using relatively heavy-handed training procedures is surprisingly weak.

The work discussed in this section suggests that individuals systematically fail to consider the cognitions of others in relatively simple environments. Improved performance requires that the focal negotiator adopt strategies for routinely examining these additional components. Further, to the extent that individuals have such a strong bias against considering the cognitions of others, negotiators need to incorporate the fact that the opponent may not be fully considering the cognitions of the focal negotiator either.

This tendency to ignore the cognitions of others can be seen in the escalation bias described earlier in this chapter. Why do bidders get involved in Shubik's dollar-auction exercise? Because people see the potential for profit early in the auction and then fail to take the perspective of what the auction will look like to other bidders.

This section has proposed that poor performance on the "Acquiring a Company" problem was due to a tendency to ignore or to simplify the cognitions of opponents. However, Carroll, Bazerman, and Maury (1988) note that this problem does not have an "opponent" in the usual sense of this term. The negotiator has no opportunity to get information about the opponent, to influence the other party, to get feedback, or to have the usual interaction that accompanies a negotiation. Based on this inactivity by the opponent, Carroll et al. argue that there must be some underlying bias that accounts for our tendency to ignore the cognitions of others. As an alternative, and more general, explanation of the evidence in this section, they propose that individuals have a tendency to make simplifying and potentially biased assumptions when faced with a task that requires incorporating knowledge about future contingent events. That is, when individuals are faced with contingencies, they make simplifying assumptions to make decision making under uncertainty more manageable.

To test this underlying explanation, Carroll et al. (1988) created a version of the Acquiring a Company problem that contained no competitive "other." The "Beastie Run" created the same contingency as the "Company" problem, but the contingency was created by nature. Specifically, this problem required subjects to choose a net size with which to catch valuable Beasties that come in sizes ranging from 0 to 100 pounds. Beasties larger than the net will escape without cost; those that are caught can be sold at $15 per pound. Nets cost $10 per pound of capacity, and are destroyed as soon as a Beastie is caught.

The Beastie problem was presented in a parallel form to the Acquiring a Company problem. Equivalent low rates of correct answers were obtained on both problems. Thus, the tendency to ignore contingencies is a viable, and more basic, explanation of our tendency to ignore the cognitions of others.

Reactive Devaluation

Reactive devaluation is the tendency for disputants to devalue each other's concessions simply because it is the adversary who offered the concession (Oskamp, 1965; Stillenger, Epelbaum, Keltner, & Ross, 1990). While Stillenger et al. note that there are a number of rational explanations for reactive devaluation, it is also assumed that devaluation occurs to a degree beyond which can be explained by rational models. In their example of reactive devaluation, 137 individuals were divided into two groups and asked how favorable an arms reduction proposal was to the United States and to the U.S.S.R. In one group, the interviewer correctly ascribed the proposal to Mr. Gorbachev. In the other group, the interviewer implied that the then President Ronald Reagan had made the proposal. Fifty-six percent of those who believed the proposal originated with Gorbachev thought that the provisions dramatically favored the Russians. Only a small percentage (16 percent) felt that it favored the United States. The other 28 percent thought that it favored both sides equally. When they believed that President Reagan had initiated the proposal, 45 percent thought that it benefitted both sides equally, 27 percent thought that the proposal favored the U.S.S.R, and 27 percent thought that the proposal favored the United States. Thus, terms that appear mutually beneficial when advanced by one's own side may seem disadvantageous when proposed by the other party, even if the terms of the proposal are equal.

A number of explanations have been offered as the basis for reactive devaluation. First, the concessions of an opponent in an adversarial negotiation can provide signals. If an adversary is willing to offer a concession, it conveys information about the value the adversary attaches to that issue. One could logically deduce that the opponent places less value on what is being given up than on what can be gained in exchange.

A second explanation is that the specific concession increases the negotiator's aspirations (Siegel & Fouraker, 1960). Third, a concession may be discounted for psychological consistency based on balance theory (Heider, 1958; Festinger, 1957). That is, the relevant concession is likely to be evaluated negatively because it was promulgated by a negative source—the opponent. Finally, the particular concession offered by an adversary may be tainted by the entire interaction. That is, once a concession is offered, it becomes highly salient and representative of the entire negotiation process—a process that is typically assumed to be adversarial, reflective of incompatible interests, and experienced as potentially disadvantageous to the individual (Thompson, 1990b; Bazerman, Magliozzi, & Neale, 1985). Further, interpretations about the basis for the concession, omissions, or ambiguities are likely to be construed malevolently (Stillenger et al., 1990).

An additional demonstration was conducted by Stillenger and her colleagues to separate out the value of a concession from the opponent making the concession. They had found that 61 percent of subjects rated a divestiture compromise plan proposed by Stanford University (as a mechanism to divest itself of holdings in several firms doing business in South Africa) as "less favorable" (after Stanford had proposed it) than they rated the same plan (as an option) three weeks earlier. Only 24 percent of the subjects rated it as more positive and the remaining 15 percent showed no evidence of change. In contrast, none of the other two plans being evaluated (and not proposed by Stanford) showed such a decline in perceived favorableness. As such, Stillenger et al. conclude that it was the specific compromise plan offered by Stanford, and not compromise plans in general, that demonstrated this decline in favorability.

Another explanation is possible if we believe that individuals go through less complex reasoning than suggested above. Reactive devaluation may be simply an effect that results from the mythical fixed-pie—what is good for them is bad for us. Stillenger et al. offer a fascinating quote in support of reactive devaluation that reflects the mythical fixed-pie. Congressional Representative Floyd Spence, a Republican from South Carolina, said in discussing the proposed SALT treaty: "I have had a philosophy for some time in regard to SALT, and it goes like this: the Russians will not accept a SALT treaty that is not in their best interest, and it seems to me that if it is their best interests, it can't be in our best interest." This quote suggests that a negotiator's preferences are not developed in isolation. Rather, the social nature of the interaction is critical to determine what is desirable or, even, acceptable. This particular argument will be developed and extended in detail in the last chapter.

As a final note, it is likely that reactive devaluation is specifically relevant to negotiations with people that we see as "the opposition." Loewenstein, Thompson, and Bazerman (1989) found that individuals, who perceive themselves to be in negative bargaining relationships, assign positive utility to personal outcomes which result in the other side receiving comparatively less. This is true whether the focal negotiator's outcomes are positive or negative. However, no such effect existed in positive bargaining relationships. These findings suggest that reactive devaluation is a direct reaction to the other side ("the enemy") getting something that it stated it wanted. This explanation is consistent with Stillenger et al.'s finding that their U.S.S.R.–U.S. effect was stronger for "hawks" than for "doves."

Stillenger et al. argue that it is usually in the best interest of a negotiator to elicit preferences from the other side before making an offer to reduce reactive devaluation. If the other party is on record concerning its payoffs, it is less likely to revise when receiving a concession. This is consistent with the asymmetric prescriptive/descriptive framework outlined in Chapter 2 that counsels the negotiator to analyze the negotiation situation before initiating talks.

While the evidence on reactive devaluation is intriguing, it would be ideal to be able to separate the rational component of reactive devaluation from the biased component. As we have noted, the offer from the other side may, in fact, provide information concerning its needs, its priorities, and opportunities for future concessions (Stillenger et al., 1990). Thus, it is not clear that the evidence provided documents nonrational behavior. A clearer test of the nonrationality of reactive devaluation would show that a change in preference occurs in the focal negotiator's priorities before and after the offer is made. However, the after-measure would have to be collected on a separate task to insure that the measure was independent of the ongoing negotiation. This might be possible by conducting two different negotiations with two opponents on the same negotiation task. Thus, the parties' preferences are obtained before the negotiation. One could assess how a party's preferences change between the two tasks as a result of concessions in the first negotiation. This evidence would separate the nonrational component of reactive devaluation from rational incorporation of information that occurs as a result of the concessions received from an opponent.

INTEGRATING OUR DESCRIPTIVE
AND PRESCRIPTIVE KNOWLEDGE
OF NEGOTIATOR DECISION MAKING

Chapters 3 and 4 have identified a large list of systematic deviations from rationality that affect negotiator judgment. Perhaps the best way to approach a negotiation is to apply the prescriptive framework outlined in the second chapter, while being cognizant of eliminating the behavioral imperfections documented in Chapters 3 and 4. The contribution of this combined framework is to provide negotiators with advice about the aspect of negotiation that they most control—their cognitions and resulting decisions. While description for the sake of description is a worthy scientific objective, the usefulness of such research is another important attribute of an optimal, descriptive model of negotiation. We argued in the first chapter that much of the descriptive research in negotiation prior to 1980 lacked this quality. While earlier descriptive research attempted to provide insight to negotiators about their behaviors, it did so without being able to document how they would perform better with some alternative behavior. The descriptions lacked any clear directions for self-improvement. The negotiator did not know whether changing a particular tactic would actually lead to improved performance.

The benchmark of rationality has been of unique value to the growth and expansion of the behavioral decision area (Kahneman, Slovic, & Tversky, 1982). The literature's focus on how decisions deviate from rationality has enabled researchers to identify the specific deficiencies that weaken an individual's decision-making abilities and to recommend solutions. Such benefits are only beginning to accrue to descriptive models of negotiation. It is easy to see that these descriptions of how negotiators actually behave could not exist without prescriptive models for defining rationality as the goal toward which all negotiators should aspire.

Consistent with our arguments in the first chapter, we are not proposing that a complete, alternative theory to the rational model must be developed. Rather, researchers should start by addressing what a rational model might suggest about future behaviors and amending those predictions to reflect more accurately actual negotiator behaviors. This and future knowledge can provide the basis for a "limitation audit" of how judgment deviates from rationality using the list of cognitive biases in the last two chapters.

These deviations from rationality can be anticipated in the focal negotiator's and the opponent's decision making. Focal negotiators can be taught to predict the other party's behavior more accurately. In addition, they can be alerted to their own tendencies toward "naive" rationality—e.g., the incorrect "train of thought" that many people take as rational in trying to solve the Acquiring a Company problem.

A current weakness of prescriptive research is the assumption that the target can realistically enact rational advice. An example of this problem occurs in accounting, where instructors teach students that ignoring sunk costs is a rational manner to analyze problems. This advice lasts until the next exam and is then forgotten. Managers trained in accounting routinely make the sunk-cost mistake and escalate commitment to previous courses of action because they have too much invested to quit.

Unfortunately, research has shown that cognitive biases are very difficult to overcome, even in trained professionals (Fischhoff, 1982; Carroll et al., 1990). However, many years ago, Lewin (1947) suggested that telling people that changes must be made is not sufficient to alter behavior. The prior behaviors are usually too well ingrained in a person's behavioral repertoire. Rather, added steps are needed. Specifically, Lewin's "unfreezing-change-refreezing" model suggests that the target must first be unfrozen from past behaviors— they must see something wrong with their current thought processes. Once this is accomplished the model for change can be introduced. Only then can the new behaviors become practiced and reinforced. The important aspect of this model for our discussion is that behavioral research must be used to show students their current limitations, before we can expect them to adopt more rational models.

5

Negotiator Experience and Expertise*

In the previous chapters, the emphasis has been on considering the impact of cognitive biases on negotiator decision making. What has been ignored in these discussions is the role that the cognitive biases or heuristics play not only in the actual decision making of the expert but also in the development of his or her expertise. That is, what roles do cognitive biases play (1) in the ability of experts to make "good" decisions and (2) in decision makers' ability to understand and incorporate feedback to facilitate their making good decisions?

Much of the research on judgmental biases identified in earlier chapters relied upon student subjects in laboratory settings negotiating or making decisions in task domains with which they were unfamiliar. Further, these subjects were not rewarded for accurate performance nor did they typically incur costs for making poor decisions. Hogarth (1981) has suggested that dismissing the research on cognitive heuristics because of its laboratory origins would be naive. However, he also cautions that decision-making researchers have not paid sufficient attention to the "continuous, adaptive nature of the judgmental processes used to cope with a complex, changing environment" (p. 189).

Experts or experienced decision makers responsible for important decisions in their area of expertise or experience may not be accurately characterized by this stream of research (i.e., they may not be subject to the systematic errors of cognitive biases). Clearly, it may be the case that susceptibility to judgmental biases disappears as

*Many of the ideas in this chapter were developed in collaboration with Gregory B. Northcraft.

experience accumulates and familiarity with the task domain increases. This raises an important question. Is obtaining experience and expertise a key to more effective decision making?

Researchers have tended to focus on the discrete process of choice and prediction, isolated from the correcting potential of environmental feedback. In the real world, negotiators make decisions that have ongoing consequences. They typically are expected to apply learning from past decision making to improve future decision making. Thus, trial-and-error learning from experience should reduce the frequency of inappropriate use of heuristics. These concerns were echoed in Berkley and Humphreys' (1982) claim that the importance of decision-bias demonstrations in the laboratory is premised on the assumption that the subjects have accepted the small (and relatively stimulus-impoverished) world of the laboratory as a naturalized reflection of the real world in which they make decisions. Experience may eliminate or attenuate decision bias as performance feedback corrects inappropriate uses of information and decision heuristics (Garb, 1989).

Learning from Experience—A Question of Feedback

Garb and others suggest that feedback is critical to learning from experience. Without feedback, there is little opportunity or reason for decision makers to adjust their behavior (Landy & Farr, 1982). Thus, individuals will correct their future decisions only if they can learn from the feedback generated from past decisions. Laboratory experiments, the setting for most of the studies of negotiation, are often criticized for not accurately representing actual negotiations, for they do not provide subjects with naturally occurring and useful feedback.

However, there are a myriad of real world situations in which feedback is either biased or ambiguous. Consider, for example, a recent review of fifty-five studies by Garb that concluded that the relationship between experience and the validity of clinical ratings was disappointingly low. He reports that experienced clinicians were never more accurate than less experienced clinicians. Further, experienced clinicians almost never made more valid judgments than graduate students.

The impact of feedback on learning varies with its specificity (Earley, 1988), credibility (Northcraft & Earley, 1989), diagnosticity (Garb, 1989), accuracy (Cummings, Schwab & Rosen, 1971) and timeliness (Einhorn, 1980). If feedback is ambiguous, nondiagnostic, misleading or poorly managed, it may not be corrective and can even reinforce inappropriate behavior (Einhorn & Hogarth, 1978). Psychological researchers have identified four barriers that prevent decision makers from learning from experience: (1) cognitive biases and inadequate cognitive processing, considered in chapters three and four; (2) poor information search techniques; (3) the inaccurate interpretation of information and feedback; and (4) the use of unaided memory for coding, storing, and retrieving information (Einhorn, 1980; Einhorn & Hogarth, 1978).

Search. As suggested in Chapter 4, decision makers often become psychologically invested in the choices they make (Staw, 1976). This investment can influence their receptivity to feedback about the appropriateness of a previous choice. Psychological investment may lead a decision maker to see ambiguous feedback about a prior decision in a more positive light than others might (Hastorf & Cantril, 1954). Research suggests that the distortion of feedback by psychological investment is more a function of subliminal direction of attention and consequent distortion of evidence than inaccurate perception (Lord, Ross, & Lepper, 1979).

Interpretation. Even if decision makers correctly perceive the nature of the feedback emanating from a previous decision, such disconfirming or negative feedback can serve a corrective function only when it correctly identifies the causes. Whether negative feedback dictates a change in strategy is typically dependent upon the source of the feedback. If the decision maker's self-esteem is involved in the outcome of the decision, he or she may find positive interpretations of ambiguous information more compelling or easier to believe. He or she may translate the potentially negative feedback into a more positive causal schema that downplays the negative and enhances the positive features of the decision. Consider, for example, the often-cited inability of faculty to hear negative feedback in contract renewal or tenure review process. Most faculty who are denied tenure, at least report being surprised by the decision, regardless of the amount and type of negative feedback previously conveyed and documented.

Memory. Even if adequately diagnostic feedback is collected and correctly construed, that feedback still must be stored and later retrieved for subsequent inclusion into a decision-making process. As discussed in Chapter 4, memory storage and retrieval are influenced by many irrelevant factors—not the least of which are commitments, prior decisions, or expectations (O'Reilly, Northcraft, & Sabers, 1987).

In addition to these three psychological mechanisms, there are also practical constraints. Along these lines, Tversky and Kahneman (1986) have argued that basic judgmental biases are unlikely to be corrected in the real world. Responsive learning requires accurate and immediate feedback, which is rarely available, because:

> (i) outcomes are commonly delayed and not easily attributable to a particular action; (ii) variability in the environment degrades the reliability of feedback; (iii) there is often no information about what the outcome would have been if another decision had been taken; and (iv) most important decisions are unique and therefore provide little opportunity for learning (see Einhorn and Hogarth, 1978). . . . Any claim that a particular error will be eliminated by experience must be supported by demonstrating that the conditions for effective learning are satisfied. (pp. 274–275)

Einhorn and Hogarth (1978) suggest that for many tasks, decision makers have great difficulty determining what types of feedback are necessary to evaluate the accuracy of their decisions. In addition, the selection of one alternative or the implementation of one set of choices often functionally precludes the decision maker from knowing the outcomes of other alternatives or choices. The results of the chosen course of action are obviously less diagnostic if there are no comparisons that can be made to the unchosen alternative outcomes.

In an examination of learning to avoid the winner's curse in the "Acquiring a Company" problem described in Chapter 4, Ball, Bazerman, and Carroll (in press) used a repeated trial version of the Acquiring a Company scenario to test the ability of individuals to learn to incorporate the decisions of others into their own decision making. Relative to the limitations outlined by Tversky and Kahneman above, this study presented the ideal conditions for learning. Subjects were playing for real money; they played twenty times; full feedback on the results of their offer was provided immediately after each trial based on a random determination of the value of the firm; and subjects could observe changes in their asset balance (that virtually always went down). The only limitation that was not eliminated, namely variability of the environment, is part of the winner's curse phenomenon. Thus, Ball et al. addressed whether the ability to consider the cognitions of the other party in a bilateral–negotiation problem can be learned in a highly favorable environment.

Remembering that $0 is the correct answer and that $50–$75 is the answer typically obtained when decision makers ignore the cognitions of others, examine the mean bids across the twenty trials in Figure 5.1. There is no obvious trend toward learning the correct response across the twenty trials. In fact, only five of seventy-two

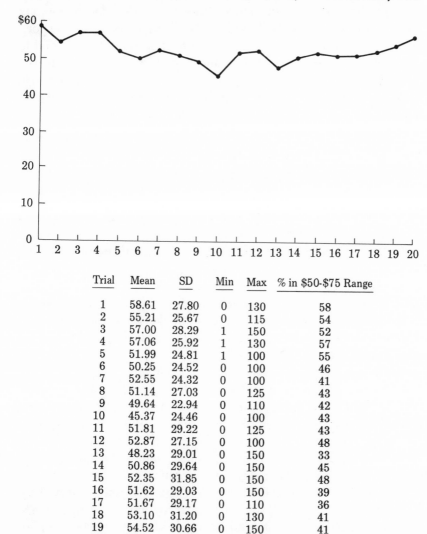

Trial	Mean	SD	Min	Max	% in $50-$75 Range
1	58.61	27.80	0	130	58
2	55.21	25.67	0	115	54
3	57.00	28.29	1	150	52
4	57.06	25.92	1	130	57
5	51.99	24.81	1	100	55
6	50.25	24.52	0	100	46
7	52.55	24.32	0	100	41
8	51.14	27.03	0	125	43
9	49.64	22.94	0	110	42
10	45.37	24.46	0	100	43
11	51.81	29.22	0	125	43
12	52.87	27.15	0	100	48
13	48.23	29.01	0	150	33
14	50.86	29.64	0	150	45
15	52.35	31.85	0	150	48
16	51.62	29.03	0	150	39
17	51.67	29.17	0	110	36
18	53.10	31.20	0	130	41
19	54.52	30.66	0	150	41
20	56.99	33.83	0	150	43

Figure 5.1 Mean Bids Across Trials for Subjects*

*Ball, Bazerman, and Carroll (1990).

subjects from a leading MBA program learned. Thus, the general conclusion from this study is that biases such as ignoring the cognitions of the competitive "other" are not fully eliminated simply by experience or even diagnostic feedback.

This and other evidence paints a very pessimistic picture of the idea that experience will, in fact, eliminate decision biases (Fischhoff, 1982; Alpert & Raiffa, 1982; Thompson, 1990a; 1990b). Thus, there is need to investigate alternative ideas for developing more rational decision-making skills. Rather than relying on experience as a sufficient teacher, perhaps attention should be turned to what other components of decision making might ameliorate the impact of judgmental biases. In the following sections, we will specifically consider how expertise influences susceptibility to cognitive biases.

Expertise—The Importance of a Strategic Conceptualization

Expertise implies so extensive a background and training in an area that both the trial-and-error and the hypothesis-testing phases of learning are complete or significantly reduced in new circumstances. A variety of definitions have been offered. Boulding (1958) suggests that expertise implies skill (i.e., the ability to produce good outcomes consistently) in a specific task or domain of tasks. Einhorn (1974) suggests that expertise is a consensual process based upon a core of knowledge with which experts should (1) cluster variables in similar ways, (2) have high inter-expert reliability, and (3) combine and weight information similarly.

Both views, though important, are incomplete. Einhorn's definition ignores the importance of being able to produce good outcomes or make good decisions. Boulding's criterion, on the other hand, focuses almost entirely on outcome quality. While trial-and-error learning will reinforce effective behaviors, those behaviors may be effective only in the limited circumstances under which the particular trial-and-error environment was encountered.

As Fiske (1961) realized, a hallmark of expertise is the ability of the expert to adjust his or her skills to be adaptive and successful even in the face of new environmental demands. Thus, expertise implies considerably more than having situationally specific skills. Experts demonstrate better performance and implement more adaptive strategies because they possess an understanding of why particular task strategies might be effective, based upon a better and more complete, and perhaps deeper and more elemental cognitive representation of the task domain (Chi, Feltovich, & Glasser, 1981; Weisser & Shertz, 1983). As such, expertise requires the capacity to generalize or transfer skills beyond a specific situation to others in the task domain. Expertise means having strategies that are sufficiently abstract or general to transfer across settings within the task domain.

The transferability of skill within a task domain, in turn, implies a causal understanding of the domain well beyond simply knowing which behaviors are effective in a particular situation. It implies knowing *why* effective behaviors are effective. This is consistent with Einhorn's (1974) comment on experts' consensual task understanding, implying that experts have internalized a common causal representation of the task. Thus, the foundation of expertise is more than having an effective strategy. The expert must possess an effective *strategic conceptualization* of the problem that explains why and when a particular strategy will be effective (Neale & Northcraft, 1990a).

A strategic conceptualization differs from other cognitive representations of tasks in terms of completeness. It includes both scripts and schemas. Scripts are well-learned behavior patterns that represent typical reactions to sets of environmental stimuli under very specific circumstances. Conceptual schemas (Taylor & Crocker, 1981) identify important features of objects or situations that may include information about how these features interrelate. For instance, a schema for negotiation might include information about bids, counteroffers, and cues about when bids and counteroffers are appropriate. Schemas also might include information about which features to monitor for feedback. Scripts, on the other hand, merely summarize "a coherent sequence of events expected by the individual, involving him either as a participant or observer" (Abelson, 1976, p. 33). Having an effective script for one situation does not imply that it will transfer effectively to another situation within the task domain. While a strategic conceptualization may certainly include script and schema information, the advantage in an effective strategic conceptualization lies in knowing why the features identified in the schema are important and why the pattern of behaviors identified by the script is effective.

Dawes and Corrigan (1974) note that expertise, particularly in prediction tasks, means knowing which environmental cues need to be monitored and which can be ignored. Even in a simple task, this is no small accomplishment. As William James has suggested, to the novice, a given task must appear as something of "a big blooming buzzing confusion" (1979, p. 32) of innumerable, potential cues.

As such, during the trial-and-error phases of strategy acquisition, the decision maker is faced with a large number of possible hypotheses to test. At this point, the function of a strategic conceptualization is to limit the universe of possibilities from which the decision maker must sample. Such constraints increase the likelihood that feedback will be sufficiently diagnostic to influence future behavior. This is consistent with the findings of Johnson et al. (1981) who suggest that experts make decisions by classifying problems into categories with which they are familiar and then applying a previously successful solution to the problem at hand. The strategic conceptualization is the perceptual set limiting which strategic hypotheses to test and dictating which environmental cues to monitor in adopting (and adapting) problem-solving strategies. The right perceptual set is what makes feedback diagnostic and what differentiates the true expert (Neale & Northcraft, 1990a). The wrong perceptual set can only interfere with a decision maker's ability to make good use of diagnostic feedback. The claim here is that negotiator expertise can lead to high-quality outcomes through one of three processes: (1) the negotiator may randomly select an effective strategy without any knowledge of what he or she has done correctly, (2) the negotiator may learn from experience a particularly effective script, but have little understanding why this particular script works in this particular situation (e.g., task-specific expertise or through ritual or superstitious behavior), or (3) the negotiator may acquire a strategic conceptualization of negotiation situations that summarizes when and why particular strategies are effective.

While the quality of outcomes of these three processes may be indistinguishable when considering a particular outcome, the differences may become obvious when the task or situation changes. The relevance of these three distinctions is enhanced in two ways—adaptability and transferability—by a consideration of the unique benefits that accrue to decision makers with well-developed strategic conceptualizations as compared to those whose claim to success is by way of experience, ritual, or luck.

Adaptability. Effective strategic conceptualizations engender adaptation. While most experienced decision makers may be effective in very specific situations, when they encounter a different context or the environment changes, experience without an effective strategic conceptualization may be quite misleading. Consider the recent history of labor-management relations in the United States. In the 1960s, there were very experienced negotiators on both sides. However, when the environment changed and the United States became less competitive, labor and management continued to use old decision-making strategies in a new, more competitive environment. This led to a disastrous period of layoffs for organized labor and declines in productivity in U.S. manufacturing. These negotiators had considerable experience, but lacked the necessary expertise to adapt their strategies to the changing global negotiating environment. While there clearly were other environmental and organizational factors that led to the decline of American industry, the rigidity of labor-management relations was certainly contributory.

The adaptability of a strategic conceptualization is illustrated in a study comparing expert and amateur negotiators (Neale & Northcraft, 1986). In this study, two samples of negotiators—one expert, the other amateur—participated in separate runs of the competitive market simulation developed by Bazerman, Magliozzi, and Neale (1985). The expert sample consisted of eighty professional corporate real estate negotiators with an average of 10.5 years of direct negotiating experience. These subjects reported spending an average of 32 percent of their typical workday in negotiations. One hundred and seventy-eight undergraduates and graduate business students composed the amateur sample.

The data indicated some striking similarities and differences among these two groups. First, experts and amateurs did not differ in their susceptibility to the framing bias. However, the performance of both experts and amateurs suggested that they did differ in their susceptibility to the fixed-pie bias described in Chapter 4. Experts were able to achieve agreements of significantly greater joint value than amateurs. While both groups became more integrative over time, the experts were able to achieve outcomes which realized more of the integrative potential of the game and use this knowledge to maximize joint gain much earlier in the market.

What this suggests is that unless the strategic conceptualization specifically includes some component directed at reducing the impact of cognitive biases, it is unlikely that experts will be immune to their effects. Second, even if there were components of the strategic conceptualization that directly addressed a bias, decision makers are still at considerable disadvantage as feedback must be both diagnostic and available to check the implementation of the strategic conceptualization.

Transferability. The second benefit of developing expertise and strategic conceptualizations rather than relying on experience, ritual, superstition, or luck concerns the transferability of expertise. If experienced decision makers are asked how they do what they do, they often report that their decision making is an art that comes from years of observation and experience. One interpretation of this is that these decision makers do not know how to convey what they do. This obviously reduces their ability to transfer their knowledge to others—a key task of management. Thus, a final drawback of experience without expertise is that it limits the ability of the decision maker to transfer knowledge efficiently to future generations.

In determining the transferability of expertise, two perspectives must be considered. First, can negotiators recognize critical variables in their decision-making process? In addition, what conditions are necessary for the transference of this expertise? Two studies begin to shed some light on these questions. Northcraft and Neale (1987) examined the ability of negotiators to identify the factors influencing their decision making. Neale, Northcraft, and Earley (1990) examined the antecedents necessary for the acquisition of a strategic conceptualization.

In the first study, Northcraft and Neale (1987) used residential real estate agents to examine the impact of the anchoring-and-adjustment bias (in the form of a listing price) on their valuation of residential real estate. Real estate agents and brokers who had been in sales for an average of eight years and completed an average of 16.2 transactions per year composed this expert sample.

Real estate agents (i.e., the experts) were provided with ten pages of information concerning a residential property currently for sale and randomly assigned to one of four conditions. The conditions were based upon the distance from the appraised value of the house of the listing price given in the ten pages of information (-11 percent, -4 percent, $+4$ percent, and $+11$ percent). After viewing the property, agents were asked to estimate (1) the appraised value of the house, (2) the price for which they would list the house, (3) the most they would pay for this house if they were a buyer, and (4) the least they would accept for the house if they were the seller. In addition, a group of students (i.e., the amateurs) were also shown the property, given exactly the same information, asked the same questions. The results of the study can be examined graphically in Figure

5.2. They suggest that both groups (amateurs and experts) were significantly influenced by the anchor of the listing price.

The analysis of the estimates indicated strong support for the experts' use of anchoring and adjustment, biasing their valuations toward the listing price provided. Interestingly, when the experts were asked to identify the factors that influenced their decisions, they denied using listing price as a consideration in their decision. However, a statistical analysis of their answers revealed that over 50 percent of the variance in their valuation responses could be accounted for by the listing price provided. Not only were the experts unaware of the impact of this critical variable in their decision, they

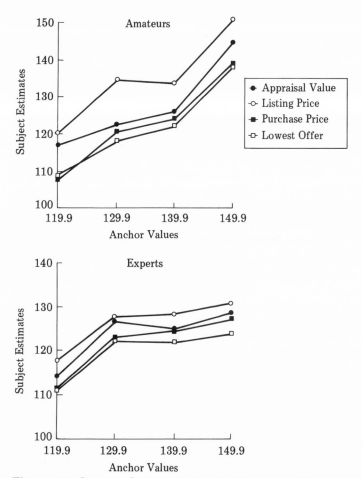

Figure 5.2 Impact of Anchoring-and-Adjustment Bias

explicitly denied even using the listing price in their calculations. While this is only one study, other researchers such as Nisbett and Wilson (1977) and Einhorn (1980) have suggested that decision makers are generally very poor in specifying how they make their decisions.

Transferring expertise may also require some form of preparation by the recipient of the strategic conceptualization. In an early test of the factors that enhance the acquisition of a strategic conceptualization of negotiation, Neale, Northcraft, and Earley (1990) suggested that having specific, assigned goals would be more effective in improving negotiator performance if decision makers had a strategic conceptualization of negotiation. They argued that negotiation was a particularly revealing arena in which to contrast the effort-enhancing and strategy-search-stimulating effects of goal-setting, because a negotiation can be viewed as either a low- or a high-complexity task.

Negotiations can be viewed as low-complexity tasks when they are considered only in their *distributive* dimension. Treating a negotiation as purely distributive may ignore the specific demands of the situation and the strategic opportunities present. Alternatively, negotiations may, in reality, be more complex when the *integrative* elements of the negotiation are considered. While Pruitt (1983) argues that integrative bargaining requires both high aspirations and a problem-solving orientation, other researchers have suggested that effective integrative bargaining also requires extensive planning, strategy development, alternative generation, and dynamic analyses (Raiffa, 1982; Neale & Northcraft, 1986).

Interestingly, whether the negotiation is viewed as a distributive or integrative task may be as much a function of negotiator perceptions as a function of the bargaining situation itself. That is, naive or amateur negotiators often assume a fixed-pie perspective on negotiations and act as if all negotiations were distributive (Walton & McKersie, 1965). Expert negotiators are more likely to see a particular negotiation as an opportunity for integrative bargaining (Bazerman, Magliozzi, & Neale, 1985; Neale & Northcraft, 1986).

The results of Neale et al. (1990) provide strong support for the notion that certain factors enhance the transferability of a strategic conceptualization of negotiation. Negotiators were more likely to benefit from the available training in negotiation when specific goals were in place. Subjects with only "do-your-best" goals who were exposed to the training were not able to maximize joint profit as were those with specific goals.

Dawes (1988) highlights the drawbacks of poor adaptability and transference of expertise that results when learning occurs from experience. He notes that Benjamin Franklin's famous quote "experience is a dear teacher" is often misinterpreted to mean "experience is the best teacher." Dawes asserts what Franklin really meant was that "experience is an expensive teacher," because he goes on to observe "yet fools will learn in no other [school]." Dawes writes:

> Learning from an experience of failure . . . is indeed "dear," and it can even be fatal. . . . Moreover, experiences of success may have negative as well as positive results when people mindlessly learn from them. . . . People who are extraordinarily successful—or lucky—in general may conclude from their "experience" that they are invulnerable and consequently court disaster by failing to monitor their behavior and its implications. (p. 101)

This view of experience and luck reiterates the relative value of expertise and the development of a strategic conceptualization. Such expertise, as defined by Neale and Northcraft (1990a), specifically avoids the danger of "mindless" learning referred to above. It does not simply rely upon the feedback of uncertain, uncontrollable, and often delayed results.

But the question still remains as to whether true expertise eliminates or ameliorates the impact of cognitive biases on important, real world decisions. There is evidence that expertise in the form of a strategic conceptualization can reduce the impact of some judgmental biases but may not have impact on other judgmental biases. In the Neale and Northcraft (1986) study, experts were susceptible to the framing bias, but did not fall prey to the fixed-pie bias. In their 1987 study, Northcraft and Neale found the real estate experts were able to elucidate a calculative strategy that should have reduced the anchoring-and-adjustment bias, but did not. The failure of the real estate agents' strategic conceptualization in the house-valuation task may be traced to the impossibility of getting appropriately diagnostic feedback from the task. Because there are no objective market values with which to compare their estimates, real estate agents may have a good sense of what they are supposed to be doing, but little idea if they are, in fact, doing it. Thus, in the absence of properly diagnostic feedback on the effectiveness of implementation, even an ostensibly well-developed strategic conceptualization, may not be sufficient.

To succeed in reducing experts' vulnerability to decision bias, the strategic conceptualization for negotiation must specifically address the causes of decision bias. This implies that the ultimate success of expertise in preventing bias via a strategic conceptualization can only be measured by the success of direct attempts to prevent such biases—attempts where the strategic conceptualization deals primarily with the prevention of decision bias.

Unfortunately, the literature on attempts to "de-bias" decision makers does not paint an optimistic picture. Using extensive training to cure biases in decision making has met with only limited success. Alpert and Raiffa (1982) used feedback linked with conceptual discussion about the potential for bias in trying to reduce overconfidence. They found that the probability for judgmental error with their subjects "fell from a shocking 41 percent to a depressing 23 percent" (p. 304).

Levenson (1975) reports an interesting finding on training clinicians and their subsequent susceptibility to overconfidence in their clinical diagnoses. He asked judges to discriminate drawings belonging to children receiving psychological treatment from those drawings belonging to normal children. Ph.D. psychologists were correct 72 percent of the time; psychology interns, 61 percent of the time; and hospital secretaries, 61 percent of the time. Thus, additional clinical training did seem to lead reliably to more appropriate judgments. While Lichtenstein and Fischhoff (1980) found appreciable improvement in judgment after ten sessions of extensive training, they noted that virtually all gains in judgment quality occurred following the first training session. Quantity of training was not the critical variable in differentiating between successful and unsuccessful de-biasing efforts. Further, Choo (1976) found almost no improvement in resistance to bias in probability assessment after training. A key to de-biasing judgments is providing a good strategic conceptualization directed toward the root cause of decision bias, plus lots of practice accompanied by diagnostic feedback. Even this does not guarantee success.

IS THERE HOPE FOR DEVELOPING RATIONAL BEHAVIOR IN NEGOTIATION?

The emphasis of this chapter has been on the development of expertise, in the form of a strategic conceptualization of the task domain, as a primary mechanism to reduce judgmental errors among negotiators. In addition to influencing the behavior of expert negotiators via their understanding of the demands of the particular problem, another important component of the negotiator's strategic conceptualization may be the way he or she decomposes and restructures a negotiation.

Raiffa (1982) identifies a series of questions a negotiator should answer prior to beginning a negotiation. These questions identify critical information to enhance a negotiator's ability to reach agreements that maximize joint profit. A similar audit could reduce the expert negotiator's susceptibility to common judgmental biases.

Including factors such as restructuring how the information will be incorporated in making the decision may make a strategic conceptualization more effective in reducing judgmental bias. Huber, Northcraft, and Neale (1990) found that changing the mode of presenting information can limit the impacts of the anchoring-and-adjustment bias. In examining the impact of simultaneous and sequential presentation of information on potential job candidates, they found that the number of available positions (one or three) anchored decision makers when they were presented twenty candidates simultaneously, but not when the twenty candidates were presented sequentially. That is, significantly more candidates were selected for interviews when there were three openings than when there was one opening, and all candidates were presented to the decision maker simultaneously. There were no differences attributable to number of openings when candidates were evaluated one at a time. Interestingly, when both groups were asked about the importance of number of openings in determining who and how many should be interviewed, they both reported that it was a relatively unimportant consideration—typically dominated by such considerations as technical ability of the applicant.

While previously cited research on training painted a rather pessimistic picture, this research on information decomposition and task restructuring may provide new ideas about the factors that must necessarily comprise an effective strategic conceptualization. Further the results of this study imply that the inputs for an effective strategic conceptualization may take many forms. In addition to restructuring the form of the task, other research has also found that decision aids, for example, have been able to offset biases of availability (Northcraft & Neale, 1986).

Recent interest in expertise has been fostered by a variety of factors from the increasing importance of good advice in times of economic scarcity to the burgeoning field of artificial intelligence. Initially, early views of the nature of expertise were based upon the belief that experts were experts because they were able to process more information than nonexperts. Termed the "power" strategy, models of expertise were developed that relied on the ability of these expert systems to process large amounts of information. More recently, however, the emphasis in this area has focused on developing systems that have "better ways to express, recognize and use diverse and particular forms of knowledge" (Minksy & Papert, 1974, p. 59).

The notion of strategic conceptualization mirrors, in many respects, this transition. It is not the expert's ability to process more information that gives him or her the edge. Rather it is the ability to know which information is important and to which cues to attend in selecting a successful course of action. Current research is only beginning to specify the structure of a strategic conceptualization. Future research on such knowledge structures is critical to our understanding of negotiator expertise and successful negotiations.

6

Group Negotiations*

The first five chapters focused primarily on two-party negotiations, consistent with the bulk of the existing literature. In contrast, much negotiation occurs in multiparty contexts. This chapter extends our perspective from the two-party case to the multiparty case. Additional parties add more complexity. A central focus of this chapter will be to examine how this added complexity affects many of the dependent variables already discussed throughout this book.

Research in group decision making typically examines how members of groups reach decisions and how decisions are influenced by factors such as group size (Komorita & Lapworth, 1982), group discussion (Moscovici & Zavalioni, 1969), and social combination rules (Davis, 1969). Researchers have examined group decisions for tasks involving logically correct answers, such as Maier's Horse Trading Problem (Maier & Solem, 1952), tasks involving factual questions, such as vocabulary knowledge (Laughlin & Johnson, 1966), human relations and value judgment tasks (Kogan & Wallach, 1967), and perceptual judgments, such as dot estimation (Thibaut et al., 1960). Researchers have compared group performance to individual decision makers or to other decision-making groups (Hare, 1976). Many of these decision tasks are characterized by *cooperative* relations among group members in which individuals are rewarded for group performance, or by *competitive* relations in which group members are dividing a fixed-sum of resources.

Despite the tendency of the group literature to focus on competitive or cooperative tasks, most group decision-making situations are neither purely cooperative nor purely competitive, but rather, in-

---

*Much of the basic research on which the ideas of this chapter are based was conducted in collaboration with Elizabeth Mannix and Leigh Thompson.

volve both goals. In past research, mixed-motive tasks typically concentrated on the consequences of parties who chose to cooperate or defect. However, little research has examined mixed-motive group negotiation as a decision-making process, in which parties reveal preferences, attempt to persuade others, adopt bargaining strategies, and exchange information with other interdependent parties. Further, little research has provided normative measures of the optimality of group decisions. Our purpose is to examine negotiation in groups as a mixed-motive decision-making process.

Group negotiation is defined as a decision-making process in which three or more persons, representing their own interests, make decisions about how to resolve conflicting preferences (Bazerman, Mannix, & Thompson, 1988). The translation of research findings from two-party to multiparty negotiation is not necessarily direct. The development of integrative solutions, for instance, may be more difficult in group situations than in dyadic situations. Two factors distinguish group negotiation from two-party negotiation: (1) increased information processing demands and (2) more complex interpersonal processes.

The dynamics of multiparty negotiations are far more complex than individual or two-party decision contexts. A simple examination of numbers makes this point very clearly. In two-party contexts, there are two sets of cognitions and one dyadic interaction to consider. In three-party contexts, the network grows to three sets of individual cognitions, three possible dyadic interactions, and one large interaction of all three players. By the time we reach five-party groups, there are five sets of individual cognitions, ten possible dyadic interactions, multiple potential three- and four-person coalitions, and a five-person interaction. As the number of parties grows, the network of cognitions and relationships becomes increasingly complex. In addition to the network complexity, other factors, such as the simultaneous and sequential interactions of the parties in their communication attempts, influence multiparty decision-making groups. These increased information processing demands can lead to systematic errors in negotiator judgment in encoding and retrieving information.

Because of the increasing number of participants and the resulting increase in information processing demands, individuals in group negotiations must implicitly or explicitly select and implement social combination rules to determine how individual preferences will be combined to yield a group decision. Negotiators have to decide what criteria will be used to select among decision alternatives. The choice of particular decision rules (e.g, unanimity, consensus, majority) influences the decision-making process, affecting the problem solving necessary for reaching integrative agreements in the multiparty context (Thompson, Mannix, & Bazerman, 1989).

The interpersonal dynamics of interaction may also be problematic. Patterns of interaction can become unbalanced, unstable, and tend toward discord as the number of players increases (Wilmot, 1980). Feedback is critical to effective group problem solving, but feedback typically decreases as the number of parties increases (Shaw, 1976). Further, interpersonal complexity increases as coalition formation becomes a strategic concern in groups of three or more members.

In this chapter, we: (1) outline a mixed-motive perspective of group decision making which builds on the framework of Bazerman, Mannix, and Thompson (1988), (2) revisit the notion of rationality in the group context and discuss how the cognitive limitations discussed earlier in the book are influenced by the group context, (3) discuss the impact of coalitions on group decision making, and (4) evaluate the structural prescriptions that exist in the group decision-making literature in terms of their ability to improve the rationality of decisions.

A MIXED-MOTIVE PERSPECTIVE
OF GROUP DECISION MAKING

The two primary tasks of a negotiator are integration (i.e., increasing the resources available to the group) and distribution (i.e., increasing one's share of those resources) (compare Lax & Sebenius, 1986; Walton & McKersie, 1965). The shift from two parties to groups changes the task's cognitive information processing demands, interpersonal dynamics, and decision rules. Consider this example:

A professional service firm is divided into three divisions (A, B, and C). Division A provides 50 percent of the firm's profit, B provides 30 percent, and C provides 20 percent. Each division head has incentives based on both firm profit and division profit. All agree that the organization can save substantially by developing a system to share information on clients. However, developing a high-quality system will require a significant investment of time and effort, i.e., approximately 2,000 work-hours. The three division heads have agreed to discuss their contributions to the system's development.

This group must negotiate a solution; all of them want what is best for the overall firm, but each division head wants the other divisions to contribute a lot to the project's development (Brett & Rognes, 1986).

Distributive Aspects of Group Negotiation

Virtually all negotiations involve the distribution of outcomes. Assume that an established client information system would save Division A about 1,600 work-hours; Division B, about 1,600 work-hours; and Division C, about 800 work-hours. Thus, the firm's total benefits exceed its costs $(1,600 + 1,600 + 800 > 2,000)$. The issue of each division's contribution to the project, however, still remains. Division heads must avoid being perceived as too greedy; they must simultaneously obtain the best agreement for their division.

Each party has a reservation point, R, which establishes a bargaining zone. A negotiator should walk away without reaching a negotiated agreement for any outcome worse than R; a negotiator should prefer to reach a negotiated agreement for any outcome at, or better than, R (Raiffa, 1982). In negotiations with three or more parties, the bargaining zone is the multidimensional space that defines the common area exceeding all the negotiators' reservation points. All agreements where Division A contributes less than 1,600 hours, Division B contributes less than 1,600 hours, and Division C contributes less than 800 hours (out of 2,000 hours) are within the three-dimensional bargaining zone. If the project required 4,500 hours of development time, then no agreement could be reached that would satisfy all three parties; no bargaining zone would exist (Bazerman, Mannix, & Thompson, 1988).

As with the two-party case, knowledge of the other negotiators' reservation points is critical information. Within large groups, the task of assessing the other parties' reservation points becomes more difficult. In attempting to cope with the increasingly large information and social demands arising from group interactions, negotiators may not have the time and resources necessary to obtain information about the parties and their constituencies. They may attempt to shortcut the information search component of the negotiation and, for example, may falsely assume that the other parties' reservation points are similar and may use their assessment of one party's reservation point as an anchor for their judgment of other parties' reservation points.

Interpersonal dynamics become more complex as the number of parties increase. Norms become increasingly important as group size increases. Norms are rules of conduct established (either implicitly or explicitly) by group members to maintain behavioral consistency (Shaw, 1976). For example, if one party makes what is perceived by the other party to be an unreasonable demand in a two-party negotiation, the other party may feel justified in directly responding to this behavior. In the multiparty case, to the extent that norms have not developed, uncertainty about appropriate behavior increases. As uncertainty increases, evaluation apprehension increases, and negotiators look to the group to determine how to behave. Social psychological research suggests that as the number of individuals in a group increases, conformity pressures also increase (Asch, 1951). Thus, individuals may be less likely to dissent and more likely to engage in behaviors designed to reach agreements (regardless of the nature or quality of those agreements) as the number of individuals increases in a negotiation context.

Norms also govern perceptions of fairness in the group. Although Fisher and Ury (1981) advocate the use of objective standards as a guideline of what is fair, there is a great diversity in definitions of what constitutes a fair resource allocation decision. Philosophers, psychologists, and others debate the standards for the distribution of scarce resources. *Equity* theory argues that outcomes should be awarded in proportion to inputs (Adams, 1963; Homans, 1961; Singer, 1978). In contrast, Rawls' (1971) egalitarian theory of justice argues that resources should be distributed *equally* except in those cases where an unequal distribution would work to everyone's advantage. A third fairness rule is that resources should be distributed according to the *needs* of the individuals (Deutsch, 1975). Finally, Kahneman, Knetsch, and Thaler (1986) and Bazerman (1985) suggest that past practice is a critical determinant of the way most people make judgments about the fairness of distribution in conflict situations.

At the very least, group negotiators should be aware of various norms of distribution. Acting in accordance with an equity norm, other group members holding an equality norm may lead to misunderstandings among members, inefficient outcomes, and harmful social relationships among parties. Negotiators must be sensitive to other parties' fairness concerns in assessing the efficacy of their proposals.

In the context described above, equality (each division contributes 666.6 hours), equity based on benefit (A contributes 800 hours, B contributes 800 hours, and C contributes 400 hours), need or ability to pay based on the divisions' profitability (A contributes 50 percent of the hours = 1,000, B contributes 30 percent = 600 hours, and C contributes 20 percent = 400 hours), and how the divisions handled a similar situation in the past are four salient and viable allocative bases for resolution of this dispute. The agreement around the appropriate norm for allocation can be critical both to how easily the dispute is resolved and to the nature of the final resolution itself. A consistent research finding in this area is that each party will select the norm that enhances its own position (e.g., Komorita & Chertkoff, 1973). Alternatively, the selection of a norm may be based upon such factors as the first party to articulate a viable norm anchoring subsequent discussions (Bettenhausen & Murnighan, 1985).

We have discussed group negotiation as if acceptance by all parties is necessary to reach a binding agreement. While this assumption is necessary in two-party negotiations, consensus in group negotiations is just one of many alternative decision rules. For example, majority rule is a common rule for making decisions in groups. The decision rule, and the ensuing coalition dynamics, are likely to have a profound effect on the complexity of the interaction and the nature of the distribution of outcomes. We will return to a discussion of the effects of decision rules later in this chapter.

Integrative Aspects of Group Negotiation

The preceding discussion limited the group negotiation to only one issue—the distribution of person-hours contributed by each division. However, as we discussed in Chapter 2, there is often the possibility of increasing the total utility to the parties through integrative negotiations. In that chapter, we also discussed Pruitt's strategies for finding integrative agreements. Three of these strategies are particularly relevant to the group negotiation context: (1) obtaining added resources, (2) trading issues, and (3) bridging (Bazerman, Mannix, & Thompson, 1988).

If the division heads realize that the benefit of the project is equal to the value of 4,000 person-hours, and that 2,000 person-hours are required to obtain this value, they can reduce the problem to a discussion of how they can distribute the 2,000 person-hours of surplus among the three divisions. However, if the parties can increase the project's benefit and/or reduce its costs, the surplus will increase the bargaining zone and they might all obtain added resources as benefit. While this last suggestion is obvious, the issue for the division heads is how to achieve such cost/benefit changes.

A second strategy involves identifying and trading issues where negotiators concede their low-priority issues for concessions on higher-priority issues. If different skills are needed to complete the system, the parties might have differential costs associated with the different skills. Thus, Division A might contribute its excess managerial talent; Division B, its excess system engineers; and Division C, its excess programmers. This would reduce each division's comparative costs. As in the two-party case, trading issues is accomplished by exploring the other negotiators' interests and preferences.

Bridging is a third relevant strategy for integrating the interests of the parties in group negotiations. Bridging involves looking outside the surface-level definition of the problem for a new approach that meets the primary interests of all parties (Pruitt, 1983). For example, the best solution may be to hire an external firm to build the system, especially if the three divisions were personnel-poor and cash-rich. If the divisions focused only on the question of dividing the 2,000 person-hours, they would miss this potential solution. Bridging requires that the parties assume that other solutions exist beyond the solutions already being considered.

Finding integrative solutions is more difficult as the number of parties increases. As a member is added to the group, he or she may bring in different interests, issues, and options that must be considered. The task of finding solutions that maximally benefit all three parties is typically more cognitively complex than the task of finding solutions that benefit two parties. In addition, the rules of group decision making can interfere with integrative negotiation by the structure they impose on the group. For example, majority rule, a distributive mechanism that does not consider differences in parties' preferences, may prevent negotiators from finding integrative agreements through logrolling or bridging mechanisms. Interpersonal aspects of behavior in groups may also hinder the integrative process. Sharing information among members is more difficult as the number of parties increases. The formation of offensive or defensive coalitions may impede the discovery of mutually beneficial solutions (Thompson, Mannix, & Bazerman, 1989; Mannix, in press).

We argue that the integrativeness of a group decision is an appropriate criterion of group effectiveness. A group decision is integrative to the extent that there exists no alternative agreement that all parties would prefer, i.e., the agreement is along the *pareto* frontier. If a better agreement does exist, the integrativeness of the actual agreement may be evaluated in comparison to this superior alternative. Both Thompson et al. and Mannix, Thompson, and Bazerman (1989) used this measure in evaluating the integrativeness of agreements in a mixed-motive group task.

More than twenty-five years ago Hoffman (1961) recognized the importance of creative problem solving and the possibility of integrative agreements in groups. There is no reason, *a priori*, to believe that group decisions escape the irrationality and subobtimality evidenced in individual decisions. In the next section, we will explicitly consider the impact of cognitive biases on the outcomes of group negotiation.

RATIONALITY AND COGNITIVE LIMITATIONS IN GROUP NEGOTIATIONS

A rational outcome of a group negotiation has at least two characteristics. First, if a (multidimensional) bargaining zone exists with full information shared among members, the group should reach an agreement. Second, the agreement will extract all the integrative potential from the issues. To the extent that groups fail to reach such agreements, are they subject to the same cognitive limitations (discussed in Chapters 3 and 4) as individuals in two-party negotiations? In this section, we develop the argument that the group context may, under most circumstances, exacerbate these deviations from rationality.

As we suggested previously, a fundamental distinction in the differences between two- and multiparty negotiation is the added cognitive complexity created by the multiparty case. This complexity should increase the parties' use of these decision-making shortcuts, resulting in an exacerbation of these biases. The large number of parties in a multiparty negotiation make it much more difficult for negotiators to develop a complete cognitive understanding of the situation (Kramer, forthcoming). Limits to negotiators' cognitive capabilities will hamper their ability to represent the negotiation problem accurately (Tetlock, 1983; Kramer, forthcoming). Because heuristics allow them to simplify their decisions much of the time, decision makers coping with information overload are more likely to rely on heuristics (and be biased as a result). One would expect these effects to occur in both the individual decision maker's judgment *in* the group, as well as in the decisions *of* the group. In the following sections, the individual and competitive biases will be considered from the perspective of multiparty negotiations.

Framing. Chapter 3 identified the negative effects that framing can have on negotiation behavior. As the number of parties increases, framing continues to affect the cognitive processing of negotiators (Kramer, 1989). In a social dilemma task dealing with a fictitious nuclear arms race, Kramer found that when decisions are framed to make initial deficits in security salient, decision makers will be more likely to increase security allocations ("arm themselves"). Conversely, when decisions are framed so that security deficits appear to be low relative to economic deficits, they will allocate fewer additional resources to security, even though the objective situation was consistent across these two conditions.

Framing can also be expected to affect the nature of the discussion of groups. Pennington and Hastie (1988) have shown that groups adopt stories that they collectively use in making decisions. It may well be the case that the story creation can have a positive or negative frame, affecting the risk propensity of the entire group.

Alternatively, groups may function to reduce the impact of biases. Neale, Bazerman, Northcraft, and Alperson (1986) studied a cooperative task and found that groups reduced the effects of framing in comparison to individuals. They argued that more members increased the possibility of multiple frames being proposed, thereby reducing the impact of the imposed frame. One factor which may determine the extent to which group decisions are influenced by frames is the cohesiveness of the group. Groups with strong, consensual norms may be more sensitive to the framing bias, as a result of using a shared definition of the situation. However, groups that lack such norms or group history (such as those in the Neale et al. [1986] study) may be less influenced by decision frames, since they are likely to adopt conflicting definitions and frames. Clearly this proposition and alternative explanations are in need of further research.

Anchoring and Adjustment. If groups tend to identify one approach to a problem, then the initial starting point can be critically important to the final resolution of group negotiations. In addition, group members have the potential to influence the outcome of a negotiation by being the first to suggest a viable norm of distribution. For example, research by both Bettenhausen and Murnighan (1985) and Mannix (in press) found that groups who formed coalitions early in a series of allocation decisions were more likely to rely on coalition formation in later rounds than groups whose early allocative mechanism was more consensual. Thus, while the other members of the group (particularly those not in the coalition) may not accept the norm, it may still provide an anchor that influences the final resolution of the dispute.

Availability. Each member of a group has more data to incorporate and absorb, particularly from other group members than do individual decision makers. Given this complexity, a typical response may be to use only readily available information. Strategically, the availability heuristic suggests that other group members can readily be influenced by the suggestion of vivid and/or salient examples. Empirical support for this increased influence of the availability heuristic is found in the recent work of Argote, Seabright, and Dyer (1986) who found that groups were more likely than individuals to ignore base-rate information in favor of salient descriptions.

Counter to this is the notion that the larger and more heterogeneous the group, the more likely members are to have conflicting perspectives, thus diluting the strength of the available information and the resulting impact of the availability heuristic on group decision making. As with the framing bias, the differences here may be a function of the relative cohesiveness of the group or some other as yet unexplored characteristic unique to groups making decisions.

Overconfidence. Sniezek and Henry (1989) used a cooperative task to examine the effects of group decision making on accuracy and confidence in assessing unknown situations. They found that groups were more accurate in their judgments than individuals. However, groups were just as susceptible to unreasonably high levels of confidence in their judgments. Some 98 percent of the individual subjects believed that their group judgments were in the top half of all group judgments with respect to accuracy. In an earlier study, Boje and Murnighan (1982) reported that groups were more overconfident than individuals, although there was no increase in decision accuracy. Thus, overconfidence seems to generalize to groups in cooperative tasks.

Mixed-motive tasks provide more reasons to expect that overconfidence will be exacerbated in groups. First, with the complexity of information in a group, individual members may be less influenced by any specific information offered by another group member; instead they focus on their own information. Second, group decisions may be influenced by coalition formation (as will be discussed in detail later in this chapter), and while group members may think about the coalitions to which they might belong, they typically fail to consider coalitions that might form without them. This is consistent with the tendency to search for confirming, rather than disconfirming, information. Each member is probably overconfident in evaluating the compelling nature of his or her position as well as his or her level of personal persuasiveness. As a result, group members should be more overconfident of their potential outcomes than individuals in comparable situations. This tendency, if empirically validated, could help explain why individual members are so often disappointed with the group decision-making process.

Mythical Fixed-Pie. The fixed-pie perspective is more likely to be a problem in group negotiations than in dyadic negotiations. In an early article, Olson (1971) argued that the level of cooperation among a group of interdependent decision makers will decrease as the size of the group increases (Kramer, forthcoming). This argument has received empirical and conceptual support from a number of studies (cf. Brewer & Kramer, 1986). An increase in group members will lower the incentives to cooperate (Olson, 1971), create individuation where no individual takes responsibility for the outcome of the group (Hamburger, Guyer, & Fox, 1975), encourage social loafing as a result of the diffusion of responsibility (Messick & McClelland, 1983), and lower the group member's perceived control over the group decision and outcome (Kerr, 1989).

Kramer (forthcoming) argues that the information requirements to form integrative agreements are sufficiently large that these higher transaction costs make it more attractive for each group member to focus simply on the competitive aspect of the negotiation. In addition, we argue that as the number of parties increases, the real likelihood of finding solutions that make everyone happier decreases, even though the number of issues and options may well increase. All of these arguments converge on the conclusion that as the number of parties increases, each party has additional reasons to focus on the distributive aspect of negotiation; and the mythical fixed-pie may become everyone's shared cognitive reaction.

Escalation. Bazerman, Giuliano, and Appelman (1984) found groups, on average, escalated commitment to a previously selected course of action as much as individuals. They also found much more variance in the behavior of groups: Fewer groups escalate, but groups that do, escalate more than individuals. In much the same way as framing may differentially affect groups, the added inputs of multiple group members may increase the likelihood of recognizing the irrationality of escalating commitment to previous, unsuccessful actions. However, if this realization does not occur, the group's value for consistency may reinforce the initial decision and increase the escalation of commitment.

Ignoring the Cognitions of Others. In Chapter 4, we argued that individuals respond to the complex task of negotiation by adopting simple characterizations of their opponent. Rather than carefully thinking through the other side's contingencies, negotiators may act based on a quick guess about the information that the other side possesses. Competitive group contexts add the burden of thinking about the contingent responses of multiple others. Obviously, this task is multiplicatively more complex in groups than in dyads, and this increases the likelihood of a negotiator simplifying the problem by ignoring the contingencies in other members' behavior.

Reactive Devaluation. Chapter 4 also argued that negotiators devalue their opponents' concessions. This behavior might also generalize to the group context as well. In addition, in the group context, members may often forget who conceded what on which issue. To the extent that this is true, concessions will not be valued by other parties, rather they will simply flow into the category of issues that "the group" has resolved.

In an analysis of multiparty negotiations of the Paris Peace Conference of 1919, Morley (1982) argues that information overload impaired the ability of negotiators to recognize concessions. Winham (1977) found that participants in a multiparty simulation failed to agree on the nature or the timing of concessions in a majority of the cases. This lack of awareness is consistent with concessions being devalued once they are made. The central argument of this section is that as extra parties are added to the negotiation, each negotiator develops a greater need to simplify the cognitive demands of the negotiation task. In some groups, the desire to reduce the cognitive demands may result in more biased decision making; while in others, the group will be less susceptible to the influences of biased information processing. Obviously, the next step in this research is to delineate the conditions under which groups are more or less susceptible to the influences of cognitive biases. With such knowledge, the responses of other parties can be better anticipated and one's arguments presented to the group in their most convincing form. In terms of the quality of group decisions, as the number of parties increases, the potential for accurate assessments of the others' preferences and values decreases while the universe of options increases; and, as such, negotiators are less likely to find mutually optimal agreements.

THE IMPACT OF COALITIONS ON GROUP DECISION MAKING

Perhaps the most fundamental difference between two-party and multiparty negotiations is the potential for two or more parties within the group to form a coalition. Mannix (in press) proposes an interesting view of coalitions. She suggests that some coalition behavior is better viewed as a type of defection, where some organization members obtain short-term gains; while other individuals, groups, and the overall organization (or global entity) may be hurt in the long run. Optimally, a group decision should have all members focusing on the same objective. In reality, members frequently focus on their own interests and those of their particular coalition to the potential detriment of efforts that benefit the overall organization. In a study of coalitional behavior in groups, Mannix found that the conditions that encourage coalitional behavior reduce the effectiveness of the larger group.

Many organizational writers do not agree with this fairly negative depiction of coalitions. Rather, they argue that coalitions are a fact of life and should be analyzed as a necessary entity in organizational life (Pfeffer & Salancik, 1978; March & Simon, 1958; Mintzberg, 1975). To understand how coalitions affect groups, a number of important characteristics can be observed (Mannix, in press; Murnighan, 1978; Murnighan & Brass, forthcoming). First, what is best for a coalition is not necessarily the best (or the worst) for the total group. Second, while there may be a large number of potential coalitions, the sequence of the communication flow may be critical to determining which coalitions form. For example, who talks to whom first establishes a pertinent reference point and this may be fortuitous. Similarly, past histories between parties can influence whether parties gravitate toward a similar coalition. Third, coalitions may be inherently unstable. Organizational coalitions often form briefly, and when a member's opportunities change, the coalition changes. We see this pattern of instability in a number of parliamentary democracies throughout the world (e.g., Italy, Israel) and do not see it in others (e.g., England).

Organizational actors need to think systematically about coalition formation and stability. However, because of biases in judgment, decision makers frequently fall short of rationality in this process. In the sections that follow, we analyze the judgmental aspects of coalition formation and the decision to maintain an existing coalition. *Coalition Formation.* Game theorists and social psychologists predict coalition formation on the basis of self-interest. For example, the most likely coalitions are predicted to be those that most directly increase the resources of coalition members. While such models have demonstrated predictive validity, we argue that the actual behavior of potential coalition members is better described by focusing on the bounds of rationality that affect coalition formation. Specifically, the concepts of availability, overconfidence, and the tendency to ignore the cognitions of others can be applied to the coalition-formation process to predict how actual coalitions form.

The availability heuristic suggests that the perceived probability of an event (e.g., forming a specific coalition) is influenced by the ease of retrieving that event from memory. Consequently, previously successful coalition members will tend to emerge as more likely future coalition members. While this behavior often leads to efficient coalition formation, it has the danger of overlooking alternative combinations of potential members by focusing on readily available coalitions. Corporate boards of directors—a coalition empowered to make many of the most important decisions within an organization—is a good example. Research has shown that directors are chosen in ways that lead to the formation of an elite group within American society (a mega-coalition) that networks through overlapping board memberships (Bazerman & Schoorman, 1983; Schoorman, Bazerman, & Atkin, 1981). Many researchers argue that elite groups create these interlocks as a coordinating force to (subversively) counter antitrust legislation limitations. We contend that existing boards are not so consciously chosen. Instead, members simply rely on available information when recommending additional board members; i.e., individuals whom they have enjoyed working with or been impressed by in the past. Consequently, the same names are more likely to be proposed repeatedly.

Overconfidence can also affect coalition formation. As suggested above, individuals are likely to be overconfident in their ability to form a powerful new coalition. For example, when William Agee of the Bendix Corporation was building a coalition among stockholders for the takeover of Martin Marietta, he may have been overconfident in his ability to form that coalition and complete the takeover. In the end Agee agreed to sell Bendix to Allied, a "white knight," to save Bendix from the hostile takeover by Martin Marietta. It can be further argued that Agee was forced into this situation because he failed to consider the cognitions of others at an early stage in the development of his coalition plan.

Coalition Stability. A variety of rational models exist to predict the stability of coalition behavior (Murnighan, 1978; Murnighan & Brass, forthcoming). For example, coalitions will be stable to the extent that there are organizational structures in place that promote their stability and continued existence. Again, the behavioral-decision-theory literature makes predictions that respond to these rational arguments. Specifically, the framing, escalation, anchoring, and mythical fixed-pie effects all provide guidance in predicting long-term coalitional stability.

Agreement by coalition members to maintain an existing coalition can be viewed as risk-averse behavior, while exploring alternative coalitions can be viewed as risk-seeking behavior. From this perspective, the framing bias predicts that coalition stability will be higher when coalition members have a positive, as opposed to negative, frame. As we earlier showed, the same objective situation can often be reinterpreted through either frame.

The escalation literature asserts that individuals tend to make decisions in ways that reinforce commitment to previously chosen courses of action. This perspective suggests that individuals will often maintain an existing coalition beyond when it is rational to pursue alternative coalitions. This point is further emphasized by a tendency to evaluate new decision alternatives (i.e., the formation of a new coalition) by previously existing anchors (i.e., the existing coalition).

Finally, the previous discussion of the mythical fixed-pie may also be relevant to explaining the maintenance of existing coalitions. Consider the situation in which a dominant coalition exists, and it is in this coalition's best interests to add new members. This view requires that existing members recognize that the additions will increase the resources available to the total coalition. The mythical fixed-pie argument would predict, however, that existing coalition members will not have a tendency to recognize the full potential of expanding the pie. Instead, they will focus on the costs of adding new members—both actual and perceived.

RE-EVALUATING STRUCTURAL PRESCRIPTIONS FOR IMPROVING GROUP DECISION MAKING

Several prescriptions and procedures for improving group problem-solving ability and performance have been developed in the group decision-making literature. For one, Bazerman, Mannix, and Thompson (1988) argue that to the extent that these prescriptions are designed for either purely cooperative or purely competitive groups, they may not serve the interests of mixed-motive groups. Prescriptions that serve the distributive motive of the negotiation may not serve the integrative motive and vice versa. For example, certain group procedures such as majority rule may encourage group members to focus on the division of resources, and discourage the search for mutually beneficial agreements. Participants may maximize their own outcomes to the detriment of the overall group. Some procedures, such as the generation of creative solutions, may facilitate achieving the integrative potential of a negotiation, but ignore the distributive aspect.

Participants have different underlying interests and priorities for the negotiation issues. Because of this, group members should trade off by conceding to other parties on issues of lesser importance and ensuring that one's more important priorities are achieved. Some group procedures may discourage negotiators from trading issues. Some procedures designed to improve group performance may encourage speed and efficiency at the expense of creative problem solving. Conflict may be suppressed, and group members may erroneously believe that others have the same priorities for issues as they. Negotiators may miss opportunities to trade issues because information about priorities is not revealed (Janis, 1982; Harvey, 1977). Suppressing useful conflict can lead group members to hesitate to disagree and to avoid the intense exploration of the problem that creative problem solving requires.

In the sections that follow, several common group decision-making procedures and techniques are reviewed. In addition, we argue that these procedures and techniques may be context-specific and, as such, inappropriate for typical mixed-motive groups. These procedures and techniques may unnecessarily restrict the ability of the group to reach integrative solutions. We make several suggestions for improving mixed-motive group decision making.

Commonly Used Group Procedures

In order to assess the quality of a group decision in a mixed-motive context, we need a set of relevant evaluation criteria. Bazerman, Mannix, and Thompson (1988) suggest the following criteria: (1) expand the focus of the group by including all viable negotiable issues in the discussion, (2) discuss priorities and preferences among issues, (3) spend time and effort problem solving, (4) consider unique and innovative solutions, and (5) be unwilling to compromise on issues reflecting high-priority interests. Many prescriptions reviewed below limit group decision making in one or more of these areas.

Decision Rule: The Normative Belief in Majority Rule. A problem that faces many small groups is whether to use majority or unanimity rule to reach a decision. Majority and unanimity are not the only methods of social choice, but they are the most common (Hare, 1976; Niemi & Weisberg, 1972; Fishburn, 1974a). We use the most common definition of majority rule: requiring that the winning solution receive more than 50 percent of the votes cast. Americans use majority rule in many diverse situations, including classrooms, city councils, federal and state legislatures, and the Supreme Court. Most individuals believe that majority rule is the most fair and efficient means of combining divergent individual preferences (Harnett & Cummings, 1980).

Groups often use majority rule because of its ease and efficiency in reaching decisions (compare Hastie, Penrod & Pennington, 1983; Harnett, 1967; Ordeshook, 1986). Computer simulation research indicates that small-group decision making on an ambiguous task is best simulated by the majority, or median opinion (Hare, 1970; Cartwright, 1971). Researchers argue that majority rule is advantageous over a unanimity system in that it is less time-consuming, less subject to simple compromise, and that individuals try harder and are more honest and problem solving (Hoffman, 1978). In a purely cooperative group, majority rule may be the most efficient way to reach a decision. In a purely competitive group, a majority vote may be the best way to avoid an impasse, and to reach an agreement which is acceptable to the largest possible number of group members.

While there are a number of advantages of majority rule to recommend it, several characteristics of majority rule make it inappropriate for the mixed-motive group. When there are more than two issues to be negotiated, majority rule is subject to numerous methods of strategic manipulation and paradoxes of voting, resulting in *pareto* inefficient outcomes (Chechile, 1984; Plott, 1976). The alternative chosen may not reflect a stable preference of the electorate. The cyclical majority problem is an example of this in which alternatives voted upon later in a sequential pairing scheme are more likely to win (May, 1982).

Majority rule systems also fail to recognize the strengths of individual preferences (Kaplan & Miller, 1983). As a result, the vote of someone who cares very strongly about an issue is weighted the same as the vote of someone whose opinion is much weaker. Group members have little opportunity to discover the strength or priorities others hold on multiple issues. This information deficit restricts the opportunity to trade off issues and search for integrative agreements. Therefore, majority rule may lead group members to compromise on rather than integrate issues. Thompson, Mannix, and Bazerman (1989) found that mixed-motive groups operating under a unanimous decision rule reached outcomes of higher gain and distributed resources more equally, than groups operating under majority rule.

Integrative strategies require group members to learn other members' preferences, and find ways to expand the pie of resources to accommodate those preferences. Unanimous decision schemes encourage group members to learn the preferences of the other members. While time consuming, encouraging negotiation groups to reach unanimous decisions may help accomplish these goals by forcing them to consider non-obvious alternatives which increase the pie and satisfy the interests of all group members. Of course, unanimous decisions will not always be feasible, for both practical and institutional reasons.

Agendas: The Need for Organization. A common way that groups organize the discussion of negotiation issues is through the use of agendas (Plott & Levine, 1978; Levine & Plott, 1977; Fishburn, 1974b). Agendas are quite useful in determining the order that issues will be raised, discussed, and decided in the decision-making process.

Typically, when agendas are followed strictly, issues are considered individually and not re-introduced once the next topic has been raised. Agendas are often viewed as an aid to rational and effective decision making. Researchers argue that groups function best when operating under agendas that set the boundaries, timing, and order of their discussion (Phillips, 1970). Groups can avoid conflict and maintain order through the use of agendas. Agendas keep the group on track, and allow members to find the most effective decision in an orderly and efficient manner. In competitive groups an agenda may be helpful in reducing hostilities and focus the group on its purpose.

In dyadic negotiation, unrestricted and simultaneous discussion of issues yields higher joint profits than sequential or issue-by-issue discussion (Fisher & Ury, 1981; Lewicki & Litterer, 1985). From a group perspective, members need to determine the preferences of others to expand resources and reach integrative agreements. To some extent, agendas limit the information available to decision makers about the pattern of preferences in the group and constrain the ability of group members to identify new issues and make trade-offs among issues. Agendas do not hinder decision making in purely cooperative or competitive tasks because integrative decisions are not possible. In one study, groups using an issue-by-issue agenda reach less integrative outcomes than groups not using a formal agenda (Bazerman, Mannix, & Thompson, 1988). Agendas may also be manipulated to yield almost any outcome (Ordeshook, 1986; Chechile, 1984). Plott and Levine (1978) found that individuals who gathered enough information about the preferences of the other group members were able to adjust the agenda to yield favorable outcomes for the self.

Agendas inhibit mixed-motive groups from discussing issues simultaneously and recognizing integrative potential. Rigid issue-oriented agendas should not be used to discuss issues in mixed-motive groups. Rather than structuring the content of discussions, negotiators should use agendas to structure the general problem-solving process: (1) identify priorities, (2) reveal individual interests, and (3) suggest creative approaches to problems (Bazerman, Mannix, & Thompson, 1988).

Group Techniques: Striving Toward Rational Decision Making

Several formal techniques have been designed to improve the group decision-making process. Some of these include: the Delphi technique, brainstorming, the nominal group technique, the program evaluation and review technique (PERT), and social judgment analysis. The goal of most of these procedures is to help individuals make rational decisions by reducing or eliminating common biases that occur in group decision making. Each of these techniques defines the problem and describes methods to take advantage of the group to generate ideas, discuss alternatives, and evaluate solutions to a problem. Below, we discuss the implications of the Delphi technique, brainstorming, and the nominal group technique (the three most common) in the mixed-motive context.

The Delphi Technique. The Delphi Technique permits a restricted exchange of opinion and information, while reducing faulty, inefficient communication that might otherwise occur during face-to-face group interaction (Huber, 1980). This technique has three features: (1) anonymity, (2) opinion revision, and (3) summary feedback. Anonymity is maintained by avoiding face-to-face interaction; group members make initial judgments on anonymous questionnaires. A moderator summarizes group members' responses and provides each member with a report, often in statistical form. Group members may adjust their judgments and respond again. This process continues until convergence or until the moderator aggregates the judgments and produces a final result.

Delphi works well in either cooperative or competitive tasks, and is most often used for obtaining quantitative responses from a panel of experts. A large number of expert opinions is often essential for forecasting a future event. Delphi allows more input with fewer logistical problems (except for time and expense); decreases time wasted on hostilities (but increases decision time); and usually results in an agreement amenable to the majority of group members in competitive tasks. It reduces the conformity pressure that may occur due to the status or personality of the other group members and decreases the reluctance to disagree, allowing group members to more readily advocate positions (Murnighan, 1981).

The Delphi technique may not be useful in mixed-motive tasks (Bazerman, Mannix, & Thompson, 1988). Because the technique does not allow direct communication between group members, there is limited opportunity to discover the preference orders and priorities of specific others. Usually only the initial dominant aggregate preferences of the other group members are discovered. Thus, the opportunity to enlarge the pie of resources is restricted, and potential trade-offs may never be revealed. Delphi results in an artificially induced pressure towards consensus, in which extreme positions are inherently discouraged (Linstone & Turoff, 1975). This feature may lead group members to compromise rather than integrate. Creative problem solving is discouraged and mutually beneficial integrative agreements may never be found.

Brainstorming. Brainstorming, an ingredient in several group decision-making techniques, was designed to encourage the uncritical generation of ideas. Group members produce as many ideas as possible, are liberal in their thinking, and hitchhike or build on the ideas of other group members (Osborn, 1957). This technique is useful in a cooperative task in which participants are searching for one "best" answer. Brainstorming techniques do not specify how to choose a solution. Thus, it does not address the potentially conflicting preferences of participants (Bazerman, Mannix, & Thompson, 1988).

Researchers have questioned the effectiveness of brainstorming in terms of the quality and quantity of ideas generated (Taylor, Berry, & Block, 1958). We believe that brainstorming may be an effective technique in mixed-motive groups, because it allows group members to expand the scope of the problem, consider issues simultaneously, and encourage creative problem solving. After the ideas have been generated, they must be discussed and evaluated. One technique for selecting among ideas is the Nominal Group Technique.

Nominal Group Technique. Nominal Group Technique (NGT) specifies a way to evaluate and select among proposed solutions through face-to-face interaction. It starts with the unconstrained generation of ideas to a specific problem. NGT is intended to assure equal participation of all group members by rigidly structuring the discussion and the voting on individual judgments (Delbecq, Van de Ven, & Gustafson, 1975). The purpose of NGT is to reduce domination by strong members and equalize the time spent on different issues. Each group member begins with a blank sheet of paper with the group problem at the top. Without discussion, everyone lists as many ideas and potential answers to the problem as he or she can. A moderator polls each person for one idea one at a time, continuing in round-robin fashion until all ideas are voiced. No one presents reasons or explanations at this time. Group members discuss their opinions, and the moderator has the power to restrict discussion. Group members anonymously vote or assign points to the alternatives, and the moderator compiles the results to produce one "best" alternative. The guidelines proposed by NGT to handle the proposed solutions may decrease the potential for mutually beneficial solutions. To the extent that the moderator is restrictive, participants' priorities among issues may never be revealed, trade-offs will not be discussed, and integrative agreements will not be reached. The moderator determines the final decision by summing points across each proposal. The voting rule of NGT is likely to result in the decision originally favored by the strongest faction in the group.

The group techniques reviewed above facilitate aspects of group decision making in specific contexts, but will often be inappropriate for mixed-motive groups. These techniques equalize participation, reduce status differences, and, in some cases, improve rational decision making. However, these techniques may reduce the likelihood of expanding the pie of resources, hamper the simultaneous discussion of issues, hinder the trading of issues, and eliminate the creative problem solving necessary for mutually beneficial agreements. Our central conclusion is that these techniques should not be used without first analyzing how they will influence the specific decision process in question. Universal acceptance of any of these procedures will reduce the rationality of the decision in many circumstances.

CONCLUSIONS

This chapter has covered a broad spectrum of issues concerning the nature of negotiations when more than two parties are involved. As we mentioned in the introduction to this chapter, multiparty negotiation contexts are inherently more complex than individual decision making or two-party negotiations. This is due, in part, to the richness of the interpersonal networks and the number of individual cognitions that are involved.

This chapter suggested two themes by which the increased cognitive complexity of group negotiations relative to dyadic negotiations are critical: increased information processing demands, and interpersonal and communication dynamics. We have argued that group negotiations are, at times, even more likely to be influenced by biased decision making, and that coalitions were an important added concern of groups. Further, the prescriptions from the existing group literature may create additional barriers to effective decision making in mixed-motive groups.

The past decade has witnessed a proliferation of interest in training people to be more effective negotiators. We believe that the group decision-making literature can benefit from some of these insights. Group negotiators need to be more aware of integrative opportunities and of cognitive barriers to effective performance. In addition, group negotiators should be concerned about the impact of decision procedures even more than their dyadic counterparts. We encourage future research on groups that focuses on their integrative potential, cognitive limitations, and group procedures as an important direction for helping to make individuals more effective performers in group negotiations. The information presented in this chapter offers a number of issues to consider in evaluating multi-party decision making.

7

Negotiated Matches in a Market Context*

Moving from two- to multiparty negotiation (as presented in Chapter 6) is one way to add complexity to broaden our understanding of the negotiation problem. An alternative is to examine dyadic negotiations in their broader social context. In this chapter, we explore negotiated matches that occur in interacting markets in which the actors on either side of the market must choose with whom to negotiate, as well as conducting the dyadic negotiation within this more complex social system.

In markets that contain many undifferentiated buyers and sellers who repeatedly trade identical goods, negotiation becomes less important. In these markets, sellers frequently become buyers, and buyers become sellers. In these perfectly competitive markets in which neither the agents nor the goods being traded have any distinguishing qualities, the market typically establishes a clearing price, and most transactions are completed at or near that price. However, in other markets, some characteristics differentiate between sellers and buyers, among individual buyers and individual sellers, and/or the good or service they are trading. In addition, some markets involve people who infrequently transact and have little opportunity to learn from their market experience. They have two tasks: finding the best match available, and negotiating an advantageous agreement. We will use the term "matching" to refer to the process by which two complementary parties select each other

---

*A primary source of input for this chapter is Al Roth's extensive theoretical and field research on this topic. In addition, much of the writing is based on collaborative work with Harris Sondak.

when other potential partners are both available and differentially valued by one or both of the parties (Mortensen, 1986). This chapter is concerned with whether the outcomes of these negotiated matches are consistent with the predictions of rational models of matching and negotiation behaviors, or can be better described by systematic deficiencies.

Economic models of markets suggest that the behavior of negotiators will converge to rational outcomes (Hoffman & Spitzer, 1982), particularly when negotiators re-enter the market and have the opportunity to learn from their mistakes (Crawford & Knoer, 1981). In addition, the economic model predicts that the market itself, in addition to the actors, will behave rationally. This chapter examines whether this market level prediction is valid in a common class of markets—those in which two sides of the market have different preferences concerning how they are matched with the other side. Examples of this include markets for residential real estate and labor. Many real markets fail to provide an opportunity for learning. When negotiators have little opportunity to learn from their mistakes, the behavior of negotiators and the aggregate behavior of markets is expected to deviate from rational expectations. Negotiators in markets that involve many players who carry out infrequent transactions and where many differentiable goods are exchanged seem particularly likely to lack the feedback properties necessary for learning. We shall refer to these particular markets as quasi-markets.

The MBA job market is a quasi-market. Each year more than 60,000 students receive MBA's from American graduate schools of business (*Digest of Education Statistics,* 1986), and seek employment in a complex job market. At the J.L. Kellogg Graduate School of Management at Northwestern University, for example, 450 students interview with 250 firms in a total of 13,500 interviews. The economic view predicts that the matches between firms and students would be rational (compare Kelso & Crawford, 1982); behavioral decision theory predicts systematically nonrational outcomes in this market (Sondak & Bazerman, 1989, in press).

Three levels of rationality can be identified for negotiations in a matching market: individual, dyadic, and market levels. From an individual's perspective, a negotiator should maximize his/her own benefit by finding the best match possible and by negotiating the optimal set of terms within that match. At the dyadic level, each match should reach an agreement that is *pareto* optimal—it should lie on the efficient frontier. The market level achieves a rational outcome if the matches are so efficient that they establish a stable equilibrium (Roth, 1985a); that is, when no two agents on opposite sides of the market prefer each other to the agents with whom they are or have been matched. Whenever two parties on opposite sides of the market both prefer each other to the parties to whom they are matched, there will be an incentive for these dissatisfied parties to defect from their current matches—a set of behaviors which augments market instability and moves the market towards a state of disorder. This third level of rationality (at the market level) is the primary focus of this chapter. Here we (1) review the history of the use of imposed mechanized rationalistic matching models in the medical labor market, (2) define the characteristics of a rational model of matching, (3) compare actual behavior in markets to that of the rational model, and (4) explain the deviations from rationality that are observed.

The History of Using Rational, Institutionalized Matching Systems

Markets that have no means to assure a good fit between firms and employees may generate potentially avoidable mismatches. Roth (1984; Roth & Sotomayor, in press) documented this problem in the job market for graduating medical students—and much of this section is based on their description of the history of this market.

The notion of a medical internship for graduates of medical schools was introduced at the turn of the century. From the beginning, the number of positions for interns exceeded the supply of graduating doctors. In competing for the best students, a hospital could obtain an advantage over other hospitals by making a limited time offer to high-caliber candidates earlier than other hospitals.* The new doctor might have the incentive to take a (moderately) high-quality, certain offer over risking the possibility of ending up with other unattractive choices. Unfortunately, as all hospitals started to follow this strategy, the hospitals continually advanced the offer date until 1944 when they were making offers to students early in their junior

---

*A parallel set of behaviors has developed in the management school marketplace, where firms make "exploding offers" which either last for only a few hours, or the salary goes *down* for every day that the candidate delays accepting. Many management schools provide sanctions against this behavior because it creates unfair stress on the candidates.

year of medical school. This practice decreased the ability of hospitals and students to judge each other's quality, and disrupted the educational process. It also led to unstable agreements; that is, parties on different sides of the market preferred each other to their current assignments, and so had incentives to continue looking for better matches.

The Association of American Medical Colleges tried to cope with this situation by imposing a number of restrictions on the timing of offers and acceptances, each of which created its own new set of problems. To solve these problems, hospitals and medical schools agreed to a more centralized system. Under this procedure, hospitals would continue to post their complete job descriptions in advance (eliminating them from any negotiation) and students and hospitals would continue to make contact and exchange information as before. Students would then rank hospital positions to which they had applied in their order of preference, hospitals would rank students who had applied to them, and all parties would submit these rankings to a centralized bureau, which would use a specific algorithm to match students with hospitals.

In the 1950–51 market, a "trial run" was conducted that was *not* used to actually match students to hospitals. Instead, parties submitted rankings so that the plan could be evaluated for future use. After some initial debate concerning the characteristics of the system, the plan was actually used for the first time in the 1951–52 market. That algorithm (originally named the National Intern Matching Program) is now referred to as the National Resident Matching Program (NRMP).

The centralized matching program was voluntary; students and hospitals were free to try and arrange their own matches outside the system. Nevertheless, over 95 percent of eligible students and hospitals participated in the system, and this level of participation continued until the mid-1970s, when the rate dropped to around 85 percent. Much of the decrease has been a result of the prior inability of the algorithm to deal with two-career couples.

Roth and Sotomayor (in press) argue that a key to the success of the NRMP was the stability of its solution. They also showed that physician couples were able to find hospitals they jointly preferred over the assigned matches. Roth and Sotomayor (in press) argue that the instability created by dual-career situations explains the decreased use of the NRMP system in the 1970s.

This case provides an example of a naturally occurring market that does not create a rational outcome at a system level. The parties were not acting irrationally. Even if each party acts in his/her own interest, a broader notion of rationality may not be achieved. The invisible hand of the market did not create a rational set of outcomes in this class of markets. We will return to the distinction between individual and market-level rationality later in the chapter.

DEFINING CHARACTERISTICS OF A RATIONAL MATCHING SYSTEM

The NRMP algorithm was designed to meet two goals (Roth, 1984): produce stable outcomes and provide no incentive for the participants to misrepresent their preferences. Roth (1985b) proved that for stable solutions in two-sided matching markets, at least two sets of stable matches exist—one solution that is preferred by all job candidates, while another that is preferred by all employers. That is, the NRMP algorithm produces stable solutions h and s such that all hospitals will agree that h is as good or better than all other stable solutions, including s, while all students will agree that s is as good or better than all other stable solutions, including h. Indeed, the best stable solution for one side of the market is the worst stable solution for the other side of the market. There is, therefore, a common interest among members of the same side of the market to secure the matching solution that is preferred by their side of the market. The NRMP algorithm gives hospitals their most preferred stable solution. In instituting such a matching system, it is necessary to decide to which side of the market that preference should be given.

The algorithm's stable solution depends upon the stated preferences of the parties being accurate. Unfortunately no stable matching procedure exists for which stating true preferences is the dominant strategy for all parties in the medical market (Roth, 1982). A stable procedure only provides an incentive to reveal their true preferences to the side of the market which the algorithm favors; the parties on the other side of the market have no incentive for misrepresenting their first choice. However, to manipulate the market by falsifying preferences would require vast information about the preferences of the other players in the market and remarkable analytical skill. In the actual absence of such knowledge, there is no practical incentive for hospitals or students to misrepresent their preferences (Roth, 1984).

ASSESSING THE RATIONALITY
OF NATURALLY OCCURRING MATCHES

Clearly, instabilities can develop in naturally occurring markets. Roth (forthcoming) has documented similar market unraveling in the corresponding medical markets in the United Kingdom. Roth and Sotomayor (1990) argued that the success of a broader number of British medical markets can also be explained by their ability to produce stability. In addition, Mongell and Roth (1988) found an identical pattern of market unraveling in the context of sorority membership. Membership in these societies had originally been reserved for college seniors, but competition for new members had advanced the recruiting season to the freshman year and even back to prep school. This advancement of the recruiting season is a likely source of the term "rush" for the membership drives of fraternities and sororities.

While the job market for graduating medical schools is now governed by the NRMP, most other job markets continue to proceed without the help of an institutionalized system. Placement officials, students, and recruiters alike stress the importance of a good fit between students and firms, and the focus of both sides of the market is on finding appropriate matches. Yet, actions are not always consistent with objectives. The matches in the MBA job market, for example, occur with minimal intervention from business schools, and are probably inefficient. Prior to the stock market crash in October 1987, the investment banking job market was moving earlier at a rapid rate. Firms were more aggressive in hiring summer interns and were making exploding offers to their interns that had to be accepted or rejected before the candidates returned to interview with other firms.

In many job markets and housing markets the terms of agreement—such as job title and starting date, or closing date and financing terms—typically are negotiated. The market for graduating medical students differs from these quasi-markets because the terms of the agreements are not subject to negotiation (Roth, 1984). In the MBA job market, some firms will negotiate salary with the graduating students, and even those that do not negotiate salary usually will discuss other conditions of employment. At Northwestern's Kellogg School, for example, students reported negotiating the starting date of the job, the payment of moving expenses, the type of work a candidate will do, job title, bonuses, geographic location, vacation time, and the date of the first performance review (Sondak, 1990). Firms in some industries are more likely to negotiate these kinds of issues than in others; while investment banks tend not to negotiate any issue of an agreement, management consulting firms and consumer products manufacturers are more likely to negotiate these issues.

Sondak and Bazerman (1989) use the NRMP matching algorithm as a normative benchmark in a laboratory simulation of the MBA job market. In their study, each experimental market contained sixteen subjects who played the role of graduating MBA students (job candidates) and eight subjects who played the role of corporate recruiters (each trying to hire two recruits). Each subject was given a rank ordering of their preferences for the eight recruiting firms as well as their preferences for three other issues: salary, starting date, and job assignment. Subjects had multiple opportunities to negotiate employment agreements with members of the opposite side of the market through structured meetings. In addition, there were periods set aside to organize their decisions concerning the offering and acceptance of proposed agreements.

The results of these Sondak and Bazerman (1989, in press) studies found that markets fall far short of a rational set of matches even within a very organized market structure. *No* stable solutions emerged in eighteen runs of a market simulation across two experiments. In addition, the naturally occurring matches obtained (on average) only 77.9 percent of the matching benefit that the NRMP algorithm could provide. This does not show irrational behavior at the individual level. However, it does show that the parties in this market could have done better, on average, by using a centralized matching mechanism.

Harrison and McCabe (1987) examined the impact of the complexity of the market (number of parties on each side) on the behavior of the parties and the rationality of the outcomes. Their study found that under very simple conditions (far easier than the 24-member market of Sondak and Bazerman [1989] or any market that one is likely to confront in the real world) stability can be achieved. However, as soon as a moderate amount of complexity is added, the stability of naturally occurring matches falls apart. In addition, they found that while parties often misrepresent their interests, this misrepresentation did not increase their outcomes—supporting Roth's (1984) earlier speculation. Finally, by repeating a market multiple times with the same participants, Harrison and McCabe found with experience, the market became *less* efficient. Thus, as the parties gained enough information to think that they could manipulate the system, the only observable result was to lower the aggregate quality of the outcomes obtained.

In a second study, Sondak and Bazerman (in press) found that altering the structure of the market could improve its efficiency. In Sondak and Bazerman (1989), students were allowed to keep an offer only for a short period of time, allowing the recruiters to make their offer to an alternative student if the first student turned down the initial offer. The second study gave candidates longer to consider an offer, decreasing their opportunity costs of searching for better alternatives. By extending the life of offers, both sides knew better whether they had found a good match: the participants could locate matches of high mutual value and improve the quality of the matching solutions at the market level. Sondak and Bazerman (in press) argue that the key difference in these markets is informational. That is, by increasing the life of the offers, the candidates are able to identify less acceptable firms. In contrast, the matches that occurred in the Sondak and Bazerman (1989) study often gave very little input to the candidates in the market because they were often forced to make decisions when they were only in possession of one offer.

Sondak and Bazerman (in press) also showed that subtle changes in the structure of the market could affect the power balance between the two sides of the market. A significant difference between Roth's examination of the medical markets and Sondak and Bazerman's examination of experimental MBA markets is the inclusion of issues to be negotiated within each dyadic match (salary, starting date, job assignment). An interesting question emerges concerning how the broader social context of a matching system affects the rationality of the dyadic negotiation. One key indicator of rational behavior in dyadic negotiation is the ability of the dyad to obtain a fully integrative solution. When negotiators are preoccupied with securing their share of readily apparent resources, negotiators tend to overlook the integrative potential that, in fact, exists (Bazerman & Carroll, 1987).

Sondak and Bazerman argue that the cognitive demands of finding a good match distract attention from the dyadic negotiating problem, leading to less efficient results than that observed in studies looking only at two-party negotiations (compare Pruitt, 1983). An important concern facing negotiators in markets is their limited information processing ability. Negotiators seem unable to cope with the demands of simultaneously finding optimal matches and negotiating integrative agreements. The fact that the agreements in this study were typically less integrative than those achieved in dyadic negotiation suggests that the complexity created by needing to find a match interferes with the rationality of the dyadic negotiating process. In fact, it may be that the matching problem encourages a distributive orientation that inhibits the integrative behaviors necessary for dealing effectively with the dyadic negotiation problem.

This section documents the substantial inefficiency that can be expected in naturally occurring markets. In addition, we have begun to highlight some of the structural mechanisms that can be altered to affect the efficiency of the resulting matches. We now turn to the question of why this inefficiency persists in actual markets.

WHAT ACCOUNTS FOR MARKET-LEVEL IRRATIONALITY?

The previous section documented that many naturally occurring markets fail to achieve rational solutions. The key puzzle that develops concerns how to explain these results. In addition, we need to deal with the question of why markets use naturally occurring mechanisms when an NRMP-like algorithm would produce superior results.

Using only a rational behavior argument, Mortensen (1986) argues that unstable matching solutions can result from the optimal choices on the part of individual market participants. The cost of match formation and the cost of gaining information about match quality can lead parties to voluntarily form matches that are unstable at the market level. In addition, a social dilemma often exists in the matching context. A social dilemma is a multiparty prisoner's dilemma, in which each party has a dominating strategy (a competitive response) that is in its rational self-interest; yet it is in the interest of all parties to collectively not choose this dominating option (to cooperate) (Dawes, 1988). In the labor-matching market, each participant may have an incentive to engage in a set of behaviors (e.g., making offers to job candidates one month earlier), regardless of the behavior of the other participants, that will decrease the rationality of the matching solution of the larger societal entity. If each participant acts in his/her self-interest, all participants may be worse off than if all participants had behaved more cooperatively. In pursuing their own individual gain, individually rational behaviors can and do make it unlikely for stable solutions to emerge. An aggressive firm/hospital can make an early offer with a short fuse (deadline) to a risk-averse student who accepts this nonoptimal match. Even one such move can have a dramatic effect on the quality of matches in the larger social system (Roth, 1984; Roth & Sotomayor, in press; Sondak & Bazerman, 1989, in press).

In the market for new MBAs, firms feel the conflicting pressures of cooperating to promote system rationality versus maximizing their self-interests. Mannix and Bazerman (1990) have observed that different industries which recruit at Northwestern's Kellogg School have developed very different sets of behaviors. Marketing-oriented firms that hire assistant brand managers, and who generally show high levels of cooperation in their industry (e.g., they do not use negative advertising), have created highly cooperative forms of re-cruiting. In contrast, investment banking firms known for their competitive culture show the same types of competitive behaviors and unraveling (slowed by the 1987 crash) observed in the hospital context. Indeed, the competition among firms in investment bank-ing has led starting salaries to increase far faster than that observed in brand management.

The above arguments clarify why efficient solutions do not emerge in naturally occurring markets. However, the next question to ad-dress concerns why individuals would prefer naturally occurring systems over the use of algorithms that would increase aggregate utility. Sondak (1990) has documented that students and firms show little interest in using such an algorithm in the MBA market context. Decentralized matching procedures allow participants to decide with whom to meet to discuss possible agreements, whether to extend or accept offers, and with whom to sign a contract. Such a market maximizes the individual's control but reduces the aggregate utility to the players. However, it is easy to imagine that the individ-ual players all believe (overconfidently) that their particular out-comes will be better when they, rather than a market-control mecha-nism, make the final choice.

Centralized procedures reduce the control and remove these decisions from the individual participant's purview. While the

NRMP algorithm offers each participant equal input into the final decision, participants generally fail to appreciate the value of a stable matching solution.

We can gain some insight into the distaste that participants report for the use of such algorithms by examining the history of using linear models to make repeated decisions. Dawes (1988) has documented Meehl's (1954) early argument that future behavior can be more accurately predicted by using an actuarial combination of scores on relevant attributes than by overall clinical prediction. Dawes' research also establishes that models based on expert judgment will outperform the judgments of those very same experts. In his work on graduate admissions decisions, Dawes (1971) modeled the average judgment of a four-person committee. The predictors in the model were (1) a score from the Graduate Record Examination, (2) overall undergraduate grade point average, and (3) quality of the undergraduate school. Dawes used the model to predict the average rating of 384 applicants. He found that the model could be used to reject 55 percent of the applicant pool without ever rejecting an applicant that the selection committee had, in fact, accepted. In addition, the weights used to predict the committee's behavior were better than the committee itself in predicting future faculty ratings of the accepted and matriculated applicants.

Research shows that linear-policy capturing models produce superior predictions across an impressive array of domains, including financial decisions, corporate personnel decisions, bank loan decisions, and routine purchasing decisions. Yet, individuals continue to doubt the predictive ability of the models and typically find their use unacceptable. Stronger resistance to the use of these linear models for decision making typically is packaged as ethical concerns (having a computer determine who is guilty or innocent). Such ethical concerns are well illustrated by a woman cited in Dawes (1979):

When I was at the Los Angeles Renaissance Fair last summer, I overheard a young woman complain that it was "horribly unfair" that she had been rejected by the Psychology Department at the University of California, Santa Barbara, on the basis of mere numbers, without even an interview. "How could they possibly tell what I'm like?" The answer is they can't. Nor could they with an interview.

Dawes argues that for decision makers to believe that they can better predict qualifications based on a half-hour interview than on the information contained in a transcript covering nearly four years of work and the carefully devised aptitude assessment of graduate board exams demonstrates unethical conceit. However conceited it may be, the pattern to distrust mechanized decision procedures is a consistent finding that is equally relevant to matching algorithms.

As with the use of linear models, the NRMP algorithm mechanically combines input to determine outcomes and as such removes control from the individuals in the market. Dislike for the use of algorithms may be explained by individuals' overconfidence in their own abilities (Einhorn & Hogarth, 1978), distrust of a "dehumanized system" (Dawes, 1979), or lack of perceived control over important job-related choices (Bazerman, 1982; Seligman, 1975). In addition, many individuals and firms believe that their recruiting strategies give them a distinct advantage over the competition. We currently lack the data to evaluate the rationality of their individualism.

Together, these psychological effects result in the acceptance of suboptimal systems in a variety of matching contexts. The unfortunate fact may be that we may need to wait until a crisis is created to get relevant actors to unfreeze their attachment to decentralized systems and to consider the use of a more optimal centralized system.

CONCLUSIONS

The choice between a centralized- versus decentralized-market mechanism can be thought of as a selection of a social-choice procedure to determine collectively a social outcome (Arrow, 1973). According to traditional economic theory, the freedom of choice of decentralized social-choice mechanisms benefits the individual making these choices (Riker & Ordeshook, 1973). According to this view, individuals know best what they prefer and will pursue what they perceive to be most valuable (Sondak, 1990). In addition, decentralized mechanisms may benefit society because they are less wasteful of resources. Many economists have a strong belief that decentralized systems generally allow goods and services to be distributed so that they are obtained by those who value them the most. We hope that the overview in this chapter documents reasons for questioning this expectation in some market contexts.

The unfortunate problem with decentralized mechanisms is that the individual choices of specific actors often lead to poor collective results (Arrow, 1963, 1974; Dawes, 1980). The task of matching is a complex, competitive task. Finding the people on the other side of the market whom you like, who also like you, is the heart of the matching task. This chapter has documented the complexity of the matching task, and clarified the conflict between individual and market rationality. In addition, we have shown that naturally occurring systems can be expected to be suboptimal at a systems level. Finally, we have argued that irrationality exists in the lack of acceptance of rational, centralized mechanisms, and discussed the psychological reasons for this rejection.

Some labor and housing markets are controlled by institutional arrangements. Many others, of course, proceed without such institutional controls. Both systems have their advantages and disadvantages. While natural quasi-markets allow some individuals to outperform the results predicted by a matching algorithm, and thus reward insight, perseverance, and luck, they create unstable matches that do not maximize aggregate utility.

Further research is needed to determine the cognitive mechanisms and limitations that are the sources of inefficiency in quasi-markets. Additional work is also needed to examine the impact of a variety of structural rules on the rationality of the solutions that emerge. Understanding the processes of matching and negotiating in these markets would help in making the decision whether to create a matching institution in a specific market context.

8

Third-Party Intervention

The general topic of assisted-dispute resolution by ostensibly neutral individuals not directly participants to the dispute (or third parties) is gaining increasing interest and support from both practitioners and scholars within and outside organizations. Until somewhat recently, the research in this area has been limited to studies of third parties whose behavior was typically limited by institutional regulation or participant expectation. In contrast, we argue that the most common use of third parties occurs in informal contexts (e.g., managerial intervention in disputes). This chapter selectively overviews the existing third-party literature and highlights how a decision perspective can help negotiators and third parties achieve more optimal outcomes in assisted-dispute resolution.

A framework for understanding third parties should address the description and prescription of: (1) behaviors and decisions of the intervening parties; (2) behaviors and decisions of the disputing parties; and (3) the selection of a procedure from among the various dispute-resolution options available. In addition, we believe intervention behaviors should be evaluated against a set of criteria defining an optimal outcome for the dispute.* An ideal procedure should increase the likelihood of parties reaching an agreement if a positive bargaining zone exists, create *pareto* optimal outcomes when agree-

---

*There may be third-party interventions in which the primary objective is to enhance the relationship between the parties, rather than to assist in the resolution of a specific dispute, e.g., when a counselor acts as a mediator for a couple experiencing a conflict. Questions regarding this type of intervention are not reviewed here.

ments are reached, and lead to "fair" resolutions. While these objectives seem straightforward, we are surprised by the extent to which the third-party literature focuses on legal, clinical, and management issues, to the exclusion of a consideration of how to help parties achieve greater rationality in their decision making.

In the sections that follow, we focus on a variety of third-party interventions. We discuss the similarities and differences between the various types of interventions. These include the amount of process and decision control held by the third parties, their institutionalized authority (and subsequent restrictions on their interventions), and their involvement with the disputants after an agreement is reached. The four types of third parties discussed are mediators, arbitrators, agents, and managers.

MEDIATION

Mediation, a form of intervention where the third party aids the disputants in the resolution process but has no authority to impose a settlement, is the most common type of third-party dispute resolution (Kolb & Rubin, forthcoming). According to anecdotal accounts of its many uses in primitive societies, it has the longest history of any intervention form (Barley, in press). Mediation is important at all levels of society and in virtually every significant area of social conflict (Pruitt & Kressel, 1985). Only recently, however, have mediation researchers from law, organization behavior, psychology, and political science begun to offer a variety of theoretical perspectives and research findings to practitioners.

Recent developments in the dispute-resolution industry have outpaced advancements in the academic literature (Ury, Brett, & Goldberg, 1989). This is probably most obvious in the mediation area. Unfortunately, there has been limited connection between basic research on dispute resolution and the practice of mediation. The chasm between mediation researcher and practitioner is similar to the one that existed between negotiation researchers and practitioners.

The importance to the practitioner of coupling prescriptive and descriptive research becomes salient when examining the current applicability of purely descriptive research. Consider the options open to a mediator upon learning that he or she is involved in a dispute in which the parties are on opposite sides of a highly emotional labor-management dispute. The academic literature typically provides little direction to the mediator for rationally choosing specific strategies. However, if we view the third party as having the superordinate goal of creating rational, *pareto* optimal agreements, a decision research perspective increases the potential applicability of research for practicing third parties. *Pareto* optimal agreements (which maximize the disputants' outcomes) can be the benchmark to evaluate the performance of the mediator.

The typical mediation practitioner is likely to have little faith in the current empirical findings of his/her academic counterparts. As Kolb (1983, p. 3) suggests:

> A certain aura of mystery shrouds the practice of mediation. Practitioners claim that mediation is an art with as many theories, philosophies, and approaches as there are mediators. Through their choice of metaphors, mediators emphasize particular features of their work: the intuitive over the systematic and the unexpected over the planned. To their way of thinking, the process of mediation is shaped simultaneously by the unique characteristics of the individual disputes and the special skills and insights of the mediators handling these cases.

Given this idiographic, clinical perspective, it is not surprising that little empirical work has influenced the training of mediators. If practitioners are convinced that mediation is an art rather than a science, it is little wonder that the available research findings are typically ignored when deciding how to structure interventions. Unfortunately, much of the current research in mediation has not been directed toward producing mediators better able to maximize the joint utility of the parties. Consequentially, it provides few clues about how to reach such an end state.

This art-form perspective is restrictive for two reasons. First, it keeps mediators from developing an understanding of their behavior that allows generalizability across contexts. To the extent a mediation is viewed as art, it is easy to argue that barriers exist which impede mediators' ability to practice across different content areas. However, if the mediator understands the conceptual process that he or she uses, it becomes viable to generalize across domains. Second, the art perspective decreases our ability to train new third parties. Transferring knowledge requires the development of a systematic understanding of the process. As the mediation literature moves from art to science, opportunities are created for the transfer of

knowledge to current and future practitioners. In a review of mediation research, Pruitt and Kressel (1985) castigate mediation researchers for the purely descriptive orientation to their research.
Writers typically rely on personal experience or case studies of
mediation (Rubin, 1981; Young 1972). Regardless of the study cited,
only a small percentage of outcome variance has been accounted for
by dispute, disputant, or situational characteristics (Thoennes &
Pearson, 1985; Carnevale & Pegnetter, 1985).

In a study of how mediators actually behave, Kolb concluded that
the intuitive orientation reflected in anecdotal accounts of mediation
does not reflect mediation in practice. Instead, she found the process of mediation "was more one of pattern and routine than creativity
and innovation" (Kolb, 1983; p. 150). Early empirical work found
that successful mediation in industrial settings was impeded if exces-
sive hostility existed between the parties (Landsberger, 1955; Carnevale & Pegnetter, 1985; Kochan & Jick, 1978). Other research
found the anticipation of compulsory mediation speeds concession-
making when conflict of interest is small but slows it down when
conflict of interest is large (Hiltrop & Rubin, 1982). While these
findings are interesting, they do little to further a scientific perspective of mediation.

To increase the understanding of third-party intervention, generally, and mediation, specifically, one needs to have a better grasp on
what factors influence how mediators select intervention strategies.
One missing factor in current research is the interaction of the
mediator's decision-making process with the disputants' needs and
objectives. For example, consider the emphasis on reaching an
agreement that permeates much of the descriptive literature on
mediation. Mediators are likely to emphasize this activity to the
exclusion of carefully considering whether or not reaching a mediated settlement is in the best interests of one or both of the parties.
The emphasis on reaching an agreement, *any* agreement, may reflect an unexamined bias that mediators possess. In some disputes,
the interests of one or more of the parties may best be served by a no-
agreement outcome. That is, sometimes the mediator may need to
facilitate the parties' *not* reaching an agreement.*

Thoennes and Pearson (1985) suggest that in divorce-mediation
cases, the actions of the mediators may be more crucial to the

---

*This is similar to the marriage counselor facilitating the couple's acceptance of the
need to dissolve the marriage.

disputants' perceptions of success than either the nature of the dispute or the characteristics of the disputants. With such impact on the disputants and the dispute, it is important that mediators be able to identify situations when their power to convince the parties to settle may not be in the best interests of the parties. What has clearly not been addressed in the current research on mediation is how the disputants' interests should interact with the mediator's decision-making processes.

Our central argument is that much of the mediation literature does not address the central task of mediation—helping the parties reach more rational outcomes to disputes. To accomplish this, mediators should have the goal of increasing the likelihood of an agreement when a positive bargaining zone exists, increasing the likelihood of impasse when a negative bargaining zone exists, and increasing the *pareto* efficiency of agreements. Further, mediators should help negotiators eliminate the decision biases that affect their decisions. This requires that mediators develop greater appreciation of prescriptive and descriptive decision models. More research should describe how mediators can help the parties achieve rational outcomes in negotiation.

While the above paragraph clarifies how we think mediation should operate, it does not describe current reality. Thus, a negotiator involved in a mediation must be armed with an understanding of how the mediator will affect the dispute-resolution process. Given the power and influence mediators can impose on disputants, it is critical to reconceptualize the mediator as more than a benign facilitator of agreements. Rather, the mediator can both fashion agreements and convince the parties to acquiesce to such agreements. To the extent that mediators have reaching an agreement as their dominant goal, they may compromise the interests of the less-informed, weaker party for the sake of the agreement. Such a disputant may find that the concessionary behavior elicited by the mediator is decidedly one-sided. As with clinicians described in Chapter 5, mediators are subject to biases and systematic influences which may work in concert with their goals to produce sub-optimal agreements for one or more of the disputants.

With the increasing popularity of mediation comes a greater need for practitioners to understand the ways in which they can help disputing parties attain rational outcomes. More descriptive research can determine the ways in which mediators deviate from this goal. Similarly, prescriptive research can begin to provide direction to third parties, and disputants electing to involve a mediator, to help them overcome biases and increase the effectiveness of mediated negotiations.

ARBITRATION

In contrast to mediation where the disputants have control over the final outcome, in arbitration, the neutral third party has control over the resolution. The two most common types of arbitration are conventional and final-offer arbitration. In conventional arbitration, the arbitrator determines the final award based on the arguments and positions of the conflicting parties (Elkouri & Elkouri, 1981), although they typically select an agreement between the final positions of the two disputants. The threat of conventional arbitration can reduce participants' willingness to compromise in negotiation; they have an incentive to exaggerate their claims and concede little (Long & Feuille, 1975; Feuille, 1975). If the arbitrator "splits the difference" between the parties' final positions, the party does best who concedes the least. Operationally, this leads to greater and greater reliance on arbitration to resolve disputes because the parties are unwilling to concede in the negotiations prior to the imposition of arbitration for fear of compromising their impasse positions (Stevens, 1966; Notz & Starke, 1978).

Final-offer arbitration was introduced to alleviate these problems. Under this arrangement, the arbitrator's decision alternatives are limited to one or the other of the parties' final offers. As such, the third party may not "fashion" an agreement. Laboratory (Grigsby & Bigoness, 1982; Notz & Starke, 1978; Starke & Notz, 1981; Neale & Bazerman, 1983; Farber, Neale, & Bazerman, 1990) and field research (Kochan, Mironi, Ehrenberg, Baderschneider, & Jick, 1979; Delaney & Feuille, 1984) provide evidence that negotiated resolution rates are higher when negotiators are threatened with final-offer arbitration than when they are threatened with conventional arbitration. In addition, negotiators are more willing to make concessions prior to final-offer arbitration than prior to conventional arbitration (Stevens, 1966).

Much research and policy making has been based on assumptions about the decision processes of arbitrators. This raises the importance of understanding these processes, which has only recently been the topic of systematic study. For example, final-offer arbitration was created as a response to the fear that arbitrators "split the difference" under conventional arbitration. A central argument in the literature concerns whether conventional arbitrators actually do split the difference between the two parties or whether they evaluate each case and make a decision based on the facts of the case.

Splitting the difference would be consistent with an equality norm of justice. This follows Rawls' egalitarian theory of justice which argues that scarce resources should be apportioned equally to all parties. In contrast, basing arbitration decisions on the facts of the case is consistent with an equity norm of justice, which argues that scarce resources should be distributed according to the merits of the situation (Adams, 1963, 1965). Arbitrators commonly argue that their decisions are based on the merits of the cases presented to them. While they claim they are not affected by the extremity of the parties' positions, research has documented that in actual arbitration cases the arbitrator's decisions are positively related to the final offer of the parties. Bloom (1986) presented arbitrators with scenarios that were patterned closely after actual cases involving public sector employees in New Jersey. Bloom found that the primary determinants of the arbitrators' decisions were the final offers of the parties, leading him to conclude that splitting the difference is a reasonable description of arbitrator behavior in conventional arbitration.

In contrast, Farber and Bazerman (1986, 1989; Bazerman & Farber, 1985) argue that Bloom's research ignores the possibility that the parties, too, hold justice norms and may set their offers to surround what they perceive to be the "fair" resolution to the conflict. If this is the case, then an arbitrator who makes the "fair" award will appear to be splitting the difference. Thus, any time the offers of the parties co-vary with the "fair" decision, arbitrators will appear to split the difference, regardless of whether the offers of the parties have any impact on their decision. In a study using actual arbitrators, where the offers of the parties were independent of the characteristics of the case, Farber and Bazerman found that arbitrators did not pay attention to the offers. Rather, their decisions were determined by the characteristics of the case.

The disagreement between Farber and Bazerman and Bloom concerned whether arbitrators pay attention to the characteristics of the case or the offers of the parties. In a study focusing on the decisions of specific arbitrators, Bazerman (1985) found a very different norm operating. Consistent with Tversky and Kahneman's (1974) concept of anchoring and adjustment, Bazerman found that the most common practice of arbitrators was to use the anchoring heuristic. Arbitrators made only minor adjustments to last year's contract, thus maintaining an approximation of past agreements.

In addition to understanding the decisions of arbitrators, it is important to understand the decisions of negotiators who face potential arbitration. Farber, Neale, and Bazerman (1990) examined the decisions of negotiators in assessing the importance of the costs of conventional arbitration for union/management contract negotiations of wage rates. Subjects were rewarded monetarily for their attained agreements. In one condition a monetary penalty was assessed if arbitration was invoked, while in the other no costs were incurred for resorting to arbitration. When subjects incurred direct costs, they were more likely to obtain a negotiated settlement than declare an impasse, even in cases were there was no *a priori* positive bargaining zone. Neale (1984) also found that when the costs of invoking final-offer arbitration were made relatively salient to negotiators, they were much more likely to reach a negotiated agreement. Neale and Bazerman (1983) also empirically compared the impact of conventional and final-offer arbitration on negotiator performance. They found that the threat of final-offer arbitration produced resolution on more issues and greater rates of concession behavior than the threat of conventional arbitration.

The fact that the arbitration process demands a set of concrete decisions by the parties makes it an ideal context for studying the decisions of parties in dispute resolution. By having a better understanding of the decisions of the parties and the arbitrator, we can provide better advice to help disputants achieve rational outcomes and devise optimal systems to resolve conflicts efficiently.

AGENTS

The previous sections assumed that the third parties were neutral. While some have questioned whether mediators and arbitrators might have political interests in a particular settlement (e.g., to maintain a reputation for being fair to both union and management), these third parties generally do not have a direct interest in the outcome of the particular dispute (Elkouri & Elkouri, 1981). In contrast, disputants often encounter third parties who have a direct interest in the outcome of the dispute. This section and the next focus on such situations. In this section, we focus on the impact of adding an agent(s) to the negotiation process.

Agents are those who act for, on behalf of, or as representatives of the disputants or principles (Arrow, 1985; Ross, 1973). They are similar to mediators in that they may have little power to impose a solution to a dispute. However, unlike mediators, they may have considerably more information about the dispute than one or both of the disputants. A potential bias of negotiators is to view third parties as acting in the best interest of the principals, or at least being neutral. In fact, third parties can act against one or both of the principals involved in a dispute. While the principal-agent problem has been a central focus of the theoretical work in the economics literature (Jensen & Meckling, 1976), virtually no empirical research has been published that examines the impact of self-interested agents on the process and outcome of negotiations.* Partially as a result of its industrial-relations heritage, the research literature on third parties has limited its focus to formal third parties who do not have a vested interest in the outcome of the dispute (e.g., mediators, arbitrators, etc.). As such, this research has considered the impact of the threat of third-party intervention on negotiator behavior *prior* to using the third party rather than on the direct impact of the third-party procedure. Such a perspective does not capture the essence of the third-party intervention, such as agent-aided negotiations, in which the third party plays a *direct* role in resolving an ongoing dispute.

Agents exist in many situations because of their specialized knowledge. Consider a typical principal agent/principal dispute represented by a buyer, residential real estate agent, and seller. The agent has specialized knowledge of the housing market. His or her skill lies in identifying and matching prospective buyers and sellers. In some cases, the agent may be passive, simply acting as a messenger who transmits information between the principals. In others, the agent may take a more active role, directly participating in the fashioning of an agreement. In this form of agency, the agent receives a percentage of the selling price from the seller. As such, the realization that the agent's incentive structure does not match the desires of *both* the

---

*A number of studies, however, are currently being conducted on the impact of biased third parties by Donald Conlon and his colleagues. See, for example, Conlon, Carnevale, and Murnighan (1990).

buyer and seller simultaneously is critical to understanding this one agent/two principals arrangement.

One obvious cost of this form of agency is that whatever the agent receives from the transaction must come from one or both of the parties. Thus, the joint surplus available in a direct negotiation between the buyer and seller will be reduced when negotiating through an agent. In a residential real estate setting, the potential buyer and seller depend upon the real estate agent(s) to represent them. The agent typically is legally responsible only to the seller, regardless of the agent-buyer relationship, since it is the seller who pays the commission (usually 6 percent of the selling price). Given that the agent receives a commission based on the selling price, the agent has a clear incentive to be biased in the direction of the seller's interests. The structure of this interest may influence both the transmitting and presenting of information in the negotiation process.

The use of an agent is expected to increase the sales price of a piece of property, since the seller pays the agent's commission out of the surplus created by the sale. However, the amount of the increase is unclear. One viable prediction is that the selling price will increase (at least) by the amount of the agent's commission. When assured of an agreement, the agent routinely has an incentive to increase the selling price of the property. This could push the price beyond the point where the additional surplus covers the commission. Such an argument is commonly used by realtors when trying to convince a seller to list with an agent rather than attempting to sell a home without one.

In contrast, when individuals or professional appraisers evaluate the market value of a home, they do not provide one figure for its value if sold by an agent and another figure for its value if sold without an agent. Rather, market value implies the objective value of a property, regardless of the mechanism by which that property is transmitted from seller to buyer. The value (and subsequently the price) of the property should not change as a result of the agent's involvement. These two perspectives on agents lead to very different conclusions. The first suggests that the buyer ends up paying the agent's commission; the second suggests that the seller incurs this cost. In one study of actual real estate negotiations, Judd and Frew (1986) concluded that sellers and buyers roughly split the cost of the realtor's commission.

Bazerman, Neale, Valley, Kim, and Zajac (in press) examined the impact of type of intermediary (no intermediary versus agent versus mediator) on (1) the selling price and (2) impasse rate in negotiations on three fictitious pieces of residential real estate—a house, townhouse, and condominium. Agents were intermediaries whose incentive structure was directly tied to the final selling price; mediators were intermediaries whose incentive structure was directly related to getting an agreement. They found that the use of agents produced significantly higher selling prices as well as significantly more impasses than did mediators or direct (i.e., no intermediary) negotiations. There were no significant differences in impasse rate or selling price when comparing mediator-assisted and direct negotiation conditions.

Bazerman et al. (in press) also examined the negotiated relationship between the principals and the agent by considering the allocation of surplus among the parties. The design simulated three different property transactions—house, townhouse, and condominium—crossed with two different manipulations of bargaining zone—$10,000 and $20,000 bargaining zones. The agent's percentage of the total pie was significantly greater when the bargaining zone was larger. However, the agent's actual dollars remained relatively unchanged regardless of the selling price of the property.

In a second study, Valley, White, Neale, and Bazerman (in press) examined the impact of agent's knowledge of buyer and/or seller's reservation points in a residential real estate negotiation. They considered the impact on selling price, percent of agent's commission, and impasse rate when four different "conditions" of knowledge existed: knowing neither the buyer's nor the seller's reservation point; knowing the buyer's reservation point, but not the seller's; knowing the seller's reservation point, but not the buyer's; knowing both the buyer's and seller's reservation points. They reported that the selling price was lowest when the agent knew only the seller's reservation price. When the agent knew only the buyer's reservation point, the agent took advantage of this knowledge and the final selling price was the highest of the four in this condition. While the four means did not differ significantly, the highest agent fee (in dollars) and percentage occurred in the buyer-knowledge condition; while the highest impasse rate occurred in the know-both condition.

This section highlights the importance of considering the decision-making processes and incentive structures of various types of third parties. Negotiators can maximize their interests if they rationally consider all the available information concerning each party at the table—not just that of the disputants. This perspective suggests that in some contexts, the intervenor should be considered a party to the dispute with his/her own set of interests.

MANAGERS AS INTERMEDIARIES

Within organizations, managers often act as third-party intermediaries in disputes. While mediators and arbitrators are normally viewed as personally disinterested in the actual dispute, primarily concerned with dispute resolution, managers are often personally involved in the conflict. As with agents, managers may be self-interested in the specific terms of the outcome. In addition, they frequently have vested interests in a specific process being used to resolve the dispute or a specific outcome of the dispute. These interests may include those of the organization, the manager, and the disputants. In contrast to most other third-party intervenors, managers have an ongoing relationship with the disputants which typically began prior to the dispute and continues after the dispute is resolved. The manager may have dealt with comparable problems or disputes in the past and is likely to be involved in similar disputes in the future (Lewicki & Sheppard, 1985).

Managers often find themselves in situations which they see as opportunities for mediation (Lewicki & Sheppard, 1985). For example, to the extent that managers attempt to resolve disputes among their peers, the manager typically takes on the role of a mediator. In other organizational disputes, the manager has power over the disputants and can impose a settlement. However, the manager may be unwilling to impose a settlement initially with the expectation that the parties can resolve the dispute among themselves. Thus, the manager may, early in his or her involvement in the dispute, intervene as a mediator; once it becomes clear that the disputants will not or cannot resolve the dispute among themselves, he or she may step in and impose a settlement. As such, the manager's behavior is reflective of neither pure mediation nor pure arbitration. Rather, it is a marriage of the two which reflects the manager's unique position as an intervenor.

Murnighan (1986) makes this distinction in his concept of *intravention*. Intravention occurs when a manager enters into a dispute between his or her subordinates (or less powerful organizational members), with or without their specific invitation for assistance. From this perspective, intravention differs from mediation in that intravenors have power over the disputants, make the decision whether and how to intervene, and can direct the final resolution of the dispute.

Because managers differ in unique ways from formal third parties, they probably do not use the pure form of mediation, arbitration, or factfinding. Kolb and Sheppard (1985) suggest that the typical institutional practices of mediation and arbitration are not likely to be common practices among organizational dispute intervenors, either because of lack of training or by design.

Given that conflict-managing behaviors are central to the role of the manager (Tornow & Pinto, 1976), it is surprising that so little empirical research has explored the specific conflict-managing procedures used by managers in organizations (Thomas, 1976). Many of the deviations from rationality discussed above that influence mediators, arbitrators, and agents are likely to affect managers' abilities to act as effective third parties also. For example, Bazerman's (1985) findings that arbitrators are prone to the anchoring bias suggests that where managers exert decision control over the resolution of disputes, they might be inappropriately prone to using past norms to guide future decisions. If future budgets are simple adjustments of past budgets, the threat of anchoring and adjustment is obvious. If we think of the performance-appraisal process as the organization's method of distributing limited resources (i.e., salary increases and promotions) through an arbitration system (i.e., the employees, themselves, are not asked to decide how to allocate these scarce resources), this system can be vulnerable to the anchoring bias in third-party decision making (Huber, Neale & Northcraft, 1987).

While no research to date has catalogued managers' strategies, several researchers have attempted to describe general taxonomies of third-party intervention techniques. Building on Thibaut and Walker's (1975) framework for categorizing procedures and the literature on institutional third parties, Sheppard's (1984) model identifies seven distinct categories of third-party intervention, differentiated by the degree of third-party process and outcome control. However, Sheppard's empirical research revealed that managers rely almost exclusively on three categories: inquisitional intervention, providing impetus, and advisory intervention. A study by Karambayya and Brett (1989) provided some corroboration of the Sheppard model. In their study, managers used four types of intervention strategies: inquisitorial, mediational, procedural marshal, and motivational control (equivalent to providing impetus in Sheppard's model). Both Sheppard's and Karambayya and Brett's intervention taxonomies are based on two underlying dimensions: (1) control over the process and (2) control over the outcome. When managers select the form of intervention, they tend to choose strategies that maximize outcome control. When disputants select the form of intervention, they are more likely to rely on procedures which maximize their control of the outcome.

Although these researchers provided interesting and useful taxonomies for classifying intervention strategies across a variety of dispute settings, deductive, theory-driven approaches necessarily result in the inclusion of some possibly irrelevant factors while excluding others that may be of importance (Rubin, 1983). As noted by Falbo, although this "top down" approach to theory construction is a "popular and respected means of studying social phenomena, such methods tend to restrict the types of [behaviors] considered" (Falbo, 1977, p. 537). Thus, it is difficult to determine whether a deductively derived taxonomy is an accurate description of reality, or merely a representation of the theorist's preconceptions or idiosyncratic perspective. Further, the peculiarities of the manager's third-party role (e.g., vested interest in the outcome, on-going relationships with the disputants) make it unlikely that general third-party taxonomies will be comprehensively applicable to both formal and informal forms of third-party intervention. These taxonomies may, therefore, be insufficient to describe the full range of third-party intervention techniques implemented by managers in organizational settings.

Because of problems inherent in traditional deductive methods, some theorists have espoused the need for better descriptions of what managers actually do in the role of a third party. While descriptive, interpretative methodologies could provide new insights in this area, this stream of research has been stymied by difficulties in observing managers acting as third parties in dispute intervention. In the past, researchers have tended to rely on qualitative, anecdotal, or journalistic methods to assess the managerial-dispute intervention techniques in realistic settings. (For a discussion of this issue, see Kruskal & Wish, 1978.)

While empirical work suggests that the choice of intervention strategy may be affected by the manager's perception of the dispute (Lewicki & Sheppard, 1985), the next step in this research stream is to determine which characteristics of disputes, disputants, and intervenor affect the manager's decision of how to intervene. Few empirical studies specifically use managers as the sample of interest in answering dispute-intervention research questions.

Lewicki and Sheppard asked thirty-five commercial credit managers and travel agency owners or managers to react to two case scenarios that differed in terms of time pressure to resolve the dispute, expectation of future relations between disputants, and range of the settlement on future conflicts. They found that these managers were significantly more likely to select outcome-control strategies when they were under time pressure, when the disputants were not likely to work together in the future, and when the settlement would have broad impact on the resolution of other disputes.

A second study (Sheppard, Blumenfeld-Jones, & Minton, 1986) was an exploratory study of 300 informal third parties (public, private, and academic managers; parents; and students) who agreed to participate in structured interviews investigating their most recent intervention in a dispute. During the interview, subjects were asked to describe their dispute on a number of factors, indicate how concerned with fairness they were when intervening in the dispute, and match their intervention strategies with those developed by Sheppard (1984). They found that the subjects' choice of intervention procedure was related to their perceptions of the characteristics of the dispute and the goals of the intervenor. That is, process consultation was used when the third party did not have authority over the disputants, when the dispute involved a personality clash, or when the third party was concerned with effectiveness and fairness of the outcome. Third parties exerted more decision control when they were concerned with fairness and efficiency, but not when they were concerned with participant satisfaction. Finally, the use of Sheppard's "providing impetus" intervention was not predicted by dispute characteristics or goal preferences of the intervenors. Kolb (1987) approached managerial dispute intervention from an ethnographic perspective. She contacted and interviewed ombudsmen in three organizations. The extensiveness of her interviews ranged from biweekly meetings for four months to one day of interviewing with the ombudsmen and eight managers in an organization for one hour each. She identified three distinct third-party roles: the advisor, the investigator, and the restructurer. In the advisor role, the manager primarily facilitates communication between the disputants. The manager, as investigator, identifies the facts of the dispute and brings them to the attention of superiors. Finally, the restructurer uses the authority of his or her position to redesign the organization or reporting relationships to handle the dispute.

Based upon the studies cited above and more general work on institutional (i.e., non-managerial) third parties, evidence suggests that informal as well as formal third parties use contingencies in selecting intervention strategies. Specifically, managers appear to vary their approaches to dispute intervention contingent on characteristics of the dispute (e.g., the nature of the disagreement or characteristics of the disputants).

Unfortunately, there has been no consistent effort to identify the determinants in the selection of a *managerial*-intervention strategy. That is, the research to date has tended to examine discrete decisions rather than investigate the underlying dimensional structure of those decisions. However, a review of previous empirical work on institutional, managerial, and informal third parties suggests that the following factors influence a manager's selection of intervention strategy: managerial-dispute intervention goals, amount of conflict, time pressure, issue importance, relative power of the disputants, and hierarchical level of intervenor. Each of these factors will be considered in the following sections in further detail. It should be noted, however, that much of what follows is speculative because of a dearth of empirical data.

Dispute-Intervention Goals

Logically, the manager's intervention strategy should be influenced by his or her goals. Sheppard (1983) identified four goals for such intervention: efficiency, effectiveness, fairness, and disputant satisfaction. Managers most concerned with efficiency should probably select an intervention strategy which maximizes outcome control. Managers more concerned with the disputants implementing the solution should be willing to give up outcome control for process control (i.e., controlling how the disputants interact rather than the solution they achieve). Lissak and Sheppard (1983) interviewed a number of managers and non-managers and had them describe recent job-related disputes as well as the criteria they considered important when selecting dispute-resolution procedures. They found that managers were less concerned with fairness than non-managers, but more concerned with efficiency. This suggests that managers had different intervention goals than non-managers and, as such, would generally prefer different forms of intervention.

When managers become involved as a third party to an organizational dispute, they may have multiple, opposing goals. For example, they may want to resolve the dispute efficiently as well as assure the acceptance of the eventual solution. The particular strategies necessary for maximizing these conflicting goals may change over time or may require more or less control as each goal gains or recedes in significance.

Amount of Conflict

The selection of a dispute-intervention technique also may be influenced by a manager's perception of the amount of conflict or the divergence of interests between the disputants. If the parties appear to be close to resolving the dispute, the manager may choose to avoid intervening or may intervene in such as way as to minimize his/her impact on the process (Carnevale & Conlon, 1987; Kressel & Pruitt, 1985). If the parties appear far apart (e.g., a high conflict dispute), the manager may choose a more controlling intervention strategy, especially if he or she wishes to maintain legitimacy as the final authority for solving disputes the parties cannot. Research shows that managers use more controlling strategies when the disputants are not likely to work together in the future (Lewicki & Sheppard, 1985).

Time Pressure

Lewicki and Sheppard also suggest that managers facing time pressure will choose intervention styles that allow them to maintain *outcome* control. They were unable to determine the factors that influence a manager's desire to maintain *process* control, but did report that intervenors also use more aggressive strategies when they face a deadline or time pressure. Carnevale and Conlon (1987) found similar results when they specifically examined the impact of time pressure on mediators.

Issue Importance

The nature of the dispute—whether it is central or tangential to the organization—may also affect the selection of intervention strategy. When the dispute is important, involving central organizational issues, more care and control of the outcome may need to be taken.

Important disputes emphasize the quality of the final outcome, as consistent with Sheppard's notion of effectiveness. Thus, if the dispute is important or central to an organization or group's survival, managers should maintain more outcome control as they intervene. If the disputes are peripheral to the organization, then the dispute process may be as important as the actual solution. The manager may choose not to intervene or may intervene to facilitate the disputants' conflict resolving skills. Lewicki and Sheppard (1985) reported that managers used more controlling intervention strategies when the resolution of the dispute had wide-ranging impact on other organizational actors (i.e., the dispute is important). In addition, Sheppard et al. (1986) found that the choice of intervention strategies differed with the degree of issue importance, and third-party control over outcome.

Relative Power of the Disputants

In a laboratory study of managerial handling of disputes, Karambayya and Brett (1989) reported that the selection of intervention techniques was also strongly influenced by the relationship of the manager to the disputants. That is, when disputants were subordinates, managers intervened in a more controlling manner than when disputants were peers or superiors. Work by Kipnis and Schmidt (1983) support the notion that the relative power of the participants plays an important role in the selection of influence strategies. Sheppard et al. (1986) also report that the choice of intervention strategies was influenced by the interdependence of the disputants.

Hierarchical Power of the Intervenor

Surprisingly, there have been few attempts to examine the impact of an intervenor's power on the selection of intervention strategies. Heller (1971, 1981) suggests that the higher a manager's level, the more likely she or he will share power and authority with subordinates. Examining the impact of hierarchical power from the point of view of the disputants reveals support for Heller's findings. Using partners from a large accounting firm in a policy-capturing study that examined the impact of disputant rank and relationship on their preferences for intervention strategies, Valley (1990) found that higher-ranking organizational members preferred less formal interventions than did lower-ranking members. Taken together, these studies suggest that managers and disputants of differing ranks may differentially prefer intervention procedures. Lower-ranked members may be concerned with fairness and impartiality while higher-ranked members may be more concerned with the cost of the procedures. Thus, more controlling dispute interventions (such as arbitration) may result in a perception of greater fairness and impartiality; but they are likely to cost considerably more than less-controlling dispute intervention procedures (such as mediation).

CONCLUSION

The central argument of this chapter is that we need to understand the decisions of each party in assisted disputed resolution better. Practitioners have made major advances in implementing assisted-dispute resolution systems across a variety of domains (Ury, Brett, & Goldberg, 1989). The underlying assumption of this work is the sometimes unexamined belief that dispute resolution is good; therefore resolution rates are the primary variable of consideration. Recent research into court-assisted arbitration and court-assisted mediation programs suggests that although participants are satisfied with these processes, they do little to reduce the backlog of court cases and, interestingly, have little impact on resolution rates (Mac-Coun, Lind, Hensler, Bryant, & Ebener, 1988). These results are certainly contradictory to the expected benefits of alternative-dispute resolution. If this is supported by additional research, it calls into question the impact these procedures are having on disputants' behavior.

Clearly, what is needed is a systematic examination of the impact of alternative third-party dispute interventions and the impact of their use on the rationality of decisions and the quality of the outcomes. It is not sufficient to assume that since this type of intervention was designed to improve both the quality and amount of agreements that it, in fact, meets these expectations. More importantly, it is not sufficient to assume that all disputes *should* actually be resolved.

What we have presented in this chapter is the basis for conceptualizing third-party intervenors as (more) active participants in the negotiation process—participants who have vested interests in particular outcomes. The belief that third parties (even institutional third parties) are, necessarily, neutral facilitators or decision makers ignores the vested interests and values these parties place on reaching agreements. Both researchers and practitioners should explicitly recognize both the ubiquitous nature of third-party intervenors and the obvious impact that including these participants can have on the resulting decision process of the primary disputants. This recognition can facilitate the improvement of descriptive models of third-party intervention as well as the development of useful prescriptions for negotiation practitioners.

9

Social Determinants of Negotiator Cognition

In Chapter 1, we argued that the situational literature on negotiation has had limited prescriptive value as a result of its focus on relatively fixed components of the negotiation. We proposed that situation variables were best understood in terms of the way in which the negotiator cognitively transforms the process. However, in that chapter, we offered little advice on how to connect the social phenomena identified in the situational literature to cognitive aspects of the transformational process (Thibaut & Kelley, 1959).

The basic thrust of this book has been to articulate the important role of negotiator cognition in explaining negotiator behavior. In this closing chapter, we extend our conception of that domain by arguing that the way in which the negotiator cognitively perceives the situation has important influences on the process and outcome of the negotiation. The cognitive effects that have been documented throughout this book are largely context-free. This chapter suggests that future research should examine how a negotiator's cognitive interpretation of a situation can explain how the negotiator systematically responds to varying social environments.

A central argument of this chapter is that the same objective negotiation situation can go through alternative cognitive transformations resulting in different decisions by negotiators. For instance, Pinkley (1990) has shown that three dimensions describe how disputants cognitively transform and represent conflict situations: relationship/task, emotional/intellectual, and compromise/win. Pinkley and Northcraft (1990) found that these distinctions among negotiators' cognitive transformations significantly influence the content of agreements. For instance, when negotiators perceived a dispute in

155

emotional terms, they tended to include apologies or statements about how the negative feelings should be handled.

This final chapter suggests that a cognitive perspective to negotiation will be more useful if it can incorporate the many situational phenomena that are known to affect negotiation. In addition, we suggest that situational influences are most useful if understood in terms of how the situation is perceived and cognitively transformed by negotiators. The study of the social determinants of negotiator cognition has the potential to provide insights that would not be viable within a purely situational or purely cognitive analysis.

While there are many possible interrelationships between situation and cognition, we will focus on three domains by which we can better understand social situations through a cognitive lens: the cognitive transformation of social roles, perceptions of fairness, and the affective (or emotional) states of the negotiator. In the four sections of this chapter, we will highlight each of these three domains as well as the interactive effects of perceptions of fairness and affective state. We will continue our focus on how cognitions lead to systematic departures from the expectations of rational models. However, the focus will change from the specific judgment of the negotiator to the social situation that surrounds these judgments. The logic of the arguments in this chapter will not be limited to dyadic negotiations. However, the dyadic case will often be used as the model for discussion.

THE COGNITIVE TRANSFORMATION
OF SOCIAL ROLES

A curious, consistent, and robust laboratory finding is that buyers tend to outperform sellers in symmetric negotiation experiments (cf. Bazerman et al., 1985; Neale, Huber, & Northcraft, 1987). Given the artificial context of the experiments, and the symmetry of the design, there is no logical reason why the social role of "buyer" should lead to higher levels of performance than the social role of "seller." This result is inconsistent with an economic analysis of the negotiation problems in these studies.

We offer the contextual argument that naturally occurring social influences frame how people process information. Neale et al. (1987) suggested that sellers frame transactions in terms of gaining resources (e.g., How much do I gain by selling the commodity?); whereas buyers frame the transaction in terms of loss (e.g., How much do I have to give up?). As a result, buyers tend to be risk-seeking and sellers tend to be risk-averse (Kahneman & Tversky, 1979). As we argued in Chapter 2, when a risk-averse party negotiates with a risk-seeking party, the latter is more willing to risk the agreement by holding out longer, while the former is more willing to concede to close the agreement. Thus, whether negotiators are in the buyer or seller role affects how they will interpret and respond to the same situation.

The context of a negotiator's role (buyer/seller) also affects the valuation of objects. Any trade between a buyer and seller depends on the willingness of the buyer to pay at least as much as the minimum value that the seller will accept. Kahneman, Knetsch, and Thaler (in press) have recently documented that the buyer and seller roles affect the valuation of an item in a way that works against trades. They tested the impact of role contextualization in a series of experiments conducted in classroom settings. In a prototype of their experiments, a decorated mug (retail value of about $5) was placed before one-third of the seats after students had chosen their places. All students then received a questionnaire. The form given to the mug recipients (the sellers) indicated that "You now own the object in your possession. You have the option of selling it if a price, which will be determined later, is acceptable to you. For each of the possible prices below indicate whether you wish to (x) Sell your object and receive this price; (y) Keep your object and take it home with you." The students indicated their decision for prices ranging from $.50 to $9.50 in steps of 50 cents, with the understanding that their responses would not affect the predetermined price of the mug (this understanding was true in all three conditions).

Another third of the students who had not received a mug (the choosers) were given a similar questionnaire, informing them that they would have the option of receiving either a mug or a sum of money to be determined later. They indicated their preferences between a mug and sums of money for varying possible levels of the sum of money from $.50 to $9.50. Finally, a final third of the students were told that they were to receive a sum of money and could potentially give up their money to obtain the mug (the buyers). These individuals also indicated their preferences between a mug and sums of money ranging from $.50 to $9.50.

The median values of the mug were $7.12 for the sellers, $3.12 for the choosers, and $2.88 for the buyers. Notice that the buyer role and the more neutral chooser role led to very similar valuations. However, owning the mug created an increased valuation in the mind of the seller. Kahneman et al. (in press) argue that the different roles created different referent points that are used to judge the value of the mug versus money. Occupying different roles may lead to different perceptual contexts that influence frames, risk propensities, and valuation. We need to know more about the cognitive effects of the buyer/seller roles as well as other role effects, such as supervisor and subordinate, friend, enemy, etc. These recent research results suggest that a more complete understanding of negotiation requires that we consider the impact of roles on the perceptual context of the negotiator.

FAIRNESS IN NEGOTIATION

The majority of research on fairness in dispute resolution has focused on decisions concerning the distribution of scarce resources (see Chapter 8) and the fairness of procedures for resolving disputes (Thibaut & Walker, 1975; Lind & Tyler, 1988). However, fairness is not an objective state. Rather, a social environment is cognitively transformed, and a state of (un)fairness is perceived. One researcher found that as soon as children were able to understand the differences between equity and equality norms, their perceptions led them to believe in, and apply, the particular allocation norm that maximized their return.

Clearly, people care about fairness; it affects their decisions in competitive environments. A number of authors have argued that fairness considerations account for the inability of economic models to explain wages. For example, Akerlof (1970) and Solow (1980) argue that fairness considerations explain why many employers do not cut wages during periods of high unemployment despite the potential offered by the supply/demand levels. Okun (1981) has made similar arguments concerning consumer behavior.

In an interesting set of experiments, Kahneman, Knetsch, and Thaler (1987) demonstrate that fairness considerations dominate economically rational choices in decision making. For example, subjects were asked to evaluate the fairness of the action in the following example:

A hardware store has been selling snow shovels for $15. The morning after a large snowstorm, the store raises the price to $20. Please rate this action as: completely fair, acceptable, unfair, or very unfair.

The two favorable and the two unfavorable categories were combined to indicate the proportion of respondents who judged the action acceptable or unfair. Despite the economic rationality of raising the prices on the snow shovels, 82 percent of 107 respondents considered this action unfair.

Many of the effects that Kahneman et al. report are intertwined with judgmental biases. For example, they found that fairness judgments were susceptible to framing effects (see Chapter 3). Consider these problems:

Question A: A company is making a small profit. It is located in a community experiencing a recession with substantial unemployment but no inflation. There are many workers anxious to work at the company. The company decides to decrease wages and salaries 7 percent this year.

Of 125 respondents, 38 percent said this was acceptable, and 62 percent called it unfair.

Question B: A company is making a small profit. It is located in a community experiencing a recession with substantial unemployment and inflation of 12 percent. There are many workers anxious to work at the company. The company decides to increase wages and salaries 5 percent this year.

Of 129 respondents, 78 percent rated this action as acceptable, and 22 percent as unfair.

Despite the real income changes being very similar, judgments of fairness are starkly different. A wage cut is coded as unfair loss; while a nominal gain which does not cover inflation is more acceptable. The context clearly affects judgments of fairness. Fairness considerations also explain deviations from the expectations of rational models in a set of studies using "ultimatum" bargaining games (Guth, Schmittberger, & Schwarze, 1982; Roth, forthcoming). In the Guth et al. study, player 1 divided a fixed sum of money any way he/she chose, by filling out a form stating "I demand DM _____" (the study was conducted in West Germany using Deutsche Marks). Player 2 could accept the offer and receive his/her portion of the money as divided by player 1, or reject the offer, leaving both parties with nothing. Game theoretic models predict that player 1 would offer player 2 only slightly more than zero, and that player 2 would accept any offer that was greater than zero. However, subjects incorporated fairness considerations in their choices. The average demand by player 1 was for less than 70 percent of the funds, both for players participating in the game for the first time and for players repeating the game one week later. In addition, individuals in the role of player 2 rejected profitable offers and took zero 20 percent of the time. Guth et al. concluded that "subjects often rely on what they consider a fair or justifiable result . . . subjects do not hesitate to punish if their opponent asks for 'too much'" (p. 384).

This result has been confirmed in a number of other experiments (Guth & Tietz, 1987; Ochs & Roth, 1989; Forsythe, Horowitz, Savin, & Sefton, 1988). Ochs and Roth, for instance, argue that the players' utilities for fairness explain the results. However, they also argue that a simple notion of fairness does not explain the data, since in most cases player 1 does ask for more than 50 percent of the resources. Rather, parties realize that the other side may very well refuse offers perceived as unfair despite the economic rationality of accepting them.

Ochs and Roth's argument is consistent with that of Forsythe et al.: Player 1 played either an ultimatum game as described above, or a "dictator" game in which player 1 could simply decide how the resources would be split without needing acceptance by player 2. They found that while many player 1's chose a 50–50 split in the ultimatum game, none proposed a 100–0 split. However, under the dictator format, 36 percent of the player 1's took 100 percent. When acceptance is required, proposals become more equal (Ochs & Roth, 1989; Roth, forthcoming). Some 64 percent of the subjects in the dictator game, however, still chose to give the other party some portion of the resources. Thus, both a concern with being fair and the realization that being unfair may have future costs lead to choices (and resulting behaviors) that deviate from rational models in systematic and predictable directions.

Fairness considerations lead to systematic departures from the predictions of economic models. Interestingly, someone who acts according to a rational model (e.g., increases the price of the snow shovels, or asks for 90 percent of the resources in the ultimatum game) may underperform those who consider norms of fairness, since other parties (e.g., the shovel customers or player 2) may punish a party for the unfairness of an economically rational action.

AFFECT

Siegel and Fouraker (1960) observed that negotiations often collapse when one party becomes angry with the other and attempts to "maximize his opponent's displeasure rather than his own satisfaction" (p. 100). Yet, the impact of affect on negotiation processes and outcomes remains one of the least studied areas of negotiation. Empirical research in other arenas has shown that positive affect influences generosity and helpfulness (Isen, 1970; Isen & Levine, 1972), enhances liking of others and improves conceptions of human nature (Gouaux, 1971; Veitch & Griffitt, 1976), and lessens aggressiveness and hostility (Baron, 1984). Isen and her colleagues (Isen, 1983; Isen & Daubman, 1984; Isen, Johnson, Mertz, & Robinson, 1985) also assert that those who are made to "feel good" will tend to solve problems more creatively.

Carnevale and Isen (1986) found that "good humor," initiated through the receipt of a small gift, facilitates creative problem solving and integrative agreements in negotiations. They also report that recently amused negotiators used less contentious tactics. Tidd and Lockard (1978) examined the influence of smiling by a cocktail waitress on the tips received from ninety-six customers. Broad smiles led to larger tips ($23.20 total from forty-eight customers) than weak or minimal smiles ($9.40 total from forty-eight customers). Positive emotions around an event are also associated with that event being more memorable (Isen & Shalker, 1982; Teasdale & Fogarty, 1979; Rafaeli & Sutton, 1989).

Other studies focus on how people are affected by their personal needs, distorting their causal attributions to allow them to feel competent and secure (Heider, 1958). Need-based illusions, like the cognitive illusions presented earlier in this book, lead to systematic departures from rational behavior. Need-based illusions make an individual's reality more palatable, while influencing decision making and negotiation (Taylor & Brown, 1988). Janis (1962), for instance, suggested that people underestimate the danger or potential risk of a threatening situation to reduce their felt needs for vigilance and reassurance.

Taylor and Brown (1988) have described three need-based illusions: illusion of superiority, illusion of optimism, and illusion of control. The illusion of superiority is based upon an unrealistically positive view of the self, both in absolute and relative terms. For instance, people emphasize their positive characteristics and discount their negatives. In relative terms, they believe that they are more honest, capable, intelligent, courteous, insightful, and fair than others. People give themselves more responsibility for their successes, take less responsibility for their failures, and hold others responsible for their own failures and not responsible for their own successes (Schlenker & Miller, 1977; Taylor & Koivumaki, 1976; Nisbett & Ross, 1980).

The illusion of optimism suggests that people are unrealistically optimistic about their future, relative to others and normative baserate. People underestimate the likelihood that they will experience "bad" future events and overestimate the likelihood that they will experience "good" future events.

Finally, the illusion of control means that people believe that they have more control over outcomes than they have in reality. This effect even exists over obviously random events such as throwing dice (Langer, 1975; Langer & Roth, 1975; Crocker, 1982). Tyler and Hastie (forthcoming) argue that while both cognitive and need-based illusions involve a cognitive component, need-based illusions are preceded by need-based, self-serving goals. These need-based goals lead us to replace the goal of seeing the world as it is with the goal of seeing the world as we would like it to be. As a result, the negotiator acts in a way that is less than fully rational because of the errors that he/she makes in assessing the true negotiation context.

The distinction between cognitive and need-based illusions helps us to understand the failure to learn from feedback in negotiation that was documented in Chapter 5. Tyler and Hastie (forthcoming) suggest that the existence of need-based illusions may prevent individuals from learning from experience because they are *unwilling* to use the information optimally. While that chapter focused on the cognitive abilities of the negotiator, Tyler and Hastie raise the possibility that the lack of learning will often be motivated by a desire to maintain a need-based illusion. They suggest that a negotiator may underuse or ignore information about his/her past decisions (particularly if failure resulted) because he/she is motivated to preserve the illusion of superiority. For a person to learn from a mistake, he/she must be willing to recognize that he/she has made a mistake. This recognition can threaten the illusion that the negotiator is competent.

THE INTERACTIVE ASPECTS
OF FAIRNESS AND AFFECT

The first three sections of this chapter have explored the cognitive transformation of three social phenomena, which may not act independently. This section explores the interactive effects of feelings toward the other party and concerns for fairness on the negotiator's decision.

Loewenstein, Thompson, and Bazerman (1989) examined the preferences for outcomes to self and to others under different affective states. They asked subjects to assess their satisfaction with different monetary outcomes for themselves and for another person in a dispute. The social utility function (Messick & Sentis, 1985) of each subject was assessed by regressing his or her satisfaction with each outcome on his or her financial outcome, advantageous inequity (i.e., how much more the subject received than the other party), and disadvantageous inequity (how much the other party received above his or her outcome). In general, disputants preferred equal payoffs over inequity. However, advantageous inequity was preferred over disadvantageous inequity (Adams, 1963, 1965). The general pattern of preferences is illustrated in Figure 9.1. The three curves represent three different payoff levels to the individual. Within each payoff level, the curve captures the disutility that the individual receives from the other party receiving more or less than the subject. The x-axis represents the difference between between outcome to self and outcome to other. The y-axis represents the subjects' rated satisfaction with the outcome. Overall, interpersonal concerns dominated subjects' concern for their own personal outcome: subjects placed much more emphasis on their performance *relative* to the disputing other, rather than the absolute value of what they attained in the negotiation.

Loewenstein et al. (1989) went on to manipulate the emotion that the disputant felt toward the other party at three levels—positive, neutral, negative. When a relationship shifted from positive to negative, disputants shifted toward selfishness: they became more concerned with their own payoffs and were more accepting of advantageous inequity (see Figure 9.2). Unlike the similar curves for

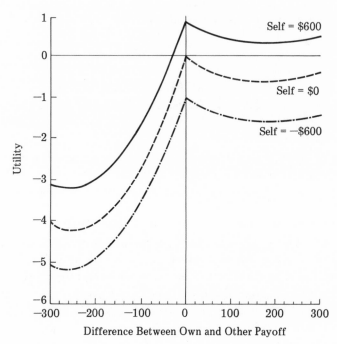

Figure 9.1 Utility as Function of Difference Between Own and Other Payoff and Payoff to Self

neutral and positive affective relationships, negative relationships generate positive utility for advantageous inequity.

An additional study by Loewenstein et al. validated these results by comparing choice behavior in individual and interpersonal decision tasks. This experiment was designed to show that the social-utility curves derived from the previous study could predict choices in risky environments that are (1) predictably different from that expected by individual decision models and (2) predictable, based on the nature of the disputing relationship.

All subjects participated in two phases of this experiment. In Phase 1, they made three binary choices, each a selection between a sure thing and a risky alternative. In Phase 2 (the phases were presented in reverse order for one-half of the subjects), subjects also made three binary choices that offered the same choices to self as the first set, but varied the implications for the other party (for half of the subjects, this order was reversed). The only difference between the decision task in Phase 1 and Phase 2 was the social context: individual versus interpersonal choice.

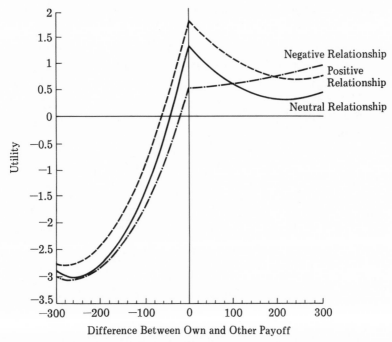

Figure 9.2 Effect of Disputant Relationship on Social Utility Function

In the intrapersonal-choice condition, the risky choice involved gains/losses only to the self. In the interpersonal-choice condition, the risky choice involved gains/losses to the self and another party. In addition, in the interpersonal condition, subjects were randomly assigned to positive- and negative-relationship conditions.

The individual questionnaire contained three choices on a single page, with the instructions: "Below you are given choices between a Sure Thing and a Gamble. Decide which option you prefer and indicate your choice to each question by circling either A or B." The three questions and resulting choices are summarized in Table 9.1.

The interpersonal choices began with the instructions: "Below you are given a description of an incident involving you and a neighbor. Please read the description and then answer each question." The description specified that either a positive or negative relationship existed between the disputants. The questionnaire then described three situations in which the subject and neighbor either jointly owed or were to be paid $10,000. Subjects were then given a choice between accepting a settlement proposed by the neighbor or

Table 9.1 Response Proportions: Individual Versus Interpersonal Choice:

| | Individual Choice ($n = 67$) | Interpersonal Choice | |
| | | Positive Relationship ($n = 35$) | Negative Relationship ($n = 32$) |
Question			
Question 1			
Sure thing	19%	85%	27%
Gamble-arbitrate	81%	15%	73%
	100%	100%	100%
Question 2			
Sure thing	73%	56%	33%
Gamble-arbitrate	27%	44%	67%
	100%	100%	100%
Question 3			
Sure thing	25%	85%	82%
Gamble-arbitrate	75%	15%	18%
	100%	100%	100%

taking a risky option of arbitrating. The three interpersonal questions in the interpersonal-choice set involved identical payoffs to the subject as the three questions in the intrapersonal-choice set. These three questions are summarized in Table 9.1.

The first choice in both conditions was either a choice between a sure $5,000 or a risky alternative offering a .7 chance of $6,000 and a .3 chance of $4,000 (expected value = $5,400). In the individual-decision condition, 81 percent chose the risky alternative and 19 percent chose the sure thing (see Table 9.2). In the positive relationship (interpersonal) condition, 85 percent opted for the sure $5,000/$5,000 split rather than a .7 chance of $6,000/$4,000 and a .3 chance of $4,000/$6,000. However, in the negative relationship (interpersonal), only 27 percent opted for the sure split. The choices in the interpersonal/positive condition were significantly different from those in the individual and interpersonal/negative relationship conditions.

This data is consistent with the predictions of the social utility curves described earlier. Subjects in the intrapersonal condition were willing to take risks to increase their expected values. However, in the interpersonal/positive condition, the social utility function of most subjects is "single peaked" around the equal-payoff point. The equal-split alternative dominated the option for arbitra-

Table 9.2 Payoffs to Self and Other

	Individual–Choice Condition			Interpersonal–Choice Condition				
	Sure Thing	Risky Choice		Sure Thing		Risky Choice		
Choice	Payoff to Self	Probability	Payoff to Self	Payoff to Self	Payoff to Opponent	Probability	Payoff to Self	Payoff to Opponent
1	$5,000	.3	$4,000	$5,000	$5,000	.3	$4,000	$6,000
		.7	$6,000			.7	$6,000	$4,000
2	$4,000	.5	$3,000	$4,000	$6,000	.5	$3,000	$7,000
		.5	$5,000			.5	$5,000	$5,000
3	−$5,000	.5	−$10,000	−$5,000	−$5,000	.5	−$10,000	$0
		.5	$0			.5	$0	−$10,000

tion; both unequal outcomes, even the one offering a greater payoff to the subject, offered lower utility than the equal split.

The social utility curves described earlier also explain the reversal of preference that results as subjects move from a positive to a negative relationship. A shift from positive to negative has two effects on the utility function: (1) it causes a "selfish shift" which increases the desirability of the high-valued risky alternative, and (2) it increases the slope of utility as a function of positive differences between the disputants' payoffs. Now, getting more than the other person is valuable; without the negative relationship, differences provided negative utility. Negative affect removes fairness barriers to selection of the option with the greater expected value.

For the second choice where the sure thing and the risky alternative had equal expected values of $4,000 to the self (and $6,000 to the other party in the interpersonal choice), 73 percent of the subjects in the individual-decision condition chose the typical risk-averse preference for a sure $4,000 over a 50–50 chance at $3,000 or $5,000 (see Chapter 3). In the interpersonal conditions, however, a significantly greater proportion of the subjects preferred the risky course of action: 44 percent with a positive relationship and 67 percent with a negative relationship. Two factors contributed to the attractiveness of arbitration in the interpersonal conditions. First, one of the risky outcomes involved a $5,000/$5,000 split, which is especially attractive given the negative utility associated with inequality. Second, the slope of utility as a function of a negative discrepancy between own and other payoff is convex: so a negative discrepancy of $2,000 is not twice as bad a negative discrepancy of $1,000. Contrary to the expectations of Loewenstein et al. (1989), subjects in the negative relationship condition were more likely to opt for arbitration than subjects in the positive relationship condition. This may reflect a generally negative attitude toward arbitrating a dispute against a friend.

The third item involved losses rather than gains. In the individual-decision condition, as Prospect Theory (Kahneman & Tversky, 1979) predicts, 75 percent of subjects preferred a 50–50 chance of losing $10,000 or losing nothing over a sure loss of $5,000. However, in an interpersonal context, 85 percent of subjects in the positive relationship and 82 percent of the subjects in the negative relationship preferred equal payments of $5,000 over a lottery giving a 50 percent chance of either side paying the full amount. The conditions of positive and negative interpersonal relationship differed significantly from the individual condition, but did not differ between each other. In this problem, we see a pattern of concern for equality of payoffs dwarfing the general preference for losses in the domain of losses.

The general pattern of results from Loewenstein et al. (1989) is that subjects care a great deal for the relative outcomes of parties in a dispute, and that these concerns can overwhelm some of the dramatic effects from the literature on individual decisions. In addition, Loewenstein et al. document the important ways in which affect changes the concern for fairness exhibited by subjects.

Prospect Theory describes a model of individual decision making in which losses and gains are evaluated in comparison to a neutral referent point. This point usually represents the status quo; in laboratory studies of choice, this is usually zero. In more natural contexts, this may represent present wealth. Loewenstein et al. argue that others' outcomes may often represent a key reference point in interpersonal decision settings. Further, while losses and gains also affect choice independently of the other party's payoff, the comparison to a relevant other will often be a more important determinant of the utility of the focal decision maker.

In a recent study, Bazerman, Loewenstein, and White (1991) have shown that while individuals in a positive relationship care far more about social comparisons than absolute outcomes when evaluating a specific outcome, absolute outcomes are more important in actual choice behavior. For example, while 70 percent rated the outcome (+ $400 for self, + $400 for other) as *more* acceptable than (+ $500 for self, + $700 for other) when they evaluated each of these outcomes separately, only 22 percent chose the outcome (+ $400 for self, + $400 for other) over (+ $500 for self, + $700 for other) when asked to choose among these options. Bazerman et al. argue that when the outcomes are evaluated separately, other's outcomes becomes the reference point. In a choice context, no referent is needed to judge outcomes to self, since such outcomes can be easily compared between the two (or more) choices. Thus, the salient attribute will be outcomes to self in a choice task. This evidence is consistent with the argument that the social context plays a critical role in formulating the frame that we used to make a variety of decisions in competitive environments.

This research provides initial support for the influential and possibly synergistic effects of social phenomena on negotiator decision making. Preferences for different norms of fairness are influenced by the affective state of the negotiator. As with other components of negotiator judgment, it may be useful to consider the interaction of these perceptual and social contexts in predicting negotiator behavior and developing normative prescriptions.

CONCLUSION

This concluding chapter extends our decision framework by integrating evidence that shows how the context of a dispute cognitively transforms and filters the information that affects a negotiator's judgments. Specifically, we have shown that aspects of the perceptual context, such as negotiation roles, common conceptions of fairness, and affect, can lead to negotiator judgments that are counter to tenets of rational decision making and are not predicted by the context-free predictions from behavioral decision theory. Thus, the social context highlights new and interesting ways in which negotiation behavior can be conceptualized and negotiated outcomes explained.

A key contribution of this chapter has been to show that the extension of a cognitive perspective that incorporates social determinants is useful in identifying negotiator behavior that is not explainable from either a purely situational or purely cognitive perspective. The future of the cognitive perspective of negotiation depends on the ability of researchers to combine the power of behavioral decision research with the complexities of social phenomena that are part and parcel of this particular decision-making context.

As described in the first chapter, the majority of the existing negotiation literature has been concerned with normative models and the descriptive study of situational and personality variables. Yet, researchers have recognized negotiation as a decision-making process in which two or more parties jointly make decisions to resolve conflicting issues (Pruitt, 1981). This book attempts to bring the study of negotiator cognition to the forefront of negotiation research. We believe and have attempted to document that a great deal of the suboptimality in negotiated outcomes is attributable to deviations from rationality in negotiators' cognitive processes. Research should continue to document the ways in which negotiator cognition deviates systematically from the predictions of normative models. This last chapter highlights one of many possible directions for future negotiation research within a decision perspective. We need to expand our identification of factors that keep negotiators from acting rationally. Further, negotiation research must move beyond individual judgment to the broader perceptual and social context of negotiation. It is through this identification that we may eliminate the cognitive imperfections that (1) reduce the outcomes that negotiators receive from competitive situations, (2) reduce the joint profitability of the parties in a dispute, and (3) decrease the ability of competing parties to reach mutually beneficial agreements.

Negotiation is a pervasive form of social interaction. The consequences of deviations from rationality in negotiation may be disastrous in many situations. The judgment requirements facing the negotiator are complex—and this complexity increases as the number of parties and issues increases. Negotiators attempt to act rationally; however, to be successful, they need to first appreciate the barriers that prevent them and others from achieving full rationality. Second, they need to develop and implement prescriptions that ameliorate or alleviate the impact of these barriers on the process and outcomes of negotiation.

This book has attempted to integrate what we know about making decisions in negotiations and the cognitive barriers that prevent negotiators from following such advice. A decision perspective to negotiation is less than ten years old, and, as such, our knowledge base is still quite limited. We are only beginning to identify the cognitive factors that lead people astray in negotiation. We still know very little about incorporating the knowledge of decision errors into better descriptive models and prescriptive frameworks. Organizing what we know may help clarify what we do not know—a critical step in directing future research.

Finally, this book highlights the importance of descriptive research in the study of negotiations. We have emphasized the benefits of examining how negotiators actually make decisions. Future research must focus on how to eliminate cognitive deficiencies and to improve negotiator judgment. As noted in Chapter 5, Lewin (1947) argues that it is necessary to "unfreeze" an individual before any real change can follow. We suggest that to improve negotiation effectiveness, researchers must recognize that normative recommendations may not be effective if unfreezing does not take place first. The cognitive perspective outlined in this book has the potential to confront negotiation practitioners and researchers with, and inform them about, the limitations that must be overcome to improve the effectiveness of negotiator performance, advice to negotiators, and negotiation research.

References

ABELSON, R. P. (1976). Script processing, attitude formation and decision making. In J. S. Carroll & J. W. Payne (Eds.), *Cognition and social behavior.* Hillsdale, NJ: Lawrence Erlbaum.

ADAMS, J. L. (1979). *Conceptual blockbusting.* San Francisco: San Francisco Book Co.

ADAMS, J. S. (1963). Toward an understanding of unequity. *Journal of Abnormal and Social Psychology, 67,* 422–436.

ADAMS, J. S. (1965). Inequity in social exchange. In L. Berkowitz (Ed.), *Advances in experimental social psychology, 2,* 422–436.

AKERLOF, G. (1970). The market for lemons: Quality uncertainty and the market mechanism. *Quarterly Journal of Economics, 84,* 488–500.

ALPERT, M., & RAIFFA, H. (1982). A progress report on the training of probability assessors. In D. Kahneman, P. Slovic, & A. Tversky (Eds.), *Judgment under uncertainty: Heuristics and biases* (pp. 294–305). Cambridge, Eng.: Cambridge University Press.

APPLBAUM, A. I. (1987). *Knowledge and negotiation: Learning under conflict, bargaining under uncertainty.* Dissertation, Harvard University.

ARGOTE, L., SEABRIGHT, M. A., & DYER, L. (1986). Individual versus group: Use of base-rate and individuating information. *Organizational Behavior and Human Decision Processes, 38,* 65–75.

ARROW, K. J. (1963). *Social choice and individual values.* New Haven, CT: Yale University Press.

ARROW, K. J. (1973). Social responsibility and economic efficiency. *Public Policy, 21,* 303–317.

ARROW, K. J. (1974). *The limits of organization.* New York: Norton.

ARROW, K. J. (1985). *Applied economics.* Cambridge, MA: Belknap Press.

ASCH, S. E. (1951). Effects of group pressure upon the modification and distortion of judgments. In H. Guetzkow (Ed.), *Groups, leadership, and men.* Pittsburgh, PA: Carnegie Press.

173

AXELROD, R. (1984). *The evolution of cooperation.* New York: Basic Books.

BACHARACH, S. B., & LAWLER, E. J. (1981). *Power and politics in organizations.* San Francisco: Jossey-Bass.

BALL, S. B., BAZERMAN, M. H., & CARROLL, J. S. (in press). An evaluation of learning in the bilateral winner's curse. *Organizational Behavior and Human Decision Processes.*

BARLEY, S. R. (forthcoming). Contextualizing conflict: Notes on the anthropology of dispute and negotiation. In M. Bazerman, R. Lewicki, & B. Sheppard (Eds.), *Handbook of research in negotiation* (Vol. 3). Greenwich, CT: JAI Press.

BARON, R. A. (1984). Reducing organizational conflict: An incompatible response approach. *Journal of Applied Psychology, 69,* 272–279.

BAZERMAN, M. H. (1982). Impact of personal control on performances: Is added control always beneficial? *Journal of Applied Psychology, 67,* 472–479.

BAZERMAN, M. H. (1985). Norms of distributive justice in interest arbitration. *Industrial and Labor Relations Review, 38,* 558–570.

BAZERMAN, M. H. (1987). Six years after getting to yes. In the *Dispute Resolution Forum,* Washington, DC: National Institute for Dispute Resolution.

BAZERMAN, M. H. (1990). *Judgment in managerial decision making* (2nd ed.). New York: John Wiley.

BAZERMAN, M. H., BEEKUN, R. I., & SCHOORMAN, F. D. (1982). Performance evaluation in a dynamic context: The impact of a prior commitment to the ratee. *Journal of Applied Psychology, 67,* 873–876.

BAZERMAN, M. H., & BRETT, J. (1988). *El-Tek simulation.* Dispute Resolution Research Center. Northwestern University, Evanston, IL.

BAZERMAN, M. H., & CARROLL, J. S. (1987). Negotiator cognition. In B. Staw and L. L. Cummings (Eds.), *Research in organizational behavior* (Vol. 9, pp. 247–288). Greenwich, CT: JAI Press.

BAZERMAN, M. H., & FARBER, H. S. (1985). Arbitrator decision making: When are final offers important? *Industrial and Labor Relations Review, 39,* 76–89.

BAZERMAN, M. H., & FARBER, H. S. (in press). Analyzing the decision making processes of arbitrators. *Sloan Management Review.*

BAZERMAN, M. H., GIULIANO, T., & APPELMAN, A. (1984). Escalation in individual and group decision making. *Organizational Behavior and Human Performance, 33,* 141–152.

BAZERMAN, M. H., LEWICKI, R. J., & SHEPPARD, B. H. (forthcoming). *Handbook of negotiation research: Research in negotiation in organizations* (Vol. 3). Greenwich, CT: JAI Press.

BAZERMAN, M. H., LOEWENSTEIN, G. F., & WHITE, S. B. (1991). *Inconsistency in subjective utility preferences: The rule of elicitation procedures.* Working paper, Dispute Resolution Research Center, Northwestern University, Evanston, IL.

BAZERMAN, M. H., MAGLIOZZI, T., & NEALE, M. A. (1985). The acquisition of an integrative response in a competitive market. *Organizational Behavior and Human Performance, 34,* 294–313.

BAZERMAN, M. H., MANNIX, E. A., & THOMPSON, L. L. (1988). Groups as mixed-motive negotiations. In E. J. Lawler & B. Markovsky (Eds.), *Advances in group processes: Theory and research* (Vol. 5). Greenwich, CT: JAI Press.

BAZERMAN, M. H., & NEALE, M. A. (1982). Improving negotiation effectiveness under final offer arbitration: The role of selection and training. *Journal of Applied Psychology, 67,* 543–548.

BAZERMAN, M. H., & NEALE, M. A. (1983). Heuristics in negotiation: Limitations to dispute resolution effectiveness. In M. H. Bazerman & R. J. Lewicki (Eds.), *Negotiating in organizations.* Beverly Hills, CA: Sage.

BAZERMAN, M. H., NEALE, M. A., VALLEY, K., KIM, Y. M., & ZAJAC, E. (in press). The effects of agents and mediators on negotiation behavior. *Organizational Behavior and Human Decision Processes.*

BAZERMAN, M. H., RUSS, L. E., & YAKURA, E. (1987). Post-settlement in dyadic negotiations: The need for renegotiation in complex environments. *Negotiation Journal, 3,* 283–297.

BAZERMAN, M. H., & SAMUELSON, W. F. (1983). I won the auction but don't want the prize. *Journal of Conflict Resolution, 27,* 618–634.

BAZERMAN, M. H., & SCHOORMAN, F. D. (1983). A limited rationality model of interlocking directorates: An individual, organizational, and societal decision. *Academy of Management Review, 8,* 206–217.

BELL, D. E., RAIFFA, H., & TVERSKY, A. (1989). *Decision making: Descriptive, normative, and prescriptive interactions.* Cambridge, Eng.: Cambridge University Press.

BERKLEY, D., & HUMPHREYS, P. (1982). Structuring decision problems and the "bias heuristic." *Acta Psychologica, 50,* 201–252.

BETTENHAUSEN, K., & MURNIGHAN, J. K. (1985). The emergence of norms in competitive decision making groups. *Administrative Science Quarterly, 30,* 350–372.

BLOOM, D. E. (1986). Empirical models of arbitrator behavior under conventional arbitration. *Review of Economics and Statistics, 68,* 578–585.

BOJE, D. M., & MURNIGHAN, J. K. (1982). Group confidence pressures in nominal and Delphi groups. *Management Science, 28,* 1187–1196.

BOULDING, K. E. (1958). *The skills of the economist.* Cleveland: Howard Allen.

BRETT, J., & ROGNES, J. (1986). Intergroup relations in organizations: A negotiations perspective. In P. S. Goodman (Ed.), *Designing effective work groups.* San Francisco: Jossey-Bass.

BREWER, M. B., & KRAMER, R. M. (1986). Choice behavior in social dilemmas: Effects of social identity, group size, and decision framing. *Journal of Personality and Social Psychology, 50,* 543–549.

BROCKNER, J., & RUBIN, J. Z. (1985). *The social psychology of entrapment in escalating conflicts.* New York: Springer-Verlag.

CAMBRIDGE, R. M., & SHRECKENGOST, R. C. (1980). *Are you sure?* The subjective probability assessment test. Unpublished manuscript. Langley, VA: Office of Training, Central Intelligence Agency.

CARNEVALE, P. J., & CONLON, D. (1987). Time pressure and mediator strategy in a simulated organizational dispute. *Organizational Behavior and Human Decision Processes, 40,* 111–133.

CARNEVALE, P. J., & ISEN, A. M. (1986). The influence of positive affect and visual access on the discovery of integrative solutions in bilateral negotiations. *Organizational Behavior and Human Decision Processes, 37,* 1–13.

CARNEVALE, P. J., & PEGNETTER, R. (1985). The selection of mediation tactics in public sector disputes. *Journal of Social Issues, 41,* 65–82.

CARROLL, J. S., BAZERMAN, M. H., & MAURY, R. (1988). Negotiator cognitions: A descriptive approach to negotiators' understanding of their opponents. *Organizational Behavior and Human Decision Processes, 41,* 352–370.

CARROLL, J. S., DELQUIE, P., HALPERN, J., & BAZERMAN, M. H. (1990). *Improving negotiators' cognitive processes.* Working paper, MIT, Cambridge, MA.

CARTWRIGHT, D. (1971). Risk taking by individuals and groups: An assessment of research employing choice dilemmas. *Journal of Personality and Social Psychology, 20,* 361–378.

CHAPMAN, L. J., & CHAPMAN, J. P. (1967). Genesis of popular but erroneous diagnostic observations. *Journal of Abnormal Psychology, 72,* 193–204.

CHATMAN, J. (1989). Improving interactional organizational research: A model of person-organization fit. *Academy of Management Review, 14,* 333–349.

CHATMAN, J., & NEALE, M. (1989). *Procedural and distributive justice in a mobile society.* Working paper, Northwestern University, Evanston, IL.

CHECHILE, R. A. (1984). Logical foundations for a fair and rational method of voting. In W. Swapp (Ed.), *Group decision making.* Beverly Hills, CA: Sage.

CHERTKOFF, J. M., & CONLEY, M. (1967). Opening offer and frequency of concession as bargaining strategies. *Journal of Personality and Social Psychology, 7,* 298–303.

CHI, M. T. H., FELTOVICH, P. J., & GLASSER, R. (1981). Categorization and representation of physics problems by experts and novices. *Cognitive Sciences, 5,* 121–125.

CHMIELEWSKI, T. L. (1982). A test of a model for predicting strategy choice. *Central States Speech Journal, 33,* 505–518.

CHOO, G. T. G. (1976). *Training and generalization in assessing probabilities for discrete events* (Tech. Rep. 76-5). Uxbridge, Eng.: Brunel Institute of Organizational and Social Studies.

CLARKE, F. R. (1960). Confidence ratings, second-choice responses, and confusion matrices in intelligibility tests. *Journal of the Acoustical Society of America, 32,* 35–46.

COKER, D. N., NEALE, M. A., & NORTHCRAFT, G. B. (1987). *Structural and individual influences on the process and outcome of negotiation.* Working paper, University of Arizona, Tucson.

CONLON, D. J., CARNEVALE, P., & MURNIGHAN, J. K. (1990). *Third parties with clout: Investigating models of mediation and intravention.* Working paper, University of Delaware, Newark.

CRAWFORD, V. P., & KNOER, E. M. (1981). Job matching with heterogeneous firms and workers. *Econometrica, 49,* 437–450.

CROCKER, J. (1982). Biased questions in judgment of covariation studies. *Personality and Social Psychology Bulletin, 8,* 214–220.

CUMMINGS, L. L., SCHWAB, D. P., & ROSEN, M. (1971). Performance and knowledge of results as determinants of goal setting. *Journal of Applied Psychology, 55,* 526–530.

DAVIS, J. H. (1969). *Group performance.* Reading, MA: Addison-Wesley.

DAVIS-BLAKE, A., & PFEFFER, J. (1989). Just a mirage: The search for dispositional effects in organizational research. *Academy of Management Review, 14,* 385–400.

DAWES, R. M. (1971). A case study of graduate admissions: Applications of three principles of human decision making. *American Psychologist, 26,* 180–188.

DAWES, R. M. (1979). The robust beauty of improper linear models in decision making. *American Psychologist, 34,* 571–582.

DAWES, R. M. (1980). Social dilemmas. *Annual Review of Psychology, 31,* 161–191.

DAWES, R. M. (1988) *Rational choice in an uncertain world.* New York: Harcourt Brace Jovanovich.

DAWES, R. M., & CORRIGAN, B. (1974). Linear models in decision making. *Psychological Bulletin, 81,* 95–106.

DELANEY, J., & FEUILLE, P. J. (1984). Police interest arbitration: Awards and issues. *Arbitration Journal, 39,* 14–24.

DELBECQ, A. L., VAN DE VEN, A. H., & GUSTAFSON, D. H. (1975). *Group techniques for program planning.* Glenview, IL: Scott, Foresman.

DEUTSCH, M. (1975). Equity, equality, and need: What determines which value will be used as the basis of distributive justice. *Journal of Social Issues, 31,* 137–149.

DIGEST OF EDUCATION STATISTICS (1985–1986 ed.). Washington, DC: U.S. Government Printing Office.

EARLEY, P. C. (1988). Computer generated feedback in the magazine-subscription industry. *Organizational Behavior and Human Decision Processes, 41,* 50–64.

EINHORN, H. J. (1974). Expert judgment: Some necessary conditions and an example. *Journal of Applied Psychology, 4,* 1–16.

EINHORN, H. J. (1980). Learning from experience and suboptimal rules in decision making. In T. S. Wallsten (Ed.), *Cognitive processes in choice and decision behavior.* Hillsdale, NJ: Lawrence Erlbaum.

EINHORN, H. J., & HOGARTH, R. M. (1978). Confidence in judgment: Persistence illusion of validity. *Psychological Review, 85,* 395–416.

EINHORN, H. J., & HOGARTH, R. M. (1981). Behavioral decision theory: Process of judgment and choice. *Annual Review of Psychology, 32,* 53–88.

EINHORN, H. J., & HOGARTH, R. M. (1986). Judging probable cause. *Psychological Bulletin, 99,* 3–19.

ELKOURI, F., & ELKOURI, E. (1981). *How arbitration works.* Washington, DC: Bureau of National Affairs.

FALBO, T. (1977). Multidimensional scaling of power strategies. *Journal of Personality and Social Psychology, 35,* 537–547.

FALEY, T., & TEDESCHI, J. T. (1971). Status and reactions to threats. *Journal of Personality and Social Psychology, 17,* 192–199.

FARBER, H. S. (1981). Splitting-the-difference in interest arbitration. *Industrial and Labor Relations Review, 35,* 70–77.

FARBER, H. S., & BAZERMAN, M. H. (1986). The general basis of arbitrator behavior: An empirical analysis of conventional and final offer arbitration. *Econometrica, 54,* 1503–1528.

FARBER, H. S., & BAZERMAN, M. H. (1989). Divergent expectations as a cause of disagreement in bargaining: Evidence from a comparison of arbitration schemes. *Quarterly Journal of Economics* (February), 99–120.

FARBER, H. S., & KATZ, H. C. (1979). Interest arbitration, outcomes, and the incentive to bargain. *Industrial and Labor Relations Review, 33,* 55–63.

FARBER, H. S., NEALE, M. A., & BAZERMAN, M. H. (1990). The impact of risk aversion and arbitration costs on disputed outcomes. *Industrial Relations, 29,* 361–384.

FESTINGER, L. (1957). *A theory of cognitive dissonance.* Evanston, IL: Row, Peterson.

FEUILLE, P. J. (1975). Final offer arbitration and negotiating incentives. *Arbitration Journal, 32,* 203–220.

FISCHHOFF, B. (1982). Latitudes and platitudes: How much credit do people deserve? In G. Ungson & D. Braunstein (Eds.), *New directions in decision making.* New York: Kent.

FISCHHOFF, B., SLOVIC, P., & LICHTENSTEIN, S. (1977). Knowing with certainty: The appropriateness of extreme confidence. *Journal of Experimental Psychology: Human Perception and Performance, 3,* 552–564.

FISHBURN, P. C. (1974a). Simple voting systems and majority rule. *Behavioral Science, 19,* 166–176.

FISHBURN, P. C. (1974b). Paradoxes of voting. *American Political Science Review, 68,* 537–546.

FISHER, R., & URY, W. (1981). *Getting to yes.* Boston: Houghton Mifflin.

FISKE, D. (1961). The inherent variability of behavior. In D. W. Fiske & S. R. Maddi (Eds.), *Functions of work experience.* Homewood, IL: Dorsey Press.

FISKE, S. T., & TAYLOR, S. E. (1984). *Social cognition.* Reading, MA: Addison-Wesley.

FORSYTHE, R., HOROWITZ, J., SAVIN, N. E., & SEFTON, M. (1988). *Replicability, fairness and pay in experiments with simple bargaining games.* Working paper, University of Iowa, Iowa City.

FRIEDMAN, M. (1957). *A theory of consumption function.* Princeton, NJ: Princeton University Press.

GARB, H. N. (1989). Clinical judgment, clinical training, and professional experience. *Psychological Bulletin, 105,* 387–396.

GOUAUX, C. (1971). Induced affective states and interpersonal attraction. *Journal of Personality and Social Psychology, 20,* 37–43.

GRIGSBY, D. W., & BIGONESS, W. J. (1982). Effects of mediation and alternative forms of arbitration on bargaining behavior—a laboratory study. *Journal of Applied Psychology, 67,* 549–554.

GUTH, W., SCHMITTBERGER, R., & SCHWARZE, B. (1982). An experimental analysis of ultimatum bargaining. *Journal of Economic Behavior and Organization, 3*, 367–388.

GUTH, W., & TIETZ, R. (1987). *Ultimatum bargaining for a shrinking cake—an experimental analysis.* Mimeographed working paper.

HAMBURGER, H., GUYER, M., & FOX, J. (1975). Group size and cooperation. *Journal of Conflict Resolution, 19*, 503–531.

HAMMOND, K. R., ROHRBAUGH, J., MUMPOWER, J., & ADELMAN, L. (1977). Social judgment theory: Applications in policy formation. In M. Kaplan & S. Schwartz (Eds.), *Human judgment and decision processes in applied settings.* New York: Academic Press.

HARE, A. P. (1970). Simulating group decisions. *Simulation and Games, 1*, 361–376.

HARE, A. P. (1976). *Handbook of small group research.* New York: Free Press.

HARNETT, D. L. (1967). A level of aspiration model for group decision making. *Journal of Personality and Social Psychology, 5*, 58–66.

HARNETT, D. L., & CUMMINGS, L. L. (1980). *Bargaining behavior* (pp. 21–80). Houston, TX: Dame Publishing.

HARRISON, G. W., & McCABE, K. A. (1987). *Stability and preference distortion in resource matching: An experimental study of the marriage market.* Unpublished manuscript, University of New Mexico, Albuquerque.

HARSANYI, J. C. (1988). *Rational behavior and bargaining equilibrium in games and social situations.* Cambridge, Eng.: Cambridge University Press.

HARVEY, J. (1977). Managing agreements in organizations: The Abilene paradox. *Organizational Dynamics* (Summer), 63–80.

HASTIE, R., PENROD, S., & PENNINGTON, N. (1983). *Inside the jury.* Cambridge, MA: Harvard University Press.

HASTORF, A. H., & CANTRIL, H. (1954). They say a game: A case study. *Journal of Abnormal and Social Psychology, 49*, 129–134.

HAZARD, T. H., & PETERSON, C. R. (1973). *Odds versus probabilities for categorical events* (Technical report. 73-2). McLean, VA: Decisions and Designs.

HEIDER, F. (1958). *The psychology of interpersonal relations.* New York: John Wiley.

HELLER, F. A. (1971). *Managerial decision making: A study of leadership styles and power-sharing among senior executives.* London: Tavistock.

HELLER, F. A. (1981). *Competence and power in managerial decision making: A study of senior levels of organization in eight countries.* New York: John Wiley.

HERMANN, M. G., & KOGAN, N. (1977). Effects of negotiators' personalities on negotiating behavior. In D. Druckman (Ed.), *Negotiation: Social psychological perspectives*. Beverly Hills, CA: Sage.

HILTROP, J. M., & RUBIN, J. Z. (1982). Effects of intervention conflict of interest on dispute resolution. *Journal of Personality and Social Psychology, 42*, 665–672.

HOFFMAN, E., & SPITZER, M. L. (1982). The Coase theorem: Some experimental evidence. *Journal of Law and Economics, 25*, 73–98.

HOFFMAN, L. R. (1961). Conditions for creative problem solving. *Journal of Psychology, 52*, 429–444.

HOFFMAN, L. R. (1978). Group problem solving. In L. Berkowitz (Ed.), *Group processes*. New York: Academic Press.

HOGARTH, R. M. (1981). *Judgment and choice*. New York: John Wiley.

HOMANS, G. (1961). *Social behavior: Its elementary forms*. New York: Harcourt, Brace.

HUBER, G. P. (1980). *Managerial decision making*. Glenview, IL: Scott, Foresman.

HUBER, V. L., & NEALE, M. A. (1986). Effects of cognitive heuristics and goals on negotiator performance and subsequent goal setting. *Organizational Behavior and Human Decision Processes, 38*, 342–365.

HUBER, V. L., NEALE, M. A., & NORTHCRAFT, G. B. (1987). Judgment by heuristics: Effects of rater and ratee characteristics and performance standards on performance-related judgments. *Organizational Behavior and Human Decision Processes, 40*, 149–169.

HUBER, V. L., NORTHCRAFT, G. B., & NEALE, M. A. (1990). Effects of decision context and anchoring bias on employment screening decisions. *Organizational Behavior and Human Decision Processes, 45*, 276–284.

ISEN, A. M. (1970). Success, failure, attention, and reactions to others: The warm glow of success. *Journal of Personality and Social Psychology, 15*, 294–301.

ISEN, A. M. (1983). *The influence of positive affect on cognitive organization*. Paper presented at the Stanford Conference on Aptitude, Learning and Instruction: Affective and Cognitive Processes, Stanford, CA.

ISEN, A. M., & DAUBMAN, K. A. (1984). The influence of affect on categorization. *Journal of Personality and Social Psychology, 47*, 1206–1217.

ISEN, A. M., JOHNSON, M. M., MERTZ, E., & ROBINSON, G. F. (1985). The influence of positive affect on the unusualness of work associations. *Journal of Personality and Social Psychology, 48*, 1413–1426.

ISEN, A. M., & LEVINE, P. F. (1972). Effect of feeling good on helping: Cookies and kindness. *Journal of Personality and Social Psychology, 21*, 384–388.

ISEN, A. M., & SHALKER, T. E. (1982). The effect of feeling state on evaluation of positive, neutral, and negative stimuli: When you "accentuate the positive" do you "eliminate the negative"? *Social Psychology Quarterly, 45,* 58–63.

JAMES, W. (1979). *Some problems of philosophy.* Cambridge, MA: Harvard University Press.

JANIS, I. L. (1962). Psychological effects of warnings. In G. W. Baker & D. W. Chapman, (Eds.), *Man and society in disaster.* New York: Basic Books.

JANIS, I. L. (1982). *Groupthink: Psychological studies of policy decisions and fiascoes.* Boston: Houghton Mifflin.

JENSEN, M. C., & MECKLING, W. H. (1976). Agency theory. *Journal of Financial Economics, 3,* 305–360.

JOHNSON, P. E., DURAN, A. S., HASSEBROCK, F., MOLLER, J., PRIETULA, M., FELTOVICH, P. J., & SWANSON, D. B. (1981). Expertise and error in diagnostic reasoning. *Cognitive Science, 5,* 235–283.

JOYCE, E. E., & BIDDLE, G. C. (1981). Anchoring and adjustment in probabilistic inference in auditing. *Journal of Accounting Research, 19,* 120–145.

JUDD, D. G., & FREW, J. (1986). Real estate brokers, housing prices and the demand for housing. *Urban Studies, 23,* 21–31.

KAGEL, J. H., & LEVINE, D. (1986). The winner's curse and public information in common value auctions. *American Economic Review, 76,* 894–920.

KAHNEMAN, D., KNETSCH, J. L., & THALER, R. (1986). Fairness and the assumptions of economics. *Journal of Business, 59,* S285–S300.

KAHNEMAN, D., KNETSCH, J. L., & THALER, R. (1987). Fairness as a constraint on profit seeking: Entitlements in the market. *American Economic Review, 76,* 728–741.

KAHNEMAN, D., KNETSCH J. L., & THALER, R. (in press). Experimental tests of the endowment effect and the Coase theorem. *Journal of Political Economy.*

KAHNEMAN, D., SLOVIC, P., & TVERSKY, A. (1982). *Judgment under uncertainty: Heuristics and biases.* New York: Cambridge University Press.

KAHNEMAN, D., & TVERSKY, A. (1972). Subjective probability: A judgment of representativeness. *Cognitive Psychology, 3,* 430–454.

KAHNEMAN, D., & TVERSKY, A. (1973). On the psychology of prediction. *Psychological Review, 80,* 237–251.

KAHNEMAN, D., & TVERSKY, A. (1979). Prospect theory: An analysis of decision under risk. *Econometrica, 47,* 263–291.

KAPLAN, M. F., & MILLER, C. E. (1983). Group discussion and judgment. In P. B. Paulus (Ed.), *Basic group processes.* New York: Springer-Verlag.

KARAMBAYYA, R., & BRETT, J. M. (1989). Managers handling disputes: Third party roles and perceptions of fairness. *Academy of Management Journal, 32,* 687–704.

KEELEY, M. (1978). A social-justice approach to organizational evaluation. *Administrative Science Quarterly, 23,* 272–292.

KELLEY, H. H., & THIBAUT, J. W. (1978). *Interpersonal relations: A theory of interdependence.* New York: John Wiley.

KELSO, A. S., & CRAWFORD, V. P. (1982). Job matching, coalition formation, and gross substitutes. *Econometrica, 50,* 1483–1504.

KERR, N. L. (1989). Illusions of efficacy: The effects of group size on perceived efficacy in social dilemmas. *Journal of Experimental Social Psychology, 25,* 287–313.

KIPNIS, D., & SCHMIDT, S. M. (1983). An influence perspective on bargaining within organizations. In M. Bazerman & R. Lewicki (Eds.), *Negotiating in organizations.* Beverly Hills, CA: Sage.

KLAR, Y., BAR-TAL, D., & KRUGLANSKI, A. (1988). On the epistemology of conflicts: Toward a social cognitive analysis of conflict and conflict resolution. In W. Stroebe, A. Kruglanski, D. Bar-Tal, & M. Hewstone (Eds.), *Social psychology of intergroup and international conflict.* New York: Springer-Verlag.

KOCHAN, T., & JICK, T. (1978). The public sector mediation process. *Journal of Conflict Resolution, 22,* 209–240.

KOCHAN, T., KATZ, R., & MCKERSIE, R. (1986). *The transformation of American industrial relations.* New York: Basic Books.

KOCHAN, T., MIRONI, M., EHRENBERG, R., BADERSCHNEIDER, J., & JICK, T. (1979). *Dispute resolution under factfinding and arbitration: An empirical analysis.* New York: American Arbitration Association.

KOGAN, N., & WALLACH, M. A. (1967). Group risk-taking as a function of members' anxiety and defensiveness. *Journal of Personality, 35,* 50–63.

KOLB, D. (1983). *The mediators.* Cambridge, MA: MIT Press.

KOLB, D. M. (1987). What are organizational third parties and what do they do? In M. Bazerman & R. Lewicki (Eds.), *Negotiating in organizations.* Beverly Hills, CA: Sage.

KOLB, D. M., & RUBIN, J. Z. (forthcoming). Mediation through a disciplinary prism. In M. Bazerman, R. Lewicki, & B. Sheppard (Eds.), *Handbook of negotiation research: Research in negotiation in organizations* (Vol. 3). Greenwich, CT: JAI Press.

KOLB, D. M., & SHEPPARD, B. H. (1985). Do managers mediate, or even arbitrate? *Negotiation Journal*, Oct., 379–388.

KOMORITA, S. S., & CHERTKOFF, J. (1973). A bargaining theory of coalition formation. *Psychological Review, 80*, 149–162.

KOMORITA, S. S., & LAPWORTH, A. W. (1982). Cooperative choices among individuals versus groups in N-person dilemma situations. *Journal of Personality and Social Psychology, 42*, 487–496.

KORIAT, A., LICHTENSTEIN, S., & FISCHHOFF, B. (1980). Reasons for confidence. *Journal of Experimental Psychology: Human Learning and Memory, 6*, 107–118.

KRAMER, R. M. (1989). Windows of vulnerability or cognitive illusions? Cognitive processes and the nuclear arms race. *Journal of Experimental Social Psychology, 25*, 79–100.

KRAMER, R. M. (forthcoming). The more the merrier? Social psychological aspects of multi-party negotiations in organizations. In M. H. Bazerman, R. J. Lewicki, & B. H. Sheppard (Eds.), *Handbook of negotiation research: Research on negotiation in organizations* (Vol. 3). Greenwich, CT: JAI Press.

KREPS, D. M., MILGROM, P., ROBERTS, J., & WILSON, R. (1982). Rational cooperation in the finitely repeated prisoners' dilemma. *Journal of Economic Theory, 27*, 245–252.

KRESSEL, K., & PRUITT, D. G. (1985). Themes in the mediation of social conflict. *Journal of Social Issues, 41*, 179–198.

KRUSKAL, J. (1964). Multidimensional scaling by optimizing goodness of fit to a nomothetic hypothesis. *Psychometrika, 29*, 1–27.

KRUSKAL, J., & WISH, M. (1978). *Multidimensional scaling.* Beverly Hills, CA: Sage.

KUHN, T. S. (1970). *The structure of scientific revolutions* (2nd ed.). Chicago: University of Chicago Press.

LAMM, H., & KOGAN, N. (1970). Risk taking in the experimental context of intergroup negotiations. *Journal of Experimental Social Psychology, 6*, 351–363.

LANDSBERGER, H. A. (1955). Interaction process analysis of professional behavior: A study of labor mediators in twelve labor-management disputes. *American Sociological Review, 51*, 566–575.

LANDY, F. J., & FARR, J. L. (1982). *The measurement of work performance.* New York: Academic Press.

LANGER, E. (1975). The illusion of control. *Journal of Personality and Social Psychology, 32*, 311–328.

LANGER, E., & ROTH, J. (1975). Heads I win, tails it's chance: The illusion of control as a function of the sequence of outcomes in a purely chance task. *Journal of Personality and Social Psychology, 32,* 951–955.

LAUGHLIN, P. R., & JOHNSON, H. H. (1966). Group and individual performance on a complementary task as a function of initial ability level. *Journal of Experimental Social Psychology, 2,* 407–414.

LAX, D. A., & SEBENIUS, J. K. (1986). *The manager as negotiator.* New York: Free Press.

LEVENSON, B. (1975). Professional training, psychodiagnostic skill and kinetic family drawings. *Journal of Personality Assessment, 39,* 389–393.

LEVINE, M. E., & PLOTT, C. R. (1977). Agenda influence and its implications. *Virginia Law Review, 53,* 561–604.

LEWICKI, R. J., & LITTERER, J. A. (1985). *Negotiation.* Homewood, IL: R. D. Irwin.

LEWICKI, R. J., & SHEPPARD, B. H. (1985). Choosing to intervene: Factors affecting the use of process and outcome control in third party dispute resolution. *Journal of Occupational Behavior, 6,* 49–64.

LEWICKI, R. J., WEISS, S., & LEWIN, D. (1988). *Models of conflict, negotiation, and third party intervention: A review and synthesis.* Working Paper Series (WPS 88-33). College of Business, Ohio State University.

LEWIN, K. (1947). Group decision and social change. In T. M. Newcomb & E. L. Hartley (Eds.), *Readings in social psychology.* New York: Holt, Rinehart and Winston.

LICHTENSTEIN, S., & FISCHHOFF, B. (1977). Do those who know more also know more about how much they know? The calibration of probability judgments. *Organizational Behavior and Human Performance, 20,* 159–183.

LICHTENSTEIN, S., & FISCHHOFF, B. (1980). Training for calibration. *Organizational Behavior and Human Performance, 26,* 149–171.

LICHTENSTEIN, S., FISCHHOFF, B., & PHILLIPS, L. D. (1982). Calibration of probabilities: State of the art to 1980. In D. Kahneman, P. Slovic, and A. Tversky (Eds.), *Judgment under uncertainty: Heuristics and biases.* New York: Cambridge University Press.

LIEBERT, R. M., SMITH, W. P, HILL, J. H., & KEIFFER, M. (1968). The effects of information and magnitude of initial offer on interpersonal negotiation. *Journal of Experimental Social Psychology, 4,* 431–441.

LIND, E. A., & TYLER, T. R. (1988). *The social psychology of procedural justice.* New York: Plenum.

LINSTONE, H. A., & TUROFF, M. (EDS.). (1975). *The Delphi method: Techniques and applications.* Reading, MA: Addison-Wesley.

LISSAK, R. I., & SHEPPARD, B. H. (1983). Beyond fairness: The criterion problem in research on dispute intervention. *Journal of Applied Social Psychology, 13,* 45–65.

LOEWENSTEIN, G., THOMPSON, L., & BAZERMAN, M. H. (1989). Social utility and decision making in interpersonal contexts. *Journal of Personality and Social Psychology, 57,* 426–441.

LONG, G., & FEUILLE, P. (1975). Final offer arbitration: "Sudden death" in Eugene. *Industrial and Labor Relations Review, 27,* 186–203.

LORD, C. G., ROSS, L., & LEPPER, M. R. (1979). Biased assimilation and attitude polarization: The effects of prior theories on subsequently considered evidence. *Journal of Personality and Social Psychology, 37,* 2098–2109.

MACCOUN, R. J., LIND, E. A., HENSLER, D. R., BRYANT, D. L., & EBENER, P. A. (1988). *Alternative adjudication: An evaluation of the New Jersey automobile arbitration program* (R-3676-ICJ). Palo Alto: RAND Institute for Civil Justice.

MAIER, N. R. F., & SOLEM, A. R. (1952). The contribution of a discussion leader to the quality of group thinking: The effective use of minority opinions. *Human Relations, 5,* 277–288.

MANNIX, E. A. (in press). Organizations as resource dilemmas: The effects of power imbalance on group decision making. *Organizational Behavior and Human Decision Processes.*

MANNIX, E. A., & BAZERMAN, M. H. (1990). *Matching and negotiation in entry level labor markets.* Northwestern University, Evanston, IL.

MANNIX, E. A., THOMPSON, L. L., & BAZERMAN, M. H. (1989). Small group negotiation. *Journal of Applied Psychology, 74,* 508–517.

MARCH, J. G., & SIMON, H. A. (1958). *Organizations.* New York: John Wiley.

MATHER, L., & YNGVESSON, B. (1981). Language, audience, and the transformation of disputes. *Law and Society Review, 15,* 775–822.

MAY, K. O. (1982). A set of independent, necessary and sufficient conditions for simple majority decisions. In B. Barry & R. Hardin (Eds.), *Rational man and irrational society.* Beverly Hills, CA: Sage.

MCGILL, A. L., (1989). Context effects in judgments of causation. *Journal of Personality and Social Psychology, 57,* 189–200.

MCGILL, A. L., (in press). The effect of direction of comparison on the selection of causal explanations. *Journal of Experimental Social Psychology.*

MEEHL, P. E. (1954). *Clinical versus statistical predictions: A theoretical analysis and review of the evidence.* Minneapolis: University of Minnesota Press.

MESSICK, D. M., & MCCLELLAND, C. L. (1983). Social traps and temporal traps. *Personality and Social Psychology Bulletin, 9,* 105–110.

MESSICK, D. M., & SENTIS, K. P. (1985). Estimating social and nonsocial utility functions from ordinal data. *European Journal of Social Psychology, 15,* 389–399.

MINSKY, M., & PAPERT, S. (1974). *Artificial intelligence.* Condensed lectures. Oregon State System of Higher Education, Eugene, OR.

MINTZBERG, H. R. (1975). The manager's job: Folklore and fact. *Harvard Business Review* (July–August), 49–61.

MONGELL, S. J., & ROTH, A. E. (1988). *Sorority rush as a two-sided matching mechanism.* Unpublished manuscript, University of Pittsburgh.

MORLEY, I. (1982). Preparation for negotiation: Conflict, commitment and choice. In H. Brandstatter, J. Davis, & G. Stocker-Kreichgauer (Eds.), *Group decision making.* New York: Academic Press.

MORTENSEN, D. T. (1982). The matching process as a noncooperative bargaining game. In J. J. McCall (Ed.), *The Economics of information and uncertainty.* Chicago: University of Chicago Press.

MORTENSEN, D. T. (1986). Matching: Finding a partner for life or otherwise. *American Journal of Sociology, 94,* S215–S240.

MOSCOVICI, S., & ZAVALIONI, M. (1969). The group as a polarism of attitudes. *Journal of Personality and Social Psychology, 12,* 125–135.

MURNIGHAN, J. K. (1978). Models of coalition behavior: Game theoretic, social psychological and political perspectives. *Psychological Bulletin, 85,* 1130–1153.

MURNIGHAN, J. K. (1981). Defectors, vulnerability, and relative power: Some causes and effects of leaving a stable coalition. *Human Relations, 34,* 589–609.

MURNIGHAN, J. K. (1986a). Organizational coalitions: Structural contingencies and the formation process. In R. J. Lewicki, B. H. Sheppard, & M. H. Bazerman (Eds.), *Research on negotiation in organizations* (Vol. 1). Greenwich, CT: JAI Press.

MURNIGHAN, J. K. (1986b). The structure of mediation and intravention: Comments on Carnevale's strategic choice model. *Negotiation Journal, 4,* 351–356.

MURNIGHAN, J. K., & BAZERMAN, M. H. (in press). A perspective on negotiation research in accounting and auditing. *The Accounting Review.*

MURNIGHAN, J. K., & BRASS, D. (forthcoming). Intraorganizational coalitions. In M. Bazerman, R. Lewicki, & B. Sheppard (Eds.), *The handbook of negotiation research* (Vol. 3). Greenwich, CT: JAI Press.

MYERSON, R. (1986). *Analysis of incentives in dispute resolution.* Working paper, Dispute Resolution Research Center, Kellogg Graduate School of Management, Northwestern University, Evanston, IL.

MYERSON, R. B. (1987). *Analysis of incentives in dispute resolution.* Working paper, Dispute Resolution Research Center, Northwestern University, Evanston, IL.

MYERSON, R. B. (1990). *Game theory: Analysis of conflict.* Cambridge, MA: Harvard University Press.

NASH, J. (1950). The bargaining problem. *Econometrica, 18,* 128–140.

NEALE, M. A. (1984). The effect of negotiation and arbitration cost salience on bargainer behavior: The role of arbitrator and constituency in negotiator judgment. *Organizational Behavior and Human Performance, 34,* 97–111.

NEALE, M. A., & BAZERMAN, M. H. (1983). The role of perspective-taking ability in negotiating under different forms of arbitration. *Industrial and Labor Relations Review, 36,* 378–388.

NEALE, M. A., & BAZERMAN, M. H. (1985a). When will externally set aspiration levels improve negotiator performance? A look at integrative behavior in competitive markets. *Journal of Occupational Behavior, 6,* 19–32.

NEALE, M. A., & BAZERMAN, M. H. (1985b). The effects of framing and negotiator overconfidence on bargainer behavior. *Academy of Management Journal, 28,* 34–49.

NEALE, M. A., BAZERMAN, M. H., NORTHCRAFT, G. B., & ALPERSON, C. A. (1986). "Choice shift" effects in group decisions: A decision bias perspective. *International Journal of Small Group Research, 23,* 33–42.

NEALE, M. A., HUBER, V. L., & NORTHCRAFT, G. B. (1987). The framing of negotiations: Context versus task frames. *Organizational Behavior and Human Decision Processes, 39,* 228–241.

NEALE, M. A., & NORTHCRAFT, G. B. (1986). Experts, amateurs, and refrigerators: Comparing expert and amateur decision making on a novel task. *Organizational Behavior and Human Decision Processes, 38,* 305–317.

NEALE, M. A., & NORTHCRAFT, G. B. (1990a). Experience, expertise, and decision bias in negotiation: The role of strategic conceptualization. In B. Sheppard, M. Bazerman, & R. Lewicki (Eds.), *Research in negotiation in organizations* (Vol. 2). Greenwich, CT: JAI Press.

NEALE, M. A., & NORTHCRAFT, G. B. (1990b). Behavioral negotiation theory: A framework for conceptualizing dyadic bargaining. In L. L.

Cummings & B. M. Staw (Eds.), *Research in organizational behavior* (Vol. 12). Greenwich, CT: JAI Press.

NEALE, M. A., NORTHCRAFT, G. B., & EARLEY, P. C. (1990). *The joint effects of goal setting and expertise on negotiator performance.* Working paper, Northwestern University, Evanston, IL.

NICKERSON, R. S., & MCGOLDRICK, C. C. (1965). Confidence ratings and level of performance on a judgmental task. *Perceptual and Motor Skills, 20,* 311–316.

NIEMI, R. G., & WEISBERG, H. F. (EDS.). (1972). *Probability models of collective decision making.* Columbus, OH: Merrill.

NISBETT, R. E., & ROSS, L. (1980). *Human inference: Strategies and shortcomings of social judgment.* Englewood Cliffs, NJ: Prentice-Hall.

NISBETT, R. E., & WILSON, T.D. (1977). Telling more than we can know: Verbal reports on mental processes. *Psychological Review, 84,* 231–259.

NORTHCRAFT, G. B., & EARLEY, P. C. (1989). Goal setting, conflict, and task interdependence. In M. A. Rahim (Ed.), *Conflict management: An interdisciplinary approach.* New York: Praeger.

NORTHCRAFT, G. B., & NEALE, M. A. (1986). Opportunity costs and the framing of resource allocation decisions. *Organizational Behavior and Human Decision Processes, 37,* 348–356.

NORTHCRAFT, G. B., & NEALE, M. A. (1987). Expert, amateurs, and real estate: An anchoring-and-adjustment perspective on property pricing decisions. *Organizational Behavior and Human Decision Processes, 39,* 228–241.

NORTHCRAFT, G. B., & NEALE, M. A. (forthcoming). Dyadic negotiation. In M. Bazerman, R. Lewicki, & B. Sheppard (Eds.), *Handbook of negotiation research: Research in negotiation in organizations* (Vol. 3). Greenwich, CT: JAI Press.

NOTZ, W. W., & STARKE, F. M. (1978). The impact of final offer arbitration versus conventional arbitration on the aspirations and behaviors of bargainers. *Administrative Science Quarterly, 23,* 189–203.

OCHS, J., & ROTH, A. E. (1989). An experimental study of sequential bargaining. *American Economic Review, 79,* 335–385.

OKUN, A. (1981). *Prices and quantities: A macroeconomic analysis.* Washington, DC: Brookings Institute.

OLSON, M. (1971). *The logic of the collective.* Cambridge, MA: Harvard University Press.

ORDESHOOK, P. C. (1986). *Game theory and political theory: An introduction.* Cambridge, Eng.: Cambridge University Press.

O'REILLY, C. S., NORTHCRAFT, G. B., & SABERS, D. (1987). The confirmation bias in special education eligibility decisions. *School Psychology Review, 18,* 126–135.

OSBORN, A. F. (1957). *Applied imagination.* New York: Charles Scribner.

OSKAMP, S. (1965). Attitudes towards U.S. and Russian actions: A double standard. *Psychological Reports, 16,* 43–46.

PENNINGTON, N., & HASTIE, R. (1985). *Causal reasoning in decision making.* Working paper, University of Chicago.

PENNINGTON, N., & HASTIE, R. (1988). Explanation-based decision making: Effects of memory structure on judgment. *Journal of Experimental Psychology: Learning, Memory, and Cognition, 14,* 521–533.

PFEFFER, J., & SALANCIK, G. R. (1978). *The external control of organizations.* New York: Harper & Row.

PHILLIPS, G. M. (1970). PERT as a logical adjunct to the discussion process. In R. S. Cathcart & L. A. Samovar (Eds.), *Small group communication.* Dubuque, IA: Wm. C. Brown.

PINKLEY, R. L. (1990). Dimensions of conflict frame: Disputant interpretations of conflict. *Journal of Applied Psychology, 75,* 117–126.

PINKLEY, R. L., & NORTHCRAFT, G. B. (1990). *Cognitive interpretations of conflict: Implications for disputant motives and behavior.* Working paper, Southern Methodist University, Dallas, TX.

PITZ, G. F. (1974). Subjective probability distributions for imperfectly known quantities. In L. W. Gregg (Ed.), *Knowledge and cognition* (pp. 29–41). New York: John Wiley.

PLOTT, C. R. (1976). Axiomatic social choice theory: An overview and interpretation. *American Journal of Political Science, 20,* 511–596.

PLOTT, C., & LEVINE, M. (1978). A model of agenda influence on committee decisions. *American Economic Review, 68,* 146–160.

PRUITT, D. G. (1981). *Negotiation behavior.* New York: Academic Press.

PRUITT, D. G. (1983). Achieving integrative agreements. In M. H. Bazerman & R. J. Lewicki (Eds.), *Negotiating in organizations.* Beverly Hills, CA: Sage.

PRUITT, D. B., & KRESSEL, K. (1985). The mediation of social conflict. *Journal of Social Issues, 41,* 1–10.

PRUITT, D. G., & RUBIN, J. Z. (1986). *Social conflict.* New York: Random House.

RAFAELI, A., & SUTTON, R. I. (1989). The expression of emotion in organizational life. In L. L. Cummings & B. M. Staw (Eds.), *Research in organizational behavior* (Vol. 11, pp. 1–42). Greenwich, CT: JAI Press.

RAIFFA, H. (1982). *The art and science of negotiation.* Cambridge, MA: Belknap.

RAIFFA, H. (1985). Post settlement settlements. *Negotiation Journal, 1,* 9–12.

RAPOPORT, A. (1959). Critiques of game theory. *Behavioral Science, 4,* 49–66.

RAWLS, J. (1971). *A theory of justice.* Cambridge, MA: Harvard University Press.

RIKER, W. H., & ORDESHOOK, P. C. (1973). *An introduction to positive political theory.* Englewood Cliffs, NJ: Prentice-Hall.

ROLOFF, M. E., & JORDAN, J. (1989). *Strategic communication within bargaining plans: Forms, antecedents, and effects.* Paper presented to the second biannual Conference of the International Association for Conflict Management, Athens, GA.

ROSENTHAL, R., & JACOBSON, L. (1968). *Pygmalion in the classroom.* New York: Holt, Rinehart and Winston.

ROSS, L., & ANDERSON, C. A. (1982). Shortcomings in the attribution process: On the origins and maintenance of erroneous social assessments. In D. Kahneman, P. Slovic, & A. Tversky (Eds.), *Judgment under uncertainty: Heuristics and biases.* Cambridge, Eng.: Cambridge University Press.

ROSS, S. (1973). The economic theory of agency: The principal's problem. *American Economic Review, 63,* 134–139.

ROTH, A. E. (1982). The economics of matching: Stability and incentives. *Mathematics of Operations Research, 7,* 617–628.

ROTH, A. E. (1984). The evolution of the labor market for medical interns and residents: A case study in game theory. *Journal of Political Economy, 92,* 991–1016.

ROTH, A. E. (1985a). Common and conflicting interests in two-sided matching markets. *European Economic Review, 27,* 75–96.

ROTH, A. E. (1985b). Conflict and coincidence of interests in job matching: Some new results and open questions. *Mathematics of Operations Research, 10,* 379–389.

ROTH, A. E. (forthcoming). An economic approach to the study of bargaining. In M. H. Bazerman, R. J. Lewicki, & B. H. Sheppard (Eds.), *Handbook of negotiation research: Research in negotiation in organizations* (Vol. 3). Greenwich, CT: JAI Press.

ROTH, A. E., & SOTOMAYOR, M.A.O. (in press). *Two sided matching: A study of game–theoretic modelling and analysis.*

RUBIN, J. Z. (1981). *Dynamics of third–party intervention: Kissinger in the Middle East.* New York: Praeger.

RUBIN, J. Z. (1983). The use of third parties in organizations: A critical response. In M. H. Bazerman & R. J. Lewicki (Eds.), *Negotiating in organizations* (pp. 214–224), Beverly Hills, CA: Sage.

RUBIN, J. Z., & BROWN, B. R. (1975). *The social psychology of bargaining and negotiation.* New York: Academic Press.

SAMUELSON, W. F., & BAZERMAN, M. H. (1985). The winner's curse in bilateral negotiations. In V. Smith (Ed.), *Research in experimental economics* (Vol. 3, pp. 105–137). Greenwich, CT: JAI Press.

SCHANK, R. C., & ABELSON, R. P. (1977). *Scripts, plans, goals, and understanding: An inquiry into human knowledge structures.* Hillsdale, NJ: Lawrence Erlbaum.

SCHLENKER, B. R., & MILLER, R. S. (1977). Egocentrism in groups: Self-serving biases or logical information processing? *Journal of Personality and Social Psychology, 35,* 755–764.

SCHOORMAN, F. D. (1988). Escalation bias in performance appraisals: An unintended consequence of supervisor participation in hiring decisions. *Journal of Applied Psychology, 73,* 58–62.

SCHOORMAN, F. D., BAZERMAN, M. H., & ATKIN, R. S. (1981). Interlocking directorates: A strategy for the management of environmental uncertainty. *Academy of Management Review, 6,* 243–251.

SEBENIUS, J. K. (1989). *International negotiation: Problems and new approaches.* Working paper, Kennedy School of Government, Cambridge, MA.

SELIGMAN, M. E. (1975). *Helplessness: On depression, development, and death.* San Francisco: Freeman.

SHAW, M. E. (1976). *Group dynamics: The psychology of small group behavior.* New York: McGraw-Hill.

SHEPPARD, B. H. (1983). Mangers as inquisitors: Some lessons from the law. In M. H. Bazerman & R. J. Lewicki (Eds.), *Negotiating in organizations.* Beverly Hills, CA: Sage.

SHEPPARD, B. H. (1984). Third-party intervention: A procedural framework. In B. M. Staw & L. L. Cummings (Eds.), *Research in organizational behavior* (Vol. 6). Greenwich, CT: JAI Press.

SHEPPARD, B. H., BLUMENFELD-JONES, K., & MINTON, J. W. (1986). *To control or not to control: Two models of conflict intervention.* Paper presented at the American Psychological Association's annual meeting, Washington, DC.

SHUBIK, M. (1971). The dollar auction game: A paradox in noncooperative behavior and escalation. *Journal of Conflict Resolution, 15,* 109–111.

SHUBIK, M. (1982). *Game theory in the social sciences.* Cambridge, MA: MIT Press.

SIEGEL, S., & FOURAKER, L. (1960). *Bargaining and group decision making: Experiments in bilateral monopoly.* New York: McGraw-Hill.

SIMON, H. A. (1957). *Models of man.* New York: John Wiley.

SINGER, P. (1978). Rights and the market. In J. Arthur & W. H. Shaw (Eds.), *Justice and economic distribution.* Englewood Cliffs, NJ: Prentice-Hall.

SKINNER, B. F. (1971). *Beyond freedom and dignity.* New York: Knopf.

SLOVIC, P., & FISCHHOFF, B. (1979). On the psychology of experimental surprises. *Journal of Experimental Psychology: Human Perception and Performance, 3,* 544–551.

SLOVIC, P., & LICHTENSTEIN, S. (1971). Comparison of Bayesian and regression approaches to the study of information processing in judgment. *Organizational Behavior and Human Performance, 6,* 649–744.

SNIEZEK, J. A., & HENRY, R. A. (1989). Accuracy and confidences in group judgment. *Organizational Behavior and Human Decision Processes, 43,* 1–28.

SOLOW, R. M. (1980). On theories of unemployment. *American Economic Review, 70,* 1–11.

SONDAK, H. (1990). *Centralized and decentralized matching procedures: A behavioral approach to social choice.* Unpublished dissertation, Northwestern University, Evanston, IL.

SONDAK, H., & BAZERMAN, M. H. (1989). Matching and negotiation processes in quasi-markets. *Organizational Behavior and Human Decision Processes, 44,* 261–280.

SONDAK, H., & BAZERMAN, M. H. (in press). Power balance and the rationality of outcomes in matching markets. *Organizational Behavior and Human Decision Processes.*

STARKE, F. M., & NOTZ, W. W. (1981). Pre- and post-intervention effects on conventional versus final offer arbitration. *Academy of Management Journal, 24,* 832–850.

STAW, B. M. (1976). Knee-deep in the big muddy: A study of escalating commitment to a chosen course of action. *Organizational Behavior and Human Performance, 16,* 27–44.

STAW, B. M. (1981). The escalation of commitment to a course of action. *Academy of Management Review, 6,* 577–587.

STAW, B. M., BELL, N. E., & CLAUSEN, J. A. (1986). The dispositional approach to job attitudes: A lifetime longitudinal test. *Administrative Science Quarterly, 31,* 56–77.

STAW, B. M., & ROSS, J. (1978). Commitment to a policy decision: A multitheoretical perspective. *Administrative Science Quarterly, 23,* 40–64.

STAW, B. M., & ROSS, J. (1985). Stability in the midst of change: A dispositional approach to job attitudes. *Journal of Applied Psychology, 70,* 469–
480.

STAW, B. M., & ROSS, J. (1987). Behavior in escalation situations: Anteced-
ents, prototypes, and solutions. In L. L. Cummings & B. M. Staw
(Eds.), *Research in organizational behavior* (Vol. 9). Greenwich, CT: JAI
Press.

STEINER, I. D. (1972). *Group process and productivity.* New York: Academic Press.

STEVENS, C. M. (1966). Is compulsory arbitration compatible with bargaining? *Industrial Relations, 5,* 38–50.

STILLENGER, C., EPELBAUM, M., KELTNER, D., & ROSS, L. (1990). *The
'reactive devaluation' barrier to conflict resolution.* Working paper,
Stanford University, Palo Alto, CA.

TAYLOR, D. W., BERRY P. C., & BLOCK, C. H. (1958). Does group participation when using brainstorming facilitate or inhibit creative problem
solving? *Administrative Science Quarterly, 3,* 23–47.

TAYLOR, S. E., & BROWN, J. D. (1988). Illusion and well-being: A social
psychological perspective. *Psychological Bulletin, 103,* 193–210.

TAYLOR, S. E., & CROCKER, J. (1981). *The processing of context information
in person perception.* Working paper, Harvard University.

TAYLOR, S. E., & KOIVUMAKI, J. H. (1976). The perception of self and others:
Acquaintanceship, affect, and actor-observer differences. *Journal of
Personality and Social Psychology, 33,* 403–408.

TAYLOR, S. E., & THOMPSON, S. (1982). Stalking the elusive "vividness"
effect. *Psychological Review, 89,* 155–181.

TEASDALE, J. D., & FOGARTY, S. J. (1979). Differential effects of induced
mood on retrieval of pleasant and unpleasant events from episodic
memory. *Journal of Abnormal Psychology, 88,* 248–257.

TEGER, A. I. (1980). *Too much invested to quit: The psychology of the
escalation of conflict.* New York: Pergamon Press.

TETLOCK, P. E. (1983). Policy makers' images of international conflict.
Journal of Social Issues, 39, 67–86.

THIBAUT, J. W., & KELLEY, H. H. (1959). *The social psychology of groups.*
New York: John Wiley.

THIBAUT, J. W., STRICKLAND, L. H., MUNDY, D., & CODIG, E. F. (1960).
Communication, task demands and group effectiveness. *Journal of Personality, 28,* 156–166.

THIBAUT, J., & WALKER, L. L. (1975). *Procedural justice: A psychological
analysis.* Hillsdale, NJ: Lawrence Erlbaum.

THOENNES, N. A., & PEARSON, J. (1985). Predicting outcomes in divorce mediation: The influence of people and process. *Journal of Social Issues, 41,* 115–126.

THOMAS, K. (1976). Conflict and conflict management. In M. Dunnette (Ed.), *Handbook of industrial and organizational psychology.* New York: Rand-McNally.

THOMPSON, L. L. (1990). Negotiation: Empirical evidence and theoretical issues. *Psychological Bulletin, 108,* 515–532.

THOMPSON, L. L. (1990a). Information exchange in negotiation. *Journal of Experimental Social Psychology,* in press.

THOMPSON, L. L. (1990b). The influence of experience on negotiator performance. *Journal of Experimental Social Psychology, 26,* 528–544.

THOMPSON, L. L., & HASTIE, R. (1990). Negotiator's perceptions of the negotiation process. In B. H. Sheppard, M. H. Bazerman, & R. J. Lewicki (Eds.). *Research in negotiation in organizations* (Vol. 2). Greenwich, CT: JAI Press.

THOMPSON, L. L., & HASTIE, R. M. (1990). Social perception in negotiation. *Organizational Behavior and Human Decision Processes, 47,* 98–123.

THOMPSON, L. L., MANNIX E. A., & BAZERMAN, M. H. (1989). Group negotiation: Effects of decision rule, agenda, and aspiration. *Journal of Personality and Social Psychology, 54,* 86–95.

TIDD, K. L., & LOCKARD, J. S. (1978). Monetary significance of the affiliative smile: A case for reciprocal altruism. *Bulletin of the Psychonomic Society, 11,* 344–346.

TORNOW, W. W., & PINTO, P. R. (1976). The development of a managerial job taxonomy. *Journal of Applied Psychology, 4,* 410–418.

TVERSKY, A., & KAHNEMAN, D. (1971). The belief in the "law of numbers." *Psychological Bulletin, 76,* 105–110.

TVERSKY, A., & KAHNEMAN, D. (1973). Availability: A heuristic for judging frequency and probability. *Cognitive Psychology, 5,* 207–232.

TVERSKY, A., & KAHNEMAN, D. (1974). Judgment under uncertainty: Heuristics and biases. *Science, 185,* 1124–1131.

TVERSKY, A., & KAHNEMAN, D. (1981). The framing of decisions and the psychology of choice. *Science, 211,* 453–458.

TVERSKY, A., & KAHNEMAN, D. (1983). Extensional versus intuitive reasoning: The conjunction fallacy in probability judgment. *Psychological Review, 90,* 293–315.

TVERSKY, A., & KAHNEMAN, D. (1986). Rational choice and the framing of decisions. *Journal of Business, 59,* 251–284.

TVERSKY, A., & KAHNEMAN, D. (1989). *Reference theory of choice and exchange*. Working paper, Stanford University, Palo Alto, CA.

TYLER, T., & HASTIE, R. (forthcoming). The social consequences of cognitive illusions. In M. H. Bazerman, R. J. Lewicki, & B. Sheppard (Eds.), *Handbook of negotiation research: Research on negotiation in organizations* (Vol. 3). Greenwich, CT: JAI Press.

URY, W., BRETT, J., & GOLDBERG, S. (1989) *Designing dispute systems*. San Francisco: Jossey-Bass.

VALLEY, K. L. (1990). *It's who you know: A network analysis of decision processes in organizations*. Dissertation proposal, Northwestern University, Evanston, IL.

VALLEY, K. L., WHITE, S. B., NEALE, M. A., & BAZERMAN, M. H. (in press). The effect of agent's knowledge on negotiator performance in simulated real estate negotiations. *Organizational Behavior and Human Decision Processes*.

VEITCH, R., & GRIFFITT, W. (1976). Good news—bad news: Affective and interpersonal effects. *Journal of Applied Social Psychology, 6*, 69–75.

VIDMAR, N. (1971). Effects of representational roles and mediators on negotiator effectiveness. *Journal of Personality and Social Psychology, 17*, 48–58.

VON NEUMANN, J., & MORGENSTERN, O. (1947). *Theories of games and economic behavior*. Princeton, NJ: Princeton University Press.

WALTON, R. E., & MCKERSIE, R. B. (1965). *A behavioral theory of labor negotiation*. New York: McGraw-Hill.

WASON, P. C. (1960). On the failure to eliminate hypotheses in a conceptual task. *Quarterly Journal of Experimental Psychology, 12*, 129–140.

WASON, P. C. (1968a). Reason about a rule. *Quarterly Journal of Experimental Psychology, 20*, 273–283.

WASON, P. C. (1968b). On the failure to eliminate hypothesis . . . A second look. In P. C. Wason & P. N. Johnson-Laird (Eds.), *Thinking and reasoning*. Harmondsworth, Eng.: Penguin.

WASON, P. C. (1969). Regression in reasoning? *British Journal of Psychology, 60*, 471–480.

WEICK, K. E. (1979). *The social psychology of organizing* (2nd ed.). Reading, MA: Addison-Wesley.

WEISER, M., & SHERTZ, J. (1983). Programming problem representation in novice and expert programmers. *Instructional Journal of Man-Machine Studies, 14*, 391–396.

WEISS, H. M., & ADLER, S. (1984). Personality and organizational behavior. In B. M. Staw & L. L. Cummings (Eds.), *Research in organizational behavior* (Vol. 6). Greenwich, CT: JAI Press.

WILMOT, W. W. (1980). *Dyadic communication.* Reading, MA: Addison-Wesley.

WILSON, M. G., NORTHCRAFT, G. B., & NEALE, M. A. (1989). Information competition and vividness effects in on-line judgments. *Organizational Behavior and Human Decision Processes, 44,* 132–139.

WINHAM, G. R. (1977). Complexity in international negotiation. In D. Druckman (Ed.), *Negotiation: Social psychological perspective.* Beverly Hills, CA: Sage.

YOUNG, O. R. (1972). Intermediaries: Additional thoughts on third parties. *Journal of Conflict Resolution, 16,* 48–53.

YUKL, G. A. (1974). Effects of situational variables and opponent concessions on a bargainer's perceptions, aspirations, and concessions. *Journal of Personality and Social Psychology, 29,* 227–236.

Index